EVERYTHING

YOU NEED TO KNOW ABOUT...

Wine

EVERYTHING

YOU NEED TO KNOW ABOUT...

Wine

TRISH AND ROB MACGREGOR

David & Charles

A DAVID & CHARLES BOOK

David & Charles is a subsidiary of F&W (UK) Ltd.,

an F&W Publications Inc. company

First published in the UK in 2004

First published in the USA as The Everything® Wine Book,

by Adams Media Corporation in 1997

Project Manager Ian Kearey

Cover Design Ali Myer

A catalogue record for this book is available from the British Library.

ISBN 0 7153 1956 6

Printed in Great Britain by CPI Bath

for David & Charles

Brunel House   Newton Abbot   Devon

Visit our website at www.davidandcharles.co.uk

David & Charles books are available from all good bookshops;

alternatively you can contact our Orderline on (0)1626 334555 or

write to us at FREEPOST EX2110, David & Charles Direct,

Newton Abbot, TQ12 4ZZ (no stamp required UK mainland).

This book is dedicated to the winemakers of the world – the men and women who earn their living growing grapes, doing battle with weather, pests and economics, in order to put affordable, quality wine on our tables. *Salut!*

Contents

Introduction

The idea for this book came when we couldn't find a good general introductory wine book that truly addresses the monetary realities of wine. This book focuses on the £8-per-bottle-and-under wine experience. The vast majority of wine sold around the world costs less than £8 per bottle. These are the wines that we usually drink.

Learning about wine is, for many people, an important rite of passage into adulthood – an enjoyable experience that has many benefits. For instance, your journey through the world of wine will entail a vicarious trip around the globe, perhaps to California, Australia, South Africa, South America and through most of Europe. In all likelihood you will become familiar with a broad range of styles of wine and find among them your favourites. In fact,

you will probably develop very definite ideas about what you find enjoyable – which grape varieties, which geographical regions or countries, and which producers. As your taste in wine becomes more sophisticated, so too will your appreciation of food; the two are not easily separated. Thus your new-found appreciation of good wine will add an extra dimension to the pleasures of the table. The ability to enjoy a good wine is an acquired one – and its own reward. But this journey is not without its pitfalls.

Most wine merchants, large and small, offer a vast array of wines – red, white and rosé wines from perhaps 15 different countries. To the wine novice this can be baffling and intimidating, and it has discouraged many people from learning

more about wine. 'Wine talk' is another common obstacle. The terminology used to describe wine can be difficult to comprehend, and all too often proves to be very subjective. To many beginners, the wine labels themselves do more harm than good, as far as describing the contents within goes. Some wines are labelled according to their region of origin; some are labelled by grape variety; and still others are sold under brand names. This confusion can easily lead to a bad experience with a wine purchase. For the novice this often means failing to decode both the label and the pompous description offered by a sales clerk, and bringing home a wine that is completely different from what was expected. Such a mistake can easily deflate one's enthusiasm for wine. To make matters even worse, wine has become associated with an unfortunate degree of social stuffiness, and a wine snob can be the most annoying snob of all. Because of such people, many wine novices have an unreasonable fear of looking foolish. As you learn about wine, you will soon find that all of these pitfalls are easily avoidable.

It is simple, really – read about wines, taste them, and make a note of what you like and dislike. If you taste without reading, your accumulated knowledge will consist of 'I like this' and 'I don't like that', without understanding the complex and wonderful reasons why wines taste the way they do. Conversely, if you read without tasting, you may well acquire a thorough working knowledge of the world of wine, but you will lack the most important information of all – what wine actually *tastes* like, the sensual experience that words cannot fully describe.

Buying and tasting wines yourself can be an expensive undertaking. Fortunately, many wine shops offer tastings on weekends. This can be a lot of fun, since you will be among other people with similar interests. Arranging group tastings with like-minded friends is a cost-effective way to sample several different wines of your own choosing. In either case, don't forget to take notes. Also, more and more restaurants and bars offer quality wines by the glass. Although you contribute greatly to the restaurant's profits by ordering wine this way, it still beats buying an entire bottle just to taste it.

There are many wine books in print, several of

which are directed at the beginner. One problem shared by many of these 'beginner' books is that they have been written by wine experts who seem to have forgotten that they, too, were once novices, and who have lost sight of the novice's perspective. The enormous wealth of wine information in these books is usually lost on someone with very little prior knowledge or experience. More often than not, these books are more suitable for someone wishing to establish a wine cellar than for someone who wants to find a good £5 red.

This book was not written by wine experts; rather, it is a unique collaboration of a relative newcomer to wine and a knowledgeable wine buff. While writing, we realized that what we decided to leave out of the book was as important as what we put in it. There is too much information about wine for any one book, let alone a beginner's book. Therefore, much of this book is written from the perspective of the inquisitive novice who might ask:

- What do I really need to know about wine in order to get started?
- What do I need to know about purchasing wine, both in shops and in restaurants, in order to get the most for my money?
- How can I maximize my enjoyment of wine?

We also thought it would be useful to give an overview of the history of wine, in order to establish the important role of wine in our culture. Understanding that you are drinking 5,000 years' worth of Western civilization will enhance your enjoyment. A grasp of the various processes by which wine is produced will give you a better understanding of the many different styles of wine available. Chapter 4, 'Varietal Wines, Grape by Grape', addresses the distinctions among wines produced from different types of grapes. Similarly, Chapter 6, 'Wine Around the World', explains the strengths and traditions of the world's leading wine-producing nations. The buying guides are intended to help you get the best wines for your money, and the 'Wine with Food' chapter should enable you to succeed at the mysterious food–wine matching game.

Although we discuss wines ranging in price from £3 to £300, the goal of this book is to allow you to enjoy as many types of wine as possible that sell for no more than £8 per bottle. Accordingly, and with the novice in mind, we focus mainly on inexpensive and moderately expensive wines. Few pleasures in this world equal that of finding an inexpensive wine that has qualities that remind us of a greater, more expensive wine.

Best wishes to you on this wonderful journey through the world of wine.

CHAPTER 1

WINE AND
WESTERN CIVILIZATION

FIRST PRIZE

The evolution and development of wine closely paralleled that of Western civilization itself. Wine was probably discovered by accident somewhere in the Fertile Crescent, the agriculturally generous expanse of river valleys extending from the Nile to the Persian Gulf. Early civilizations in the region (4000–3000 BC) owed their existence to the rich soils, and it is here that the wine grape first thrived. As primitive agricultural settlements gave way to powerful city-states, the seafaring and territorially ambitious peoples of the ancient world – the Phoenicians, then the Greeks, then the Romans – distributed grape vines and winemaking know-how throughout the Mediterranean and Europe.

After the Roman Empire finally collapsed in the 5th century AD, Christian monasteries in the Frankish Kingdom (France, northern Italy, part of Germany) kept detailed accounts of their grape cultivation and winemaking. This meticulous record-keeping helped to match the optimal grape varieties with the appropriate regions. The powerful influence of Charlemagne, who ruled the Frankish Kingdom from 768 to 814, extended to wine. The great emperor oversaw the establishment of vineyards from southern France to northern Germany, and the *grand cru* Corton-Charlemagne vineyard of Burgundy was once his property.

Under the rule of Elizabeth I, England emerged as a naval power with a substantial merchant-marine fleet. Her seaborne international trade brought wine throughout Britain from several wine-producing nations of Europe, and the English thirst for fortified wines – Sherry, Port, and Madeira – is largely responsible for the development of these wine types.

By the closing years of the 17th century, France was becoming recognized as being the greatest of the wine-producing nations. In 1663, Samuel Pepys wrote in his famous diary about tasting the wines of Ho Bryan (today's Haut-Brion) and, by 1784, Thomas Jefferson, who drafted America's Declaration of Independence and was one of its earliest presidents, enthusiastically wrote of their wine quality in correspondence to friends and encouraged the planting of European wine grapes in the New World. These early attempts at wine cultivation in the American colonies were largely unsuccessful, and the transplanting back and forth of European and native American vines inadvertently brought a destructive vine louse to Europe. The result was the *phylloxera* blight of the late 1800s, which destroyed most of the vineyards in Europe. This disaster, however, was not without a silver lining – the ravaged vineyards inspired new cultivation techniques and a redistribution across Europe of winemaking expertise.

The beneficial development in agricultural sciences after the turn of the century enabled winemakers everywhere to protect their crops from common grapevine afflictions such as moulds and pests. Grape-growing and winemaking became increasingly scientific. The 20th century has also seen the widespread enactment of wine laws that guarantee authenticity and quality. Today wine is produced in temperate climates around the world, and a great variety of wines is available to the consumer.

Ancient Wine

The discovery of wine was almost certainly an accident. Although the grape was known to early man – grape seeds have been discovered in ancient cave dwellings – the juicy, sweet fruit of the vine was probably a nutritious staple in the prehistoric diet long before it was known to ferment. Inevitably, the skins of some grapes held in storage were accidentally split, and wild yeasts worked their magic. Legend has it that an ancient king kept his beloved grapes in an earthen jar labelled 'poison', and a discontented member of his harem drank juice from the jar in a suicide attempt. Instead of dying, she found her spirits rejuvenated, and she shared the drink with her king, who took her into his favour and decreed that, henceforth, grapes would be allowed to ferment. Men have been buying drinks for women ever since.

Mesopotamia (Persia) and Egypt, the end-points of the Fertile Crescent, were the twin cradles of ancient winemaking. Both kingdoms were producing wine around 3000 BC. Ironically, neither area has produced any wine of note for hundreds of years, although Egypt is in the process of restoring her winemaking capacity.

The ancient Egyptians cultivated grapes and made wine in a surprisingly modern fashion. Vines were carefully tended in the fertile Nile delta, and grapes were stamped and fermented in large wooden vats. As scientifically advanced as the Egyptians were, they could not have understood the biological mechanism of fermentation.

The wine of ancient Egypt was mostly sweet white wine, probably made from the grape now known as the Muscat of Alexandria, and it was considered to be a gift from the god Osiris. As a form of respect to the gods, the Egyptians used wine in their funeral rites. Depending on the status held by the deceased, his body and belongings were anointed with wine before entombment.

The wines of Egypt found their way abroad in the ancient world. Many centuries after the decline of the Egyptian dynasties, her wines still enjoyed a fine reputation and were roundly praised in Roman writings.

The Mesopotamian culture in Persia was advanced in mathematics, commerce and agriculture. Around 3000 BC the Persians were producing wine from vines probably originating in the Caucasus foothills to the north. Like the Egyptians, the Persians regarded wine as a divine gift, and made toasts of praise to their gods. The Persians loved their wine, and rightly so – the grape varieties they used are believed to be the precursors of the finest *Vitis vinifera* species.

Situated between Egypt and Mesopotamia along the Fertile Crescent were the Phoenicians, who sailed the Mediterranean from what is now the coast of Lebanon. Thus the grapevine – and wine – found its way to Greece, Sicily and north central Italy. Here the Etruscans, immigrants from the Caucasus, began to make fine wines in the region that is now Tuscany.

That the Old Testament mentions wine so frequently is an indication of the importance of wine in early Hebrew culture. Noah is said to have established a vineyard after the flood. Much to the chagrin of his maker, he also got drunk out of sheer relief for being saved from death.

When Moses led his people out of Egypt, they regretted leaving behind the delicious wine produced there. Their fears were calmed, however, when Moses's spies returned from the Promised Land with a giant cluster of grapes they found growing there. Jewish Law requires Kosher wine – pure, unadulterated and produced under rabbinical supervision – to be used for Passover rites and other religious ceremonies.

When Greek civilization expanded to the many islands in the Aegean and the Mediterranean, the Greeks found grapes already there, brought centuries earlier by the Phoenicians. Wine played an important role in Greek civilization. Dionysus was the native god of fruitfulness and vegetation, especially with regard to vine-growing. Wine was considered to be a gift from Dionysus, and one of the semi-annual feasts to the god, known as Dionysia, was held in late December to celebrate the new wine of the vintage.

For the most part, the wines of the ancient world would not be well received by modern wine drinkers. Greek wine was typically stored in clay vessels lined with pine pitch, a flavour component found in modern-day Retsina. Additionally, wines in ancient Egypt, Greece and elsewhere were flavoured with additives such as herbs and seawater. Romans returning from Marseilles bemoaned the 'smoked' wine they found there, and it was not uncommon for wine to be smoked in a fire-house or boiled down to a syrup.

How to Enhance Your Wine-Drinking Experience

1. Sit on comfortable furniture.

2. Exercise during the day to help heighten your senses.

3. Let your wine breathe if it needs to. Ten minutes often goes a long way.

4. Use crystal wine glasses, if you have them, to add a little to the wine and a lot to the ambiance.

5. Make sure the lighting isn't too dim or too bright. Poor lighting can stress your senses.

6. Have some food in your stomach so you don't get 'buzzed' prematurely – have time to really taste the wine .

7. Have a glass of water readily available, and don't be thirsty when you drink wine.

8. Keep the wine you are drinking in your mouth long enough to really taste it. Don't be afraid to move it around a bit with your tongue.

9. Don't drink your wine, especially white, so slowly that it warms up too much.

10. Drink wine with good and appropriate food.

11. Drink wine with good and appropriate people.

The Roman Empire: The Beginnings of Quality Wine in Europe

The Roman Empire covered, at its greatest outward expansion, most of the Mediterranean lands and a good part of Europe. The Romans found grapes already under cultivation in many conquered lands, the wine culture having been widely distributed by their Greek and Phoenician predecessors. The Romans, too, loved wine and fostered its development throughout the Empire. Whereas the Romans initially shared the taste of their predecessors for adulterated wines, it is likely that pure, fine wines, both red and white, were being produced in Spain, France and northern Italy. Rome was devoted to the cult of Bacchus (the god of wine), and the methodical Romans developed sophisticated vine-growing and wine-making techniques that were unequalled until the 18th century.

The Empire was awash with wine – so much so that in 92 AD Emperor Domitian ordered that the great vineyards of France be uprooted. Fortunately, that order was not fully executed, and it was rescinded two centuries later. When the Roman Empire fell for good in 476, the great wine regions of Europe – in northern Italy, in Germany and in France – were under vine.

What we have come to think of as the European grape species actually originated in Asia Minor; however, the wine culture diminished in its birthplace and elsewhere outside of Europe due to the rise of Islam. In 634 the prophet Mohammed conquered the Meccans in the first jihad, or Islamic holy war. At its zenith (around 900), the Islamic Empire stretched from Spain to northern India. The Islamic code of law and theology forbade the consumption of alcohol, and wine production effectively ceased in these lands. The responsibility for the further development of wine culture thus fell to the rulers of the successor states (Germany and France) and the increasingly powerful Catholic Church.

1989
CASTELLO DI AMA®
DRY RED TABLE WINE OF TUSCANY
VIGNA IL CHIUSO

Da uve raccolte nel 1989 nella vigna Il Chiuso,
del vigneto San Lorenzo.

ESTATE BOTTLED BY CASTELLO DI AMA SpA.
GAIOLE IN C. - ITALY

NET CONT. 750 ML· PRODUCT OF ITALY · ALC. 12.5% BY VOL

Wine in Europe

The grapevine was introduced to southern Gaul (France) long before the Romans arrived. The Romans, however, taught their sophisticated cultivation methods to the native Gauls and introduced hardier varieties to the northern regions. Monastic orders thrived in the duchies of France and Germany, and often owned considerable vineyards. Many centuries of keeping records – of rainfall, crop yields and grape varieties – enabled the medieval monks to plant ideal grape varieties in major regions.

At the request of Pope Urban II, armies of Christian soldiers set out from Europe to liberate the Christian Holy Land from the hands of the Islamic Empire. Seven crusades and 200 years later, the European Christian soldiers had succeeded only in bringing chess and new strains of *Vitis vinifera* back to Europe. During this period the two most important regions of France, Bordeaux and Burgundy, further developed their reputations for producing quality wines.

In 1152 Henry II of England married Eleanor of Aquitaine (whose lands included most of southwest France), and her dowry included the vineyard areas of Bordeaux and neighbouring Gascony. The light-red wine of these regions gained favour in England, where it became known as Claret. By 1350, the port city of Bordeaux was shipping out the equivalent of 1,000,000 cases of wine per year. Though Bordeaux red wines are now among the most ageworthy, Claret in this era was drunk young: long-term ageing was not possible until the development of proper bottles and corks in the late 1700s.

As England's seafaring capacity grew, so too did her taste for wines from the faraway vineyards of the Mediterranean. Many wines, however, did not ship well and spoiled during their voyage. Some ingenious shippers in Spain and Portugal added brandy to the wine barrels prior to shipment, with the intention that the wines be rewatered upon arrival in England. The journey at sea jostled and heated these fortified barrels. But the wine, immune to bacterial activity at the higher alcohol content, actually improved greatly along the way. Rather than redilute them, the British preferred to drink these fortified wines at full strength. Port from Portugal, Sherry from Spain and Madeira from the Portuguese island of the same name became very popular as soothing tipples in cold and foggy England.

The wine grape was propagated by the Romans in the northerly Champagne region long before Champagne had bubbles. The delightful fizziness we associate with the beverage was probably another accidental discovery. It gets very cold in the

Champagne region; red grapes struggle to mature fully and to develop colour in such a climate. It is conceivable that a cold spell after the harvest might have arrested the fermentation process of a still wine from the region. Then after a few warm spring days the yeast left in the bottle may have awakened from its dormancy, and – boom! – the bottle exploded from the buildup of carbon dioxide. Actually, probably quite a few bottles exploded, over who knows how many years, before they worked it out.

Legend credits Dom Pérignon, the blind cellarmaster at the Benedictine Abbey of Hautvillers until his death in 1715, with harnessing the second fermentation. In the late 1600s he is reputed to have introduced to the production of sparkling wine replaceable cork stoppers, thicker glass and the concept of blending. However, another Champagne producer, Nicole-Barbe Ponsardin (the widow of François Clicquot), is credited with developing the technique for removing dead yeast from the bottle. Along with fortified wine and Claret, Champagne found favour with the English.

The French Revolution in 1789 had a negative impact on wine production in Burgundy. The vineyards there were seized from the Church and the noblemen, and were given instead to the people – few of whom were given enough acreage to produce their own wine. Most growers had to sell their grapes to *négociants* (shipper-bottlers) who did very little to maintain Burgundy's reputation for quality.

When native American vines were brought to France – perhaps to help

growers determine whether American soil was somehow to blame for the problems associated with growing the European grape varieties – the destructive *phylloxera* louse came with them. This contagious vine malady destroyed vineyard after vineyard in Europe, and eventually spread to other continents when vines were transplanted.

The solution to the *phylloxera* problem was to graft European vines onto American vine roots, which are naturally resistant to *phylloxera*. The positive side during all this turmoil was the flushing out of French winemakers from France. These craftsmen took their talents to vineyards in other European countries. In particular, the Rioja region of Spain owes its reputation for high-quality, affordable red wines to the displaced winemakers of Bordeaux.

In an effort to establish consistent standards for all of the important aspects of wine production – including region of origin, grape varieties, minimum alcohol content and maximum vineyard yields – France enacted a series of laws, beginning in 1905 collectively known as the *appellation d'origine contrôlée* (AOC) laws. These laws guard the famous place-names of France and guarantee that wines bearing their names have met rigorous government standards. In 1963 Italy followed suit with her own set of laws – *denominazione di origine controllata* (DOC) and *denominazione di origine controllata e garantita* (DOCG), by name. With these laws, Europe set the standard for the entire wine world in legislating the integrity of wine.

Wine in the New World

The European explorers who discovered the New World were delighted to find a landscape practically smothered with grapevines. Upon closer inspection, however, the vines turned out to be unlike the Old World varieties they were familiar with. Just imagine the French Huguenots trying to make wine from the native scuppernong grape in Florida. This native variety looks more like some carnivorous plant from *Star Trek* than it does a European grapevine. The grape, twice the size of a European wine grape, grows in clusters, not bunches, on a gigantic vine capable of producing, quite literally, a ton of fruit!

Needless to say, the resulting wine bore little resemblance to Old World vines. But gradually, thanks to the gradual importation and plantation of traditional Old World vines right across the newly discovered lands, many countries began to produce wines in their own right.

In the southern part of what is now the USA and right across South America, Spanish missionaries began to cultivate vines to produce sacramental wine for the church. Grapes were grown in countries we now recognize as producers of quality wines in their own right – Chile and Argentina, for example – as well as a few that may come as a bit of a surprise. Anyone for a drop of Peruvian or a tot of Mexican, by any chance?

Further north, grapes thrived in the sunny warmth of California. Would-be wine-makers in the cooler eastern states weren't so lucky, and often resorted to 'taming' the native grapes when the more familiar strains fell prone to a range of diseases.

Missionaries were also responsible for the first vines planted in New Zealand, back in 1819, but it took the Kiwis another 150 years or so to discover that high-quality grapes could be grown in both the North and the South Islands. The Australians were quicker off the mark – the first bunches of grapes were picked in the Governor's garden in 1791, grown from vines transplanted from South Africa's Cape three years earlier.

By then, the South Africans had had a headstart of almost 150 years: the Cape Province's first vineyard was planted in 1655 by its first governor, Jan van Riebeeck. But although van Riebeeck was clearly keen on his plonk, encouraging the farmers to grow vines, the Dutch had little wine tradition and it was left to the arrival of the Huguenots, some 30 years later, to dig the roots of today's industry.

Initially, of course, these wines were often of pretty low quality and were intended for domestic consumption. But during the 20th century, improvements in transport techniques and a growing appetite for wine resulted in a growing demand for the wines of the New World, particularly in the UK. It wasn't just that the wines were here – it was also the fact that they were more affordable than ever before – and more understandable to a generation that hadn't grown up on top-class claret.

While Old World producers carried on making their blended wines and wines named after the areas were they were made (for instance, Chablis or Chianti), their New World competitors were making what are known as varietal wines, where the grape variety that goes into the wine takes pride of place on the label. You no longer needed to have a master's degree in wine snobbery to buy a decent bottle of wine – all you needed was to know that you rather liked the taste of a Chardonnay or a Merlot. So popular have these wines proved that Aussie wine-makers get the largest share of our business –

a fact the French are not happy about in the slightest.

Within the past ten years, we've seen our supermarket shelves become a United Nations of the wine world. Wander down any aisle worth its salt and you'll see wines from France, Portugal, California and Chile stacked alongside bottles from more exotic origins, such as Canada, Greece, Morocco and Uruguay. And, given the investments currently being made all around the world, don't be surprised to find a cheeky little number from China or India making its way onto the shelves within the next ten years or so.

FIRST PRIZE

CHAPTER 2

AN INTRODUCTION TO
WINE AND WINEMAKING

What Makes Wine Enjoyable?

We drink wine to stimulate our taste buds, alter our brains (via alcohol), and/or quench our thirst. If you are drinking wine to enhance your image, you need therapy, not wine. The human animal is designed to crave intellectual and physical stimulation. Stimulating the taste buds via food and beverages is a significant part of the so-called human experience.

Human taste is comprised of five basic components: sweetness, saltiness, acidity, bitterness and the recently discovered *umami* (savoury). Of major importance in both the production and enjoyment of wine is its natural acidity, the component against which the other taste components are balanced. In particular, the precise balance of acidity and sweetness – from natural sugars, 'fruity' flavours and/or alcohol – is the key factor that makes wine pleasant-tasting. Too much acidity makes a wine taste unpleasantly sharp, whereas a lack of sufficient acidity results in an uninteresting wine that is neither clean-tasting nor thirst-quenching.

Flavours are detected by different taste buds in your mouth that individually perceive the components of taste. The area most sensitive to sweetness is on the tip of the tongue, and the sensation is immediate. Taste buds that react to saltiness are on the sides of the tongue, with the acidity taste buds located toward the middle. The taste buds that detect bitterness are located at the back of the tongue, and are therefore the last to get involved with the food or beverage in your mouth. This is why people often note a bitter aftertaste when eating and drinking certain foods.

When tasting wine, a little stimulation of the bitterness-sensing taste buds is pleasant. Of course, what constitutes 'too much' varies from one wine drinker to another, and also from day to day for any individual. People's mouths vary from day to day, depending on what they ate today or yesterday, their physical health, the time of day, etc. If you burn your mouth on a hot slice of pizza, the acidity of any wine isn't going to feel good.

There are several different acids that occur naturally in wine – tartaric, malic, lactic, citric and acetic acids. Therefore, when we speak of acidity in wines, we really mean the 'acidity profile', the total and often complex acidic impression of the wine on the palate. The acidity profile and its corresponding balance of complementary components are of primary importance in white wines. Red and white wines with excessive acidity taste harsh, especially without food. Wines with too little acidity do not have an interesting taste, and their flavour doesn't linger in the mouth very long. Although red wine is typically no less acidic than white wine, the acidity profile is often less apparent in reds because red wines usually display a more complex array of flavour components than do white wines. The difference is in the skins – white wine grape skins are removed and discarded early in the winemaking process, whereas red wine grape skins are generally kept in the fermenting vats long enough to give red wine its colour, flavours and tannin.

Tannin is an important component of red wine. Have you ever bitten into a grape seed? That dry, bitter taste is tannin. In moderate amounts tannin gives red wine an added taste dimension as well as a natural preservative. Great red wines are often quite tannic in their youth; with ageing the tannin softens and lends complexity to the mature red wine. In most red wines,

tannin adds a pleasant, slightly bitter taste that is best balanced by rich fruit flavours. If you find it difficult to imagine bitterness as pleasant, think of expensive dark chocolate or rich espresso coffee; bitterness is an important part of their flavours.

Red wine with too much tannin is bitter and unpleasant, and its fruit flavours may be hidden beneath the tannins. The correct amount of tannin doesn't mask other tastes, but gives the wine a little 'grip' in the mouth and seems to hold all the flavours together. A low measure of tannin makes simple, fruity red wine more suitable for quaffing than sipping.

Generally speaking, a high level of tannin is an indication of a long shelf life, since tannin is a natural preservative.

How Wine Happens

Although winemaking has been raised to a fine art and an increasingly precise science over the last 5,000 years, it remains, in essence, a relatively simple process. Wine grapes, *Vitis vinifera*, can grow with great ease in most warm-to-temperate climates. Ripe grapes contain a solution of natural sugar and water, with more sugar than in most other fruits. Additionally, the skin of the grape is an ideal medium for the accumulation of natural yeasts, one-celled plants that consume the natural sugar and convert it to ethyl alcohol and carbon dioxide. It is as if grapes *want* to become wine. Had we not evolved into humans, it is conceivable that apes could have learned to make wine – it is that simple. Of course, in the thousands of years since this process was first observed, technology has played an ever-increasing role in winemaking.

There are many technological options available to the modern winemaker. Equipment such as crushers, de-stemmers and fermentation tanks come in so many shapes and varieties that each and every vineyard in the world might well have a unique configuration of them. However, whether the end product is red, white or pink, and whether it is cheap or expensive, there are some principles common to all winemaking.

First of all, air is the enemy. Exposure to oxygen robs wine of its fresh-tasting qualities and also encourages the activity of acetobacters, naturally occurring microbes that consume ethyl alcohol and discharge acetic acid (vinegar). It is an ironic twist of nature that just as grapes wish to become wine, wine in turn aspires to become vinegar – again, with minimal effort. The winemaker, therefore, must take care to prevent air from ruining the wine. These precautions begin in the fields at harvest time.

It is crucial that the grapes are picked and transported to the winery without prematurely splitting the skins. While hand-picking is considered the best by many, mechanical harvesting machines have been developed that can handle grape bunches with sufficient care. A judicious sprinkling of powdered sulphur dioxide (a sulphite), an effective antioxidant, is often applied to protect grapes prior to crushing.

Exposure to air is also minimized during fermentation, and nature lends a helping hand in this stage of winemaking. Carbon dioxide, which is discharged by the yeasts along with ethyl alcohol, provides a cushion of protection against the ambient air. This is especially important in the fermentation of red wine, which usually takes place in an open vat.

As a final precaution against the ill effects of exposure to air, many inexpensive wines are pasteurized – that is, heated to a high-enough temperature to kill the aceto-bacters. This is an effective way at least to delay the effects of oxidation, and it is the reason why box wines enjoy such a long shelf life after opening. Inevitably, a new wave of acetobacters will find its way into the wine and begin the process of vinegar-making if the wine is kept too long. Because pasteurization is a harsh process that prevents the long-term evolution of wine in the bottle (*some* oxidation is actually beneficial!), this process is rarely used for high-quality wines. A famous exception is Château Corton-Grancey, a *grand cru* red from France's Burgundy region.

Clarity is another goal common to all winemaking, and the brilliant transparency of both red and white wines does not come naturally. Wine is, by nature, cloudy with dead yeast and tiny particulate matter. Several processes, including fining, centrifuging, filtration, racking and cold stabilization, may be used to clarify wine.

Fining is one of the few processes in which foreign matter is introduced into the wine. Whipped egg whites have long been used as a fining agent for quality wines. Shortly after fermentation is complete, the wine is transferred to a large settling tank. When added to the tank of young, unfinished wine, the mass of whipped egg whites slowly sinks to the bottom, electrostatically attracting undesirable particles along the way. The clear wine is then drawn off, leaving the coagulated meringue at the bottom of the barrel. In addition to egg whites, other fining agents are casein (milk protein) and bentonite clay (aluminum silicate).

Centrifuging and filtration are two quick and effective methods of clarifying wine. To centrifuge wine, a container of unfinished, cloudy wine is rapidly rotated so that heavy particles are separated from the wine by centrifugal force. However, this process tends to strip wine of some desirable qualities as well, and centrifuging is being used less and less frequently for quality wines. Filtration is the simple and straight-forward process of screening out unwanted particles from the wine by passing it through layers of filter paper or synthetic fibre mesh. Though less harsh than centrifuging, there are some fine wines with the term 'unfiltered' on the label – the implication being that filtration strips wine of some desirable qualities.

Compared to fining, centrifuging and filtrating, the process of racking is a relatively passive means of clarifying wine. Racking works because unwanted particles are heavier than the wine itself and eventually sink to the bottom if the wine is left undisturbed. The clear wine may then be 'racked', that is, drawn off to another

POOF

barrel. Air is the enemy, and unwanted exposure to air during the racking process must be avoided. Red wines in particular, often held for many months in the barrel prior to bottling, may undergo multiple rackings.

Cold stabilization is a relatively harsh treatment used to clarify inexpensive wines. This process involves chilling a tank of wine almost to freezing point. At this low temperature, minerals such as potassium acid tartrate (cream of tartar) become less soluble and precipitate out as crystals. Have you ever seen 'wine crystals' on a cork? Though often mistaken for unwanted sediment, this accumulation of wine crystals is actually a good sign – it means that the wine has *not* been cold-stabilized, which would have eliminated the crystals prior to bottling.

HOW WHITE WINE PRODUCTION AND RED WINE PRODUCTION DIFFER

Although the prevention of oxidation and some process of clarification are common to all winemaking, there are fundamental differences between the production of red wine and that of white wine. In short, white wine is fermented grape juice – that is, the juice is extracted from the grapes prior to fermentation. Red wine, by contrast, is the juice of fermented grapes, which are crushed into a thick mush – the 'must' – from which the juice is extracted after fermentation. Interestingly, the finest rosés are often produced from red grapes handled like white grapes: The red grape skins, which provide color, are removed prior to fermentation, leaving only a slight blush of colour.

The differences between the production of red wine and that of white wine begin in the vineyards. Most of the classic red wine grape varieties – for example, Cabernet Sauvignon, Merlot and Syrah – thrive in climates warmer than those that are ideal for the important white-wine varieties. Full ripeness is so crucial for red-wine grapes because the essential components of quality red wine – rich fruit flavours, tannin, body and colour – develop in the grape in the final stage of ripening. Paradoxically, these grapes must not ripen too quickly. If that happens, the resulting wine often lacks depth and harmony of flavours. The longer the growing season, the more complex the wine, and a prolonged growing season that doesn't bring the grapes to full ripeness until early autumn is ideal. Although most of sunny California's vineyards are planted in the warm valleys, the finest California reds usually come from grapes grown on the cooler slopes overlooking the valleys.

High-quality red and white grapes can often grow side by side, but in general the important white varieties perform best in climates too cool for great reds. Chardonnay, Sauvignon Blanc and especially Riesling grapes tend to make uninteresting, low-acid wines in the same climates in which the great red grapes may thrive. But Chardonnay is made into the great white wine of the chilly Chablis region of France, an area whose red grapes rarely mature fully. Germany's Rieslings are among the finest wines in the world, yet German red wines are often of little more than curiosity value. Riesling, along with an increasing amount of Chardonnay, have been the only *Vitis vinifera* successfully grown in the northern USA, where winter can be brutally cold.

Although the climates in which red and white wine grapes thrive may vary, the cultivation techniques are not that different. The real differences between red and white wine production begin after harvest.

White Wine

As soon as possible after picking, white wine grapes are fed into a crushing machine that gently splits the skins. For most white wines, prolonged skin contact after crushing is not desirable, so the skins and other grape matter are quickly separated from the juice. However, in making some of the great white wines of the world the skins are allowed to remain in the juice for a day or so in order to lend additional body and character to the wine. A juicing machine uses pressurized sulphur dioxide gas to squeeze out the juice, which then goes to a settling tank, where undesirable solids such as dirt and seeds settle to the bottom. The juice might be centrifuged at this stage, but the centrifuge can remove the good with the bad. The clarified white grape juice is now ready for fermentation... well, almost.

Some doctoring of the grape juice might be deemed necessary by the winemaker. Although regulations vary around the world, adjustments in acid and sugar levels are often called for. In cooler regions, where even white-wine grape varieties struggle to achieve full ripeness, sugar may be added to the juice. This is called chaptalization. Without enough sugar, the wine might not attain the desired alcohol level. Fully ripened grapes usually ferment to an alcohol content of 12 per cent by volume. The acidity might also

be adjusted at this point. Calcium carbonate may be added to reduce acidity, and tartaric or other acids may be added to raise it. In the final analysis, the sugar and acid must be in balance at the desired levels in order to make good wine. Now fermentation may begin.

Although wild wine yeast naturally accumulates on grape skins during the growing season, almost all winemakers prefer to control fermentation and therefore introduce carefully cultivated yeast to the juice. Fermentation proceeds – slowly, it is hoped, because a rapid fermentation might raise the temperature to a level that kills the yeast. Also, the yeast itself imparts character to the wine, so a slow fermentation, with longer contact with the yeast, is desirable. Most winemakers control the temperature of the fermentation by refrigeration and recirculation. The carbon dioxide that is produced during fermentation is permitted to escape from the enclosed vat without allowing ambient air back in – yet another precaution against oxidation.

Through this process, the white grape juice has become white wine – rough, unfinished wine that still needs some tinkering, including a filtration to remove any remaining sugar and particles. Just prior to fining, the winemaker may deem it necessary to add some sweet, unfermented grape juice in which the yeasts and acetobacters have been killed. This is done to add roundness to the flavour and to take the acidic edge off a harsh-tasting wine. However, the new wine has its own way of reducing its acidity: malolactic fermentation.

This process, like alcoholic fermentation, occurs naturally but is usually controlled by the winemaker. In the spring following the harvest, warm weather activates microbes in the wine that convert malic acid into lactic acid and carbon dioxide. Malic acid, which is naturally present in apples, is sharply acidic. Lactic acid, which develops naturally in dairy products, is only half as acidic as malic acid. Thus malolactic fermentation softens a wine's acidity profile. This process can be controlled by the winemaker to such a degree that one may find in the shops clean, crisp white wines that have not undergone any malolactic fermentation; soft, fleshy white wines that have undergone full malolactic fermentation; and wines somewhere in the middle. Some wines have been known to undergo an unintended malolactic fermentation after bottling, resulting in a funny-tasting wine with an unwelcome trace of fizziness.

Up until a few decades ago, oak casks were the most economical storage vessels available. Oak imparts flavours to a wine, mainly vanilla and tannin. Because of the long history of wine storage in oak, these flavours have become accepted as basic components of wine. It is even likely that the style of certain wines, notably the Chardonnay-based white Burgundy wines, evolved in such a way that oak flavours are a necessary and expected facet of the wine's flavour; without oak, such wines might taste incomplete. Now that less expensive storage vessels are available, such as those made of stainless steel, oak flavour is an additive of sorts. In fact, some producers of inexpensive wines circumvent the great expense of oak barrels by adding oak chips to wine held in stainless-steel tanks.

Virtually all wines benefit from a resting period after fermentation and clarification. A few months of ageing, either in oak or steel, allows the flavour components in white wine to become more harmonious. A resting period in the bottle is also beneficial. An unfortunate consequence of the wine boom is that most wines are consumed long before they are at their best. Although red wines generally undergo a much more gradual evolution in the bottle than do white wines, a well-made white wine can improve for five or more years in the bottle. Chardonnays and Rieslings are known to age more gracefully than other white wines.

Red Wine

Red wine is not necessarily 'better' than white wine, but well-made red wines have more flavour components and are typically more complex than white wines. Enjoyable white wine has a prominent acidity profile counterbalanced with a hint of sweetness, restrained fruit flavours and maybe a touch of oak. That is why white wines are best served chilled – acidic beverages, such as lemonade, taste better at lower temperatures. If served warm, both lemonade and white wine are less enjoyable because the prominent acidity becomes unpleasantly sharp at higher temperatures. Although red wine may be nearly as acidic as white, red wine usually has a wider range of fruit flavours, as well as a noticeable amount of tannin, qualities best appreciated at warmer temperatures. The difference is skin deep.

Whereas most grapes contain the same greenish pulp, the skins of red-wine grapes give red wine its colour, tannin and assorted fruit flavours. So white grape skins, which add little to white wine, are removed early in the winemaking process, but red grape skins are kept in the fermenting vat for an extended period of time. It is thus necessary to remove the stalks from red wine grapes as they are crushed, so the stalks do not give excessive tannin to the wine. Thus a combination crusher/de-stemmer is used to prepare red grapes for fermentation rather than the simple crusher used for white grapes.

The image of half-naked men stamping grapes in an open vat is familiar to many. Although technology has replaced the human foot in most corners of the wine world, the open vat is still occasionally used in some parts of the world, but these days most are kept closed. The reason open vats were used in the past is because grape skins tend to rise to the top of the fermenting must, forming a 'cap' on top of the juice. In order to extract the desirable qualities from the skins, this cap must be continuously mixed back into the juice. This may be accomplished by pumping juice from the bottom of the barrel over the cap (called 'pumping over'), or by manually punching the cap back into the juice with a special paddle (called 'punched cap fermentation'). It is said that a punched-cap wine reflects the physical character of the winemaker – a big, strong winemaker will force more extract from the skins, resulting in a big, strong wine. As in white wine production, temperature control is important, although red wines benefit from a fermentation temperature a little higher than that which is ideal for whites.

After fermentation is complete, perhaps one to three weeks later, the new wine is drawn from the vat. This first run of juice, called 'free-run' juice, comes forth voluntarily; forcibly squeezing the juice from the must would extract excessive tannin. Only after the free-run juice is removed is the remaining must squeezed, yielding 'press wine', a portion of which might be blended with the free-run juice in order to adjust the tannin level carefully. The wine is then clarified in much the same manner as white wine and transferred to ageing barrels, where it can slowly mature. Racking may be necessary every few months if the wine is held in the cellar for a length of time. Prolonged barrel ageing before bottling is desirable for most types of red wine, since the broad array of flavour components generally needs more time to harmonize in red wines than in white wines.

The Final Stages

Many wines, both red and white, are blends of several different grapes. Even in the case of wines made entirely from one variety, a winemaker may blend different 'lots' (separate barrels) of wine in order to make the best possible wine. The 'recipe' for such wines may vary from year to year, depending on the characteristics of the available lots in a given vintage.

When wine is deemed ready for release, it is transferred to bottles in a mechanized process notable for its sanitation. Once again, air is the enemy, and care is taken not to allow its contact with the wine during bottling. Germs and impurities are also mortal enemies, and the bottling process is often the most highly mechanized step in the entire operation, as sparkling-clean bottles are filled, corked, capped and labelled with minimal human contact. For the finest wines, it is often advantageous for the winery to then keep the bottles in storage for two or more years. This makes for better wine when it finally reaches the shop, and in many cases the value of the wine will also have increased greatly during its slumber.

Components of Wine

Water

Wine is mostly water – not added water, but water gathered naturally in the grapes. Wine has long been consumed with food in regions where the local water is not reliably pure and safe. Wine may be described as 'watery' when the other components, particularly acids, seem too understated.

Alcohol

Wine is ethyl alcohol (C_2H_5OH), 9–15 per cent by volume. Fortified wine is usually 18–20 per cent. Alcohol is an important flavour component – compare vodka to water if you don't think alcohol has flavour.

Tannin

This is a family of complex organic compounds extracted mainly from the grape skins (and thus a characteristic of red wines more than whites). Oak barrels also infuse wine with a touch of tannin. You can taste tannin when you bite into a grape seed. A wine with excessive tannin tastes like biting into a woolly jumper. Tannin acts as a natural preservative, affording some wines the opportunity to improve with age. A moderate level of tannin also gives wine an added flavour dimension, albeit one that is often unpleasant to newer consumers of wine.

Fruit

The beauty of the noblest grape varieties, both red and white, is their ability to produce wine with a complex aroma of fruits other than grapes, particularly when young. Each noble variety of grape has its own set of typical fruit associations. During the winemaking process, the interaction of organic acids and alcohol forms compounds that imitate the aroma of other fruits.

Acid

There are several types of acid in wine. Together they form the wine's 'acidity profile', which is balanced by sweet components. Tartaric, malic and citric acids naturally form in grapes. After fermentation the malic acid may be converted to lactic acid (malolactic fermentation) through bacterial activity. The alcohol in wine may be converted to acetic acid (vinegar) by acetobacters, another bacteria to be found in wine.

Sugar

Not all the natural fruit sugar in grapes is completely fermented. The residual sugar in dry wine is usually undetectable, but sweetness becomes noticeable in wines approaching 1 per cent residual sugar.

Glycerine

This is the component that gives wines a desirable degree of viscosity (thickness). It is a complex alcohol, a by-product of the fermentation process.

Carbon Dioxide

This gas is produced during fermentation, and it is allowed to escape in the production of table wines. However, intentionally or not, some dissolved CO_2 may remain in the wine, giving a slight 'fizz' to it. This can be a good thing in, say, an otherwise uninteresting rosé. Sometimes a minor second fermentation takes place after bottling, and the wine is ruined by the undesirable prickle. Sometimes a trace of fizz thus formed goes away with time. CO_2 is, of course, a very important component of sparkling wines.

Oak

Once a necessity, now an option, oak treatment – barrel fermenting; barrel ageing; new oak or old, charred oak; French, American or Slavic oak; oak chips – adds a taste component to wine. Vanilla and tannin are two flavours given to wine by oak. Judicious use of oak complements the other components; too much oak can overpower the fruit. Just as a chef might try to dress up a mediocre fillet of fish with an interesting sauce, a winemaker might decide to dress up an everyday, ordinary vat of Chardonnay with heavy-handed oak treatment.

These components – water, alcohol, tannins, fruit esters, acidity, sweetness, glycerine, carbon dioxide and oak – are the ingredients that comprise wine as a finished product. It is up to the winemaker who manages the process from vineyard to bottle to manipulate these components as he or she desires. For example, a gentle squeezing of the grapes extracts significantly less tannin than a powerful crushing. Acidity may be lowered by encouraging a malolactic fermentation, the process by which malic acid ('apple acid') becomes lactic acid ('milk acid'), and the wine consequently becomes less acidic.

Variety, Soil, Weather and Winemaking Technique

There are five fundamental factors that endow wine with its characteristics: grape variety, soil, weather and viticultural and-winemaking technique. Most winemakers would agree that luck is the sixth factor, since the art of winemaking is never completely subject to scientific controls.

GRAPE VARIETY

Think of white wines as cats and red wines as dogs. There are many different breeds of each, just as there are many types of grapes within the species *Vitis vinifera*. Each breed of dog or cat has unique identifiying characteristics. Just as Golden Retrievers typically have long, orange-brown fur, Cabernet Sauvignon–based wines tend to display aromas of blackcurrants, green pepper and chocolate. We use the term 'varietally correct' to describe wines whose qualities are consistent with their predominant grape variety. Some great wines, notably the whites of Alsace (France), are sometimes more identifiable for their region of origin than for their grape variety. However, there are some generally accepted varietal characteristics associated with the popular grape varieties. Here are two examples.

Cabernet Sauvignon
Aromas: blackcurrants, green pepper, chocolate, mint; jammy fruit when young, cedar and tobacco with age
Colour: deep purple/red
Flavours: moderate acidity balanced by fruit flavours, firm tannin, long progression of flavours on the palate.

Sauvignon Blanc
Aromas: cut grass or nettles, gooseberries and asparagus in cooler climates, warmer climate examples often have tropical fruit, particularly passion fruit
Colour: pale gold, sometimes greenish
Flavours: crisp, prominent acidity, herbaceous as much as fruity flavours.

It would be a boring world of wine if all Cabernet Sauvignons and all Sauvignon Blancs were identical. That there are so many different styles of each is testimony to the importance of the other three factors. It is really a 'nature vs nurture' debate. Grape varieties have inherent characteristics that can be altered or reinterpreted by the soil, the weather and the winemaker's technique.

TERROIR

The sad fact is that 'terroir', a French term, cannot be translated directly into English. The reason this lack of translatability is so unfortunate is that it's a key word in the wine world. Generally speaking, it's understood to mean the combination of factors that influence the wines produced by any vine –factors, that is, other than those that are a result of human interaction with the plants or their fruit. By and large, terroir comes down to the total natural environment a grape is grown in, which comes down to three key factors.

First there's the soil that the vines grow in – for instance, soil can be chalky, as it is in Champagne; slatey, as it is in Germany's

Mosel, or full of pebbles, as it is in the Médoc area of Bordeaux. Then you have to take into account the macroclimate of any region: how much rain falls each year? How hot does it get in summer? Finally there's the microclimate, the particular weather conditions in any given vineyard – vines planted on south-facing slopes in the northern hemisphere get more sun than vines planted on north-facing slopes, for instance.

All of these factors combine together to create a sense of place, a 'terroir', which many experts can taste in the finished wines. And it's this that the experts get particularly worked up about – whether you put it down to tradition or whether you chalk it up to science or canny marketing, there's no doubt that grapes grown in some parts of the world develop a particular character you wouldn't find anywhere else. In the past, the concept of terroir was seen to have more importance in the Old World, where particular styles of wines have been associated with particular landscapes for centuries. These days, however, the producers of the New World are on the hunt for their own terroirs, with increasing success.

THE SOIL IN WHICH GRAPES GROW

The rich, low-lying valley floors and river deltas where so many crops thrive are not the best locations for growing wine grapes. The grapevine grows well in rocky hillsides where no other crops will and seems to prefer gravel to earth. Abundant water, so vital to other crops, can be anathema to wine grapes. The vine will dig deep for its water, sometimes as much as 3m down. Irrigation is a pretty common practice in the New World, but is seldom found in the Old World.

California wineries tend to emphasize grape variety and weather, whereas the French stress the importance of the geographical region of origin. Soil, they believe, is a vital part of terroir,. and helps to give wine its distinctive character. The established French wine-growing estates are not permitted to bring soil from elsewhere into their vineyards. Ironically, the soil in the Romanée-Conti estate, perhaps the most highly esteemed parcel of vines in France, was imported from France's Saône River banks 200 years ago!

Each of the major wine regions of France has unique soil characteristics. For instance, the Graves subregion of Bordeaux gets its name from the notably gravelly soil deposited along the Garonne River by the most recent glacial advance. The red wines of the Graves are among the most powerfully flavoured reds of Bordeaux, and the crisp, acidic whites are among the finest white wines in the world. The *goût de terroir* is evident in both.

Limestone and chalk are common components of the soil in which Chardonnay performs well. Such soil is found in the Champagne region and the Burgundy subregions of Chablis and the Côte de Beaune. The Gamay grape is not highly regarded in the heart of Burgundy, where Pinot Noir holds court as king of the red grapes. However, south of Burgundy proper is the Beaujolais subregion, where the soil is especially rich in granite. In this medium, the otherwise lowly Gamay produces the fruity red wines of Beaujolais. The soil of Châteauneuf-du-Pape in the southern Rhône valley is notable for its large white rocks that retain and reflect heat toward the vines. As a result, the red grapes grown there – Grenache, Syrah and others – achieve a degree of ripeness not found elsewhere in France, and the wines from this area are matchingly bold.

Weather

Soil is the most constant factor in winemaking; the mineral composition of a vineyard barely changes in a human lifespan. Although the weather is different in every growing season, general trends such as annual rainfall and temperature ranges may be somewhat constant. Thus the vineyard locations in France were probably chosen for their climate as well as their soil.

Geographically, soil and long-term weather trends are inextricably linked. Yet wine grapes grow for only about six months. The weather in a given growing season, though somewhat predictable (based on historical trends), is the reason that we have good years and bad years for wine. So soil is one-half of the 'nurturing' process, and weather is the other half.

New vineyard sites are usually selected for their 'microclimate', the weather trends in the vineyard plot itself. In the hilly regions where the grapes are grown, the weather can vary from one corner of the fields to the other. Viticulturalists, especially those in the New World, have made an obsession of seeking the ideal climate (both macro and micro) for growing grapes.

THE VINEYARD YEAR

Spring

It is best that early springtime remain cool, with no early heat waves. Otherwise, leaf buds might prematurely develop, only to be killed by a cold night's frost. This period is one of the few opportune times for abundant rain, which becomes less desirable as the growing season progresses. Grape leaves unfurl in late April, followed by flower buds in late May. (Of course, we are referring to the Northern Hemisphere, where the vast majority of wine is produced. The vineyards of the Southern Hemisphere – in Australia, South Africa, New Zealand and South America – harvest six months earlier.) Hail, obviously, is a dreaded enemy of the vine during the critical month-long flowering. High winds and heavy downpours can also interfere with pollination during this period.

Summer

After the bees have completed their work of pollination, the grapes themselves require about three months to ripen completely. An occasional gentle rain is welcome in early summer, as it helps to fill the grapes with liquid to plump them up to the proper size. A drought year would result in small grapes with a high skin-to-pulp ratio, which in turn would make it a tannic, intensely flavoured wine. As the grapes mature, dry and cool breezes are a blessing because they help to keep the grapes free of disease and to slow the ripening process. Grapes that ripen too rapidly tend to develop less flavour. As during the flowering stage, hail is a dreaded summertime enemy.

Autumn

September is a critical month. A warm and dry September can rescue a terrible vintage, and a cold and rainy September is sure to ruin a previously perfect growing season.

All of the grapes in a vineyard do not ripen simultaneously – a good thing! If they did, it would be impossible to pick and crush them simultaneously. A perfect September would be without rain while the pickers make pass after pass through the rows of vines, picking only the grapes at the exact point of ripeness. An impending rainstorm leaves a vineyard manager with a difficult choice – either to pick the grapes a few days shy of perfect ripeness, or alternatively to pick rain-swollen grapes after the storm and run the risk of rot.

After the harvest is complete, the weather can still be a factor. Cool weather is welcome during the fermenting period, especially for small wineries that don't have sophisticated, temperature-controlled fermenting tanks. The cool drafts around the tanks help to prolong the fermenting process and prevent overheating. In Germany and Canada, a timely winter freeze makes *eiswein* (ice wine) possible. When crushed, the frozen grapes yield a nectar of incredible richness.

Phylloxera

Phylloxera is a disease that attacks and destroys the roots of *Vitis vinifera* grapevines. In the 1800s, this disease nearly wiped out most of the vineyards of Europe. Fortunately, the wine grapes indigenous to North America, *Vitis labrusca*, were resistant to *phylloxera*. Scientists in Europe were able to graft *vinifera* vines to the roots of *labrusca* vines. Not only did this work, but the characteristics of the individual *vinifera* grapes were not compromised by foreign roots.

Phylloxera helped spread the art of winemaking throughout the world by forcing French winemakers to leave France for *phylloxera*-free pastures. Many winemakers from Bordeaux brought their expertise to the Rioja region of Spain when their own vineyards were destroyed.

Like germs that evolve into new forms that are resistant to conventional treatments, new strains of *phylloxera* have emerged to which the native American rootstock is not resistant. *Phylloxera* destroyed many of the California vines in 1996. This will cause the price of many California wines to continue to increase into the 21st century. Undoubtedly, the wine industry will team up with science and respond to the latest strain of *phylloxera* with another genetically engineered solution.

WINEMAKING TECHNIQUE

The skill of the winemaker is admirably utilized in solving problems associated with less than ideal weather, and the winemaker's ingenuity is often required early in the growing season. A frost following an early warm spell could well destroy the first vine buds, but a clever sprinkling of mist on the vines covers them with a protective shield of ice, which paradoxically insulates them from colder, more harmful temperatures.

Frequent rainfall later in the season invites grape rot of various sorts, which can be combatted with a sensible use of chemicals. Each and every vintage will yield grapes of unique character, and it is the task of the winemaker to make the best use of each harvest. This is undoubtedly a delightful task after an ideal growing season; in the real world, however, there are usually problems to be overcome.

A cold, damp summer – very rare in California and Australia, but common enough in France and Germany – is not conducive to full ripeness. Under-ripe grapes, both red and white, usually lack sufficient sugar to ferment to the desired alcoholic strength. The addition of sugar prior to fermentation is called chaptal-ization; it is permitted in some European countries, but is unnecessary in California and other New World regions. In addition, under-ripe red grapes usually lack the concentration of desirable components in the skin-pigment, tannin and fruit flavour. A skilled winemaker might compensate for this deficiency by allowing the skins to macerate in the juice for a longer time than is usual.

After fermentation it may be desirable to adjust the acidity of the wine. The addition of calcium carbonate will soften the acidity associated with under-ripeness, whereas natural wine acids (tartaric, malic, etc.) may be added to sharpen a flaccid, over-ripe wine.

With one eye on quality and the other on cost, the winemaker has to make many choices: stainless steel or oak? New oak or old oak? Oak costs money; will the wine be worth it? How much press wine should be blended back into a wine made from free-run juice? Ideally, in making these and other choices, the winemaker brings out the best in the grapes, and from them crafts a wine that reflects the hereditary qualities of the grape variety and the unique composition of the soil, and addresses any problems caused by the weather.

CHAPTER 3

QUALITY ISSUES: HOW TO
TELL GOOD WINE FROM
BETTER TO BEST

The winemaker, part artist and part scientist, manages the winemaking process from vineyard to bottle. There are variables at every step of the way, and it is here that the relationship between the quality of wine and the cost of producing it is clearly seen.

Let's look at the grapes. There are mediocre grapes, picked, perhaps, from very young vines growing in regions too warm or too cold for that particular variety. Maybe they were picked a few days too early to avoid a predicted thunderstorm. Or maybe they were picked after the storm and their rich fruit was diluted by an infusion of water.

Mediocre grapes in the hands of a skilled winemaker can make enjoyable, pleasant wines, priced for everyday drinking. These wines may even constitute a bargain. But they can *never* be great wine, any more than an expertly driven Ford Focus can win the Monaco Grand Prix'.

Then there are good grapes, well grown in good regions under favorable conditions. These might be blended with lesser grapes to produce a decent wine at a particular price and quantity. Or they may be used alone to make a higher quality wine.

Great grapes, carefully tended to maturity in well-known vineyards, command the highest price and produce the most expensive wines. The labels on these bottles might proudly display the name of the vineyard.

Now grapes, whether purchased on the market or picked from the winery's own acres, must be crushed. The cheapest way is to press the grapes along with the leaves, stems and whatever else has been picked by the machines (used because it's cheaper than hand-picking) and squeeze them until no more liquid remains. This extracts the most juice, of course, but it draws harsh tannins from the grapes as well. The most expensive method is to virtually let the grapes crush themselves with their own weight. The resulting 'free-run juice' is prized and accordingly expensive. Again, wine from each process can be blended or not – choices must be made.

Other choices must also be made – such as new oak barrels versus old (new oak imparts more oak flavour, and is often considered to be more prestigious), and barrel or steel-vat fermentation. Such decisions are made with one eye on quality and the other on cost. Each of these components contributes to the broad spectrum of wines costing from £3 to £500 per bottle.

The Quality Spectrum

CATEGORY 1: BOX WINES ((£2–5 PER 750ML)

These wines are named for the boxes they're sold in (which usually contain 3 litres). The bag inside the carton is full of wine that can be dispensed with the turn of a tap. Often bought for parties, wine boxes are also popular with those who just fancy the occasional glass in the evening. Thanks to the way the bags are sealed, the wine inside will last a week or two before deteriorating.

The downside, of course, is that these wines are often made from less expensive grapes and are designed for early drinking, so they're not ideal tippling material for wine buffs. Having said that, these wines tend to be inexpensive but good-tasting – two qualities in any beverage. In fact, these wines can be excellent value when the occasion calls for a simple wine.

CATEGORY 2: FIGHTING WINES (£3–6 PER 750ML)

Public perception says that the best value in this price range comes from the varietal wines of the New World, but there are plenty of decent European varietal and *appellation contrôlée* wines in the shops if you know what to look for.

As this is the price most of us pay for a regular bottle of wine, there's fierce competition between the major retailers to make sure there's plenty of choice and quality on the shelves. You're likely to find bargains on one brand or another due to price wars, and deep deals on high-quantity purchases at the wholesale level. True, you won't get the very best Chardonnay or Rioja (or whatever tickles your fancy) at this kind of price, but even if the wines aren't great, that doesn't mean they won't taste good.

CATEGORY 3: MID-RANGE WINES (£6–14 PER 750ML)

At this kind of price, wines can either be seen as being the best bargains in the wine world or a huge waste of money – depending on your perspective and the kind of choices you make when you're in a wine shop.

If you're hoping to buy a bottle of classy Bordeaux red, for instance, your search had better start at the top end of the price range – and even then, you have to be pretty picky about what you buy. On the other hand, if you're tempted to purchase a Chilean or South African Cabernet blend for a tenner instead, the chances are you'll end up with a bottle of something fairly special. You'll also pay far more for a really good bottle of white Burgundy than you would for, say, a really good bottle of Australian Chardonnay.

While certain kinds of wine – and certain wine-growing regions or wine producers – are sold at a premium because of their history, their prestige or their sheer marketing skills, there's great value in this section of the market. To take advantage of this, however, you either need to know a little bit about wine or find a wine retailer you can really trust. Don't be afraid to ask for advice – wine buffs are usually keen to share their knowledge.

CATEGORY 4: HAND-CRAFTED, PREMIUM WINES (£12–SKYWARDS PER 750ML)

'Hand-crafted' refers to wines made by small ('boutique') wineries where the winemaker enjoys a close, 'hands-on} relationship with the wine throughout the winemaking process. Production is typically small, and a producer of hand-crafted varietals usually doesn't mind if they sell out of wine in a given year. In contrast, volume-oriented producers usually have stockholders to satisfy, and selling out of wine would present a business problem. Such wineries have been known to purchase bulk, unfinished wine, even from other countries, and blend, bottle and sell it under their own label.

Hand-crafted wines also differ from those from large producers in terms of consistency from year to year. Whereas the large producer is inclined to strive for a uniform product from each vintage, hand-crafted wines may vary from one vintage to the next because the wine reflects the idiosyncracies of each vintage.

Vintages

Because wine is an agricultural product that can keep for several years, most quality wines give the year of harvest on the label. Yet the vintage date is a frequently misunderstood piece of information. The year of harvest tells you two things: how old the wine is, and, because climate conditions vary from year to year, whether or not the wine was produced in a 'good year'. But a 'good' year can be many things: an abundant harvest, a high-quality harvest, or both. Growing conditions might have been excellent in one area but below average in a neighbouring area; that's why we call them *micro*climates. Also, growing conditions might have been terrific for one grape variety but not another.

The vintage date, especially for inexpensive wines, can serve as a 'freshness date'. Most white and rosé wines are best drunk before their second or third birthday. Even inexpensive red wines are made to be consumed straight away, rather than aged for several years. It is a truism yet to be refuted that red wine is either enjoyable in its youth or enjoyable in full maturity, but not both. Great Chardonnays, especially those from Burgundy, and great Rieslings can improve for several years in the bottle, as can sweet dessert wines. Apart from a very few exceptions, younger is probably better for inexpensive wines.

The year 1964 was a split-personality year in Bordeaux. In Pomesol and Saint Emilion, where the earlier ripening Merlot grape predominates, the wines were outstanding. However, across the river in Medoc and Graves, heavy rains fell before the Cabernet Sauvignon was harvested, and the Cabernet Sauvignon-based wines from these districts were rather thin. It is likewise true elsewhere in the world that the quality of a vintage may vary somewhat from one microclimate to another and from one grape variety to another.

The New World, especially the warmer countries, have remarkably consistent growing weather, and 'bad years' just don't seem to happen. Some years, however, are better than others.

So, unless you are shopping for expensive wine of the 'vintage-sensitive' type ,– Piedmontese and Tuscan red wines from Italy, Red Bordeaux, or Red and White Burgundy – do not place too much stock in the vintage date. Do use the vintage date to make sure that the wine you are buying is still young enough to enjoy as it was intended to be.

The Price Components of Expensive Wines

An expensive wine doesn't start out like ordinary wine. By this we mean that it isn't just discovered, nor does it develop by chance. It is expensive to make, and it is made to be expensive.

The best grapes grow in the best vineyards. The best vineyards don't have the most fertile soil, but they do have the best soil for growing wine grapes. These soils pass on elements of mineral flavour to the grapes and thus to the wine. These vineyards also have good climates for growing wine grapes. The concept of microclimate is very big in the wine world. The amount of sun and cooling breezes can vary from acre to acre in areas with hilly terrain.

These differences contribute to the differences in grape flavours. The better the vineyard, the more expensive the land. Vineyards worthy of individual recognition are few in number, so the cost associated with a limited resource in demand certainly comes into play. Unlike the contrived scarcity of diamonds, the scarcity of top vineyard acreage is quite real.

In addition to the vineyard factor is the vine factor. Older vines produce fewer but better grapes. So it is more expensive to have older vines in the ground because they yield fewer bottles. Some wine labels that claim old vines are stretching the truth. There is no accepted standard as to just what constitutes 'old vine'.

All grape juice isn't created equal. The best wines are made from the best juice. This juice costs more than lesser juice, especially when it is bought on the open market. Free-run juices come from grapes that are lightly crushed or are allowed to crush themselves under their own weight. Often grapes whose best juice has been drained off are then more thoroughly crushed. That juice is used for lesser wines.

The top juice is often put into the best oak barrels that money can buy – made from French oak. A new oak barrel can add a few pounds to the cost of producing each bottle of wine from that barrel. After the best juice is allowed to ferment and/or age in the best barrels, the winemaker comes along and chooses the best of the best to be his top wine. The rest of the best will probably become the second-string wine, which is still going to be very good and quite expensive, but not the best.

Many top wines are crafted to be aged many years to bring out the best a grape has to offer. This cellar ageing in a barrel or a bottle certainly doesn't help cash flow. This, therefore, is another factor in pricing.

Top wines from top winemakers have a loyal following who support the pricing of these wines. If the quality falls off, then these winemakers lose the necessary buyers. They can't afford to cut quality, even if it means producing far fewer bottles of these expensive wines in an off year. Some of these top wines may not be produced at all in some years, yet much of the costof production is still incurred.

£18–30 Bottles of Wine Worth Buying and Worth Saving

1. *Champagne on sale.* Champagnes are often discounted by as much as 20 per cent. If you like Champagne, you may want to splurge on a £30 bottle marked down.
2. *White Burgundy.* There are some wonderful and ageworthy French Chardonnays. If you like to have good Chardonnay with good food, these are worth it.
3. *Riesling from Alsace, France.* Bottles in this price range will make you realize what the Riesling fuss is all about. Trimbach and Hugel are two of the top producers.
4. *Dessert Wines from Germany or France.* Dessert wines aren't for everyone, but if they are for you, then try a half bottle of German dessert wine or a Sauternes from France for £25.
5. *Super-Tuscans.* These blends of Sangiovese and Cabernet Sauvignon from Italy can be aged for a long time. If you like a big mouthful of red wine, and you also like some subtlety and complexity, then you'll like these reds.
6. *Nebbiolo-based Piedmont wines.* Also worth the money in this price range, these wines are fairly big reds and are terrific with Northern Italian cuisine.
7. *Châteauneuf-du-Pape red wines.* These can be made from any or all of 13 wine grape varieties. French quality really shows in the finest examples.
8. *Good-quality Cru Bourgeois wines from Bordeaux.* At these kinds of prices, you can expect to get a very good bottle of wine indeed. Go to a specialist merchant and get some in-depth advice before buying.
9. *Vintage Port.* These are a treat, especially during the colder months. Dow and Croft are two excellent producers. Vintage Port is available in half and full bottles.

Why Expensive Wines Are Worth It to Some People

If you've ever been to a good wine shop, you probably have looked at the expensive wines and wondered a few things. The biggest puzzle to you might be why on earth anyone would spend hundreds of pounds for a bottle of wine.

Getting a wine neophyte to understand this practice is like trying to get an atheist to believe in God. It takes a leap of faith. If you have never tasted a good £15 bottle, the leap to a £75 bottle is gigantic. Think of it as listening to a symphony orchestra performance in person versus listening to the same music on your home stereo. Going from a £7 bottle to a £15 bottle is like buying better speakers for your stereo. When you get to a certain level of wine quality, buying a great wine becomes like buying tickets to a live performance.

However, just because the music sounds better doesn't mean you will enjoy it any more. The same is true for wine. Just because you are drinking a better wine, it doesn't mean you are going to enjoy the wine-drinking experience more. If you love music, you know that just being able to listen to your favourite song on any music system can be one of life's most enjoyable experiences.

There are a lot of expectations when one goes to the symphony, and there are a lot of expectations when one pulls the cork on a £75 bottle of wine. It is hard to enjoy anything in life if you aren't relaxed, receptive and prepared to enjoy it to the fullest.

Now that we all feel good about not being able to justify spending £75 on a bottle of wine, let's talk about such precious bottles.

In April 1984 we sat in a £140-per-month student flat and drank a £120 bottle of wine. It was La Tache 1978, a Pinot Noir from France's Burgundy region.

Was this wine worth the money? Wine like this is a luxury item. Six £20 bottles may make more sense to you. Maybe six £7 bottles and a great new spring jacket would be the best use for your £120. But we both enjoyed that bottle more than any other bottle of wine we have ever had. Two factors were what made this wine-drinking experience so phenomenal. (Actually three, if you count the fact that neither of us had to pay for the wine.)

The first factor was the startling evolution of the wine during the 60 minutes from the time we opened the bottle until the last delicious mouthful. Upon opening the bottle, the wine tasted quite harsh, as if it had gone bad in the bottle. But after five minutes the flavours snapped into focus. It seemed that the flavours, ever wonderful, changed dramatically every ten minutes or so. The experience in its entirety was like tasting five or six very good wines.

The second factor was the flavour (or flavours!) of the wine itself. A gentle framework of soft tannins with an overlay of a fleshy, mouthfilling, glycerine body supported a palette of nuances – raspberry, cherry, smoke, coffee and soil, among others. And the flavours lingered in the mouth.

Good wines have structure (firmness without harshness), balanced components (so the wine isn't 'too' anything), complexity in the mouth (so it thoroughly stimulates the taste buds on both a sensual and an intellectual level), and body (not too thick, not too thin) – and they taste good. A great wine does all of these things, but it is the level of balanced complexity in its flavours and components that puts it into a different league, a league most people will never know exists (and may not ever care to know).

Sticking with the music analogy, let's take a shot at this complexity thing. Think of the components of a good wine as if they were the instruments in a six-piece ensemble.

Maybe you can pick out the violin, the cello and the other instruments while you listen to and enjoy the music, both as a total entity and as six individual entities.

When you have a symphony orchestra, you up the ante. Rather than one violin, there are many violins. This gives the music a fuller sound, and it adds a thickness to it. It's like going from a two-dimensional world to a three-dimensional world. The violin section plays as one, yet the sound is quite different from that of a single violin. It has an underlying richness. It's the difference between a square and a cube. That is why large orchestras exist. A great wine is like a great orchestra, with its components having a thickness of dimension – a thickness that can be better savoured than described.

Wine and the Internet

The Internet is a great resource for people who have an interest in wine. Why? Because in addition to the advertisements from various producers of wine, there is an amazing amount of free, specific and accurate information.

Web pages come and go, but it looks like www.winevin.com, a computer industry Web site award winner, will be around for a while. This is a good place to start in your on-line wine odyssey.

The Internet may become the first place the wine industry ever seriously attempts to target younger adults. The Internet is cheap, hip and unstuffy – adjectives people don't usually use to describe the wine world.

We don't recommend that you order wine on-line and have it shipped, because of the cost of shipping and the uncertainties of temperature and handling of your wine. You may also encounter legal consequences if the wine is shipped across boundaries.

What you can do is to find a review of a good wine on-line, and then go out and get it. If you want a good wine from Zimbabwe, however, you may want to risk the shipping and handling consequences rather than spend the time trying to track down such a wine in the real world.

CHAPTER 4

VARIETAL WINES, GRAPE BY GRAPE

Wine is made from grapes unless otherwise labelled as pear

wine, blueberry wine, etc. Grape varieties vary greatly in colour and character as well as in winemaking potential. Although there are many species of grapes, most of the world's wines come from the *Vitis vinifera* family, the classic European grape family.

The *vinifera* family of grapes, which come in red, black and green varieties, is used to make the vast majority of the world's wine. It is believed that these grapes originated in Asia Minor. The wine world has a term for a small subset of the *vinifera* family that produces the world's top wines: noble grapes. Cabernet Sauvignon, Pinot Noir, Merlot, Syrah, Sangiovese and Nebbiolo are some of the noble red grapes. Riesling, Chardonnay and Sauvignon Blanc are among the noble white grapes.

Varietal wines—those labeled and sold according to the grape variety from which they are made – must meet government-determined minimum varietal percentages, which vary from country to country. This is the minimum percentage of a wine that must be made from the grape variety under which it is being sold. Although your bottle says Chardonnay, there is a good chance that juices from other grapes are also in the bottle. These minor-percentage grapes are not usually credited on the bottle.

Varietal Correctness

Wine grapes have certain signature characteristics. Body, flavors, and textures are the most obvious. If you buy an inferior wine made from inferior grapes, you will not be able to recognize the grape because its signature characteristics are missing. When you drink the following wines, have your tongue and nose on the lookout for their signature flavor characteristics:

Cabernet Sauvignon: Blackcurrants, green peppers, chocolate, mint, cedar
Merlot: Plums, blackberries, spice, chocolate, green peppers
Pinot Noir: Cherries, rasberries, strawberries, game, rotting vegetation
Zinfandel: Berries, black pepper
Gamay: Strawberries, cherries, bubble gum, bananas
Chardonnay: Melon, grapefruit, pineapples, butter, toast, vanilla, nuts
Gewürztraminer: Lychee nuts, rose petals, spices
Semillon: Citrus, lime, honey, sweet marmalade

Cabernet Sauvignon

Main growing regions: Bordeaux (France), Australia,
California (USA), Chile, South Africa and Tuscany (Italy)
Aromas and flavours: Blackcurrants, green peppers, chocolate, mint and cedar
Acidity: Moderate
Tannin: Moderate to prominent
Body: Moderate to full
Major mixing partners: Merlot (Bordeaux),
Shiraz (Australia), Sangiovese (Tuscany)

Cabernet Sauvignon is indeed a noble variety. Although its precise origins are unknown, Cabernet Sauvignon first became note-worthy as a grape variety in Bordeaux in the late 1700s. Today this variety is at or near the top of every connoisseur's great red varietal list. Appearing either alone or in combination with other varietals, Cabernet Sauvignon generally makes rich, tannic wines capable of com-manding high prices. The most expensive and well made of these tend to need a few years of ageing in order to openly display their fine qualities – multiple layers of fruit flavours and a smooth but firm tannic structure. Typical tasting comments on young Cabernets usually praise the blackcurrant, green pepper, chocolate and spice flavours. With its forthright fruit flavours, Cabernet Sauvignon benefits from contact with new oak, which lends balance and complexity.

There are several exquisite versions of Cabernet Sauvignon from the New World, some of which (particularly those from California) fetch astronomical prices. Many top New World pro-ducers have begun to combine Cabernet Sauvignon with other grapes offering complementary flavours.

As a blending grape, Cabernet Sauvignon successfully shares a bottle with Syrah (Shiraz) in wines from Australia, and with Sangiovese in 'super-Tuscan' wines from Italy. In Bordeaux, Cabernet Sauvignon is usually blended with a combination of Merlot, Cabernet Franc (a relative) and Petit Verdot. This Bordeaux blend has found favour across the New World, too, with certain regional accents. In Chile, for instance, Cabernet Sauvignon is often blended with Carmenère, a relative of Merlot, that used to thrive in Bordeaux's vineyards but is now more commonly found in South America. In the USA, Bordeaux-style blends are often labelled 'Meritage', a term coined in California to distinguish these fine blended wines from ordinary table wines.

In any wine shop one might find varietal Cabernet Sauvignon from Chile, Australia, the USA, Italy, Spain, France or South Africa, among others. Expensive as great Cabernet Sauvignon can be, the bargains are out there. Look for varietal wines from the southwest of France (labelled *vin du pays d'oc* or Languedoc) and also from Chile. The Cabernet/Shiraz blends from Australia are often excellent value. The most sought-after versions of Cabernet Sauvignon come from several countries.

There are a handful of ultra-expensive premium Cabernet Sauvignons and Meritage wines from California's Napa Valley, among which you'll find names like Screaming Eagle, Caymus Special selection, Heitz Cellar Martha's Vineyard and Stag's Leap Cask 23. From Penfolds in Australia comes the noteworthy Cabernet Sauvignon Bin 707. Winemakers Miguel Torres and Jean Leon are producing high-quality Cabernet Sauvignon in the Penedés region of northeastern Spain, and the iconoclastic

Good Cabernet Sauvignon in Ascending Order of Price

1. Montes Alpha Cabernet Sauvignon (Chile)
2. Santa Rita Floresta Cabernet Sauvignon (Chile)
3. Cape Mentelle Cabernet Sauvignon (Western Australia)
4. Katnook Coonawarra Cabernet Sauvignon (South Australia)
5. Shafer Cabernet Sauvignon (California, USA)

winemaker Gaston Hochar planted Cabernet Sauvignon in Lebanon, where it is blended with Syrah and Cinsault in his famous Château Musar wine. Chile has also hit the heights with Santa Rita's Floresta Cabernet Sauvignon and Seña, a joint enture between Errazuriz and California's Mondavi winery

It is in the Bordeaux subregions of Médoc and Graves where the most elegant, ageworthy and expensive Cabernet Sauvignon-based wines are produced. Two of the top-rated Bordeaux châteaux, Château Mouton-Rothschild and Château Latour, rely on Cabernet Sauvignon for 70 per cent of their blends. These and other highly rated Bordeaux châteaux produce wines that can age well for many decades and command hundreds of dollars for a bottle from a great year.

The assertive flavours of Cabernet Sauvignon – young or old – match nicely with lamb, beef and other red meat dishes. Young Cabernet Sauvignon is especially well paired with meats from the grill because the youthful fruit flavours are a perfect counterpoint to the pleasantly bitter scorch imparted by the open fire.

Pinot Noir

Main growing regions: Burgundy (France), California (USA),
New Zealand and cooler parts of Australia
Aromas and Flavours: Cherries, raspberries, strawberries, game, rotting vegetation
Acidity: Moderate to high
Tannin: Low to moderate
Body: Light to medium
Major mixing partners: Chardonnay and Pinot Meunier

If it were not so difficult to grow, Pinot Noir would enjoy a reputation for greatness equal to that of Cabernet Sauvignon. It is the noble red grape of France's Burgundy region where, under ideal conditions, it yields ruby-coloured wines whose velvety richness has seduced wine lovers for centuries. Whereas the great Cabernet Sauvignons of Bordeaux may be predictably excellent, great Pinot Noirs of Burgundy overwhelm one's senses every time with their striking beauty.

Cabernet Sauvignon travelled with ease from Bordeaux to the New World's warmer climates, where it thrives in the sunshine. Pinot, however, is a trickier proposition, and only really thrives in a few small pockets. It's most at home in cooler areas, thriving up north in Oregon or down south in New Zealand. In these places, the long, cool growing season allows the Pinot Noir fruit flavours to develop slowly. Pinot Noir that ripens quickly in hotter climes tends to be jammy and uninteresting.

Less pigmented than most red grapes, Pinot Noir has a brick-orange cast rather than a deep purple colour. At its best, Pinot Noir is low in tannin and high in glycerine (hence, the 'velvet'), and has a lively acidic backbone that gives length and focus to the typical Pinot Noir flavours of raspberries, cherries, game and strawberries. Such structure makes Pinot Noir a highly versatile food wine.

Minimum Varietal Percentages by Law

Australia 85%
California, USA 75%
France 85%
Germany 85%
Italy 85%
Oregon, USA 90%
Portugal 85%
Spain 85%
South Africa 75%

Full-bodied red Burgundy from the Côte de Nuits subregion is made entirely from Pinot Noir and is a classic accompaniment to beef roasts. The lighter red Burgundies from the Côte de Beaune are perfect with game birds such as pheasant and partridge. The Pinot Noirs from Oregon and New Zealand can be very Burgundian in structure, and range from a light Côte de Beaune style to a richer Côte de Nuits style; they match with food accordingly. The light, clean acidity and modest tannin of typical Pinot Noir makes it suitable with all but the lightest of seafood dishes. Open one of the jammy Californian interpretations of Pinot Noir – from Santa Barbara, Carneros or the Russian River Valley in Sonoma – in place of Merlot. You'll find that these generously fruity and mildly acidic wines might be more enjoyable.

Perhaps one of the most surprising uses of Pinot Noir is in the making of Champagne. Although Champagne looks like a white wine with bubbles, of the three grapes traditionally used to make it, two (Pinot Noir and Pinot Meunier) of them are actually red. Pinot Noir gives Champagne its biscuity richness and weight that enhances the delicacy of the Chardonnay grapes with which it's blended. Pinot Noir is also what gives Rosé Champagne its lovely coppery pink tinge.

In warmer parts of the New World, particularly in California and Australia, the Pinot grows to full ripeness thanks to the sunshine levels. More ripeness means more colour in the skin and more fruit flavours as well. Several of the French Champagne houses, in order to widen their options, have invested heavily in vineyards in the New World, producing much good-quality sparkling wine. Some of these are great value.

Decent Pinot Noir is never cheap. A good way to get to know this grape is by trying varietal-labelled Pinot Noir from the big, reputable Burgundy (Bourgogne as it's known in France) houses. These will usually be labelled 'Bourgogne Pinot Noir'. If you feel like paying for it, move up-market from there to the better red Burgundies, although this region is very difficult (and

ADELSHEIM VINEYARD

OREGON PINOT NOIR 1995

ALCOHOL 13.5% BY VOLUME

expensive) to get to know. The Chalonnais subregion of Burgundy offers two inexpensive and enjoyable Pinot Noir–based appellations: Givry and Mercurey.

Good Pinot Noir in Ascending Order of Price

1. Ninth Island Pinot Noir (Tasmania, Australia)
2. Viña Leyda Pinot Noir Cahuil (Chile)
3. Felton Road Cornish Point Drystone Pinot Noir (New Zealand)
4. Domaine de la Vougeraie Premier Cru Les Cras, Vougeot (Burgundy, France)

Merlot

Main growing regions: Bordeaux (France), California (USA), Australia, Chile
Aromas and flavours: Plums, blackberries, spice, chocolate and green peppers
Acidity: Low
Tannin: Low to moderate
Body: Medium
Major mixing partner: Cabernet Sauvignon (Bordeaux)

It is difficult to discuss Merlot without mentioning Cabernet Sauvignon. Just as Cabernet Sauvignon gained recognition in the Médoc subregion of Bordeaux in the late 1700s, so too did Merlot become prominent in the cooler Bordeaux subregions of Pomerol and Saint-Emilion. These areas are cooler and wetter than the Médoc, and their soils tend to be clay, rather than the Médoc's stony gravel (which helps reflect the sunshine back onto the plants). Merlot grows better in cooler climates than does Cabernet Sauvignon, although not too cool (Merlot has yet to gain a foothold in chilly regions where Pinot Noir is king).

Merlot is a distant relative of Cabernet Sauvignon. The biggest difference is that the skin of the Merlot grape is thinner than that of Cabernet Sauvignon; therefore Merlot is the earlier ripening and less tannic of the two. Merlot has a reputation for making soft, round and drinkable wines with low acidity and generous fruit flavours, along with a pleasantly round texture.

Until fairly recently, Merlot has rarely been a soloist, except for in Pomerol. Its primary role has been to be blended with Cabernet Sauvignon. In the past couple of decades, however, the Merlot grape has made the transition from being an assistant to Cabernet Sauvignon in blended wine to being a star in its own right. Now examples of varietal Merlot are grown right around the world, particularly in the USA, Australia, Chile and the Languedoc. How did this happen?

When the word went forth from the medical journals that red wine was good for your heart, the resulting boom in red-wine sales was equivalent to sales of Beatles records upon rumours of Paul McCartney's death. The wine-drinking public switched en masse to red wine. Non–wine drinkers, perhaps mindful of an unpleasant experience with dry, tannic, red wine, wanted a soft, supple, drinkable red wine. These consumers turned to Merlot, due to its reputation for low acid and its softness.

It seems that every winery so capable planted additional Merlot acreage as soon as possible, and the resulting wines were often disappointing. Too often, one buys a Merlot shaped more by market forces than by the winemaker's art. Grapes from very young vines growing in marginal areas are usually pressed too hard (the better to extract every drop of pricey nectar, with the inevitable concentration of unwanted tannin).

In the meantime, the best bargains in varietal Merlot are the Languedoc and *vin de pays* wines of France. South America (Chile and Argentina) produces good, affordable Merlot as well. If you like soft and fruity red wines, experiment with Pinot Noir or perhaps *cru* Beaujolais made from Gamay. *Cru* Beaujolais comes from ten villages in Beaujolais. Unlike ordinary Beaujolais, these wines can improve with a couple of years of ageing. Pinot Noir and Gamay are both relatively easy to match with food.

What are the characteristics of a good Merlot? Look for rich, plum-like fruit, almost jammy in its concentration, and low levels of acid and tannin. Merlot does not get particularly complex; yet because of its soft tannin and gentle acidity profile, its pleasing fruit flavours are more accessible than those in sturdier reds.

The soft tannin also makes Merlot an enjoyable match with a broad variety of foods. Even seafood, especially from the grill, can be a lovely pairing with Merlot's unobtrusive flavours. Its somewhat bland personality allows Merlot to fit nicely with all types of well-seasoned ethnic dishes.

Good Merlot

1. First Step Merlot (South Australia)
2. Errazuriz Max Reserva Merlot (Chile)
3. Casa Lapostolle Cuvée Alexandre Merlot (Chile)

Syrah/Shiraz

Main growing regions: Rhône and Languedoc (France), Australia, South Africa, Chile and California (USA)
Aromas and flavours:: Leather, pepper, smoke, spice and dark berries
Acidity: Low to moderate
Tannin: Moderate to prominent
Body: Medium
Major mixing partners: Grenache (Rhône) and Cabernet Sauvignon (Australia)

The Syrah grape, known as Shiraz in many parts of the New World, is a noble grape variety held in high esteem by many red-wine lovers. The great and age-worthy wines of the northern Rhône – Hermitage, St. Joseph, and Cornas – are produced from unblended Syrah. The finest wine produced in Australia is Penfold's Hermitage, another example of unblended Shiraz at its finest. Australian varietal Shiraz is as common as Shiraz/Cabernet Sauvignon blends; the latter are remarkable wine bargains.

Although its exact origin is not known, the Syrah grape is believed by some to have originated in ancient Persia. It gets its name from the city of Shiraz in the foothills of the Zagros Mountains in what is now Iran.

Syrah seems to have brought along a whiff of exotic Eastern spices in its travels to France, Australia, the USA, South Africa and Chile. The subtle spiciness in its aroma, often a combination of cinnamon, rose petals and orange rind, complements flavours of blackberry and black pepper. These qualities require bottle ageing in order to emerge; youthful Syrah wines usually exhibit more power than finesse. Well-aged Syrah is rare in the wine market, but experience shows that mature Syrah is well worth the wait.

Some of the New World Shirazes are pretty good, but Australia, with a 100-year head-start, is the source for both bargains and top-of-the-range Shiraz. In general, however, the French version is higher in acid and better with food than the Australian version, which shows more fruit. This is because of the difference in climate. The warmer weather of Australia leads to a more thorough ripening of the grape, which in turn leads to more fruitiness and a lower acidity in the wine. Whereas the French Syrahs tend to display raspberry-like fruit aromas, the Australian versions are often more suggestive of raisins.

Good Syrah (Shiraz) in Ascending Order of Price

1. Peter Lehmann The Barossa Shiraz (South Australia)
2. Concha y Toro Lot 3 Syrah (Chile)
3. Villa Maria Cellar Selection Syrah (New Zealand)
4. Montes Alpha Syrah (Chile)
5. Penfolds Grange (South Australia)
6. Guigal La Mouline, Côte Rôtie (Rhône, France)

Nebbiolo

Main growing regions: Piedmont (Italy)
Aromas and flavours: Tar, rose petals, truffles, violets and smoke
Acidity: High
Tannin: Prominent in youth, 'dusty' with age
Body: Medium
Major mixing partners: None (Some minor, local grapes are blended with
Nebbiolo in certain Piedmont wines.)

Named for the dense fogs so prevalent in the vineyards of Piedmont, Italy, the Nebbiolo grape is responsible for several of Italy's – and the world's – finest red wines. The great red wines of Piedmont – Barolo, Barbaresco – are regarded by aficionados as members of the exclusive club of the greatest wines in the world. Nebbiolo grapes have not as yet done well when grown away from their native soil. Somewhere outside Italy there is perhaps a piece of land just waiting to be converted into a great Nebbiolo vineyard.

In the past the best of these wines, like many Cabernet Sauvignons, were too tannic to drink in their youth and required a decade or so of mellowing. Perhaps more than any other variety, Nebbiolo rewards patience. However, more Nebbiolo-based wines are being vinified to be enjoyable in their youth. If you want an affordable way to get to know Nebbiolo, try an entry-level Barolo or a Nebbiolo d'Alba selected by a wine merchant or reviewer you trust. Unfortunately, entry level for these wines is £10. If you see one of these wines it may be a bargain, even if it is a little out of your normal price range.

Despite their powerful flavours, Barolo and other Nebbiolo-based Italian wines need to be served with food because they are quite acidic. Indeed, most Italian wines, red and white, belong at the dinner table, not the bar. The Italian Nebbiolos are a natural match with rich, earthy dishes such as game and red meat with mushrooms. Even chicken can hold its own with most of these wines.

Because Nebbiolo has not been transplanted with widespread success from its native Piedmont, it is difficult to differentiate between the characteristics of the grape and those of the region. Look for Nebbiolos to be very dry, tasty but not heavy on the palate, and surprisingly subtle and complex.

Sangiovese

Main growing regions: Tuscany (Italy)
Aromas and flavours: Cherries, plums, bay leaves, violets and game
Acidity: Moderate to high
Tannin: Moderate
Body: Light to medium
Major mixing partners: Cabernet Sauvignon (Italy) and Cannaiolo Nero (Italy)

Sangiovese is an Italian grape that, like the Nebbiolo, hasn't made a significant impact on the wine world when grown outside of Italy. It is the most important grape variety in central Italy, especially in Tuscany. It is in this region that the surprisingly sophisticated Etruscans made delicious wine well before the rise of the Roman Empire. The Sangiovese grape tends to generate closely related mutations – for example, the Brunello and Sangiovetto grapes are close enough relatives of Sangiovese that they are usually considered to be Sangiovese itself.

It might be said that, in terms of style, Sangiovese is to Nebbiolo as Pinot Noir is to Cabernet Sauvignon. Like the great Pinot Noirs of Burgundy, great Sangiovese-based wines from Tuscany – Chianti Classico, Brunello di Montalcino—are somewhat light in body and colour, yet can improve for many years in the bottle. Also like these great Burgundies, many of these same great Sangiovese wines can be perfectly enjoyable before their fifth birthday.

Like all great varietals, Sangiovese can be a prince or a pauper, and the pauper, a varietal-labelled Sangiovese from one of Italy's many regions, is frequently a bargain. Early attempts at this varietal in the New World tend to cost like the prince but taste like the pauper. So far, New World winemakers have had a difficult time getting Sangiovese acclimated to the warmth and sunshine of their vineyards. However, a few producers have produced some good Sangioveses.

Sangiovese with a varietal label can be surprisingly inexpensive. Look for the typical cherry fruit, high acid and low tannin and glycerine. Because of this combination of characteristics, Sangiovese has few equals as a red wine to accompany seafood. When matching food and wine, remember also to match price along with other characteristics. In this sense, inexpensive, varietally labelled Sangiovese is a good pizza and spaghetti wine. These wines are usually better than those inexpensive, silly-looking, straw-covered bottles of cheap Chianti you see at Italian restaurants.

In Chianti wines, the Sangiovese grape was historically blended with the local Cannaiolo grape as well as two white grapes, Trebbiano and Malvasia. Presently, the top producers are omitting these in favour of more Sangiovese.

The 'super-Tuscan' red wines that first came onto the market in the 1980s are often a blend of Sangiovese and Cabernet Sauvignon. These superior wines lie outside of Italy's wine classification system, but they are more intensely flavoured than Chianti and are worth a try if you want to splurge.

The great Chianti Classico and Brunello di Montalcino wines go well with veal, beef, lamb and hearty chicken dishes. Sangiovese-based wines also stand up well with tomato sauce. Super Tuscans, with their sturdy framework of Cabernet Sauvignon, are generally best reserved for red meat and game.

Good Sangiovese in Ascending Order of Price

1. Brolio Chianti Classico (Tuscany, Italy)
2. Villa Antinori Chianti Classico (Tuscany, Italy)
3. Isola e Olena Chianti Classico (Tuscany, Italy)
4. Castelgiocondo Brunello di Montalcino (Tuscany, Italy)

Grenache

Main growing regions: Spain, Rhône and Languedoc (France)
Aroma and flavour: Raspberry and herbs
Acidity: Moderate
Body: Medium to full
Major mixing partners: Syrah, Carignan and Mourvèdre (France)
and Tempranillo (Spain)

The southern part of France is famous for its sturdy, drinkable and affordable red wines. Many different grape varieties are grown here, but Grenache is an important part of the mix and is the primary grape among the many used to make Côtes-du-Rhône rouge. This popular wine has ample body, meaty structure, and a straightforward fruit flavour of raspberry jam. Côtes-du-Rhône is a genuine bargain among French red wines, usually retailing for around £5–10 a bottle. The dry rosés of the neighbouring Provence region are also made primarily from the Grenache grape, and are considered by many experts to be the finest pink wines in the world.

Under the local name Garnacha, Grenache is extensively planted in Spain and Portugal.

It lends fruit to the relatively austere Tempranillo grape in the red wines of Rioja (Spain). In California it is vinified in bulk for use in rosés and cheap red wines. Elsewhere in the world, rosés, both dry and less so, are often based on Grenach.

To experience Grenache in its purest state, look for Château Rayas from Châteauneuf-du-Pape. Although AOC law

allows the use of as many as 13 different grape varieties for Châteauneuf-du-Pape red, most such wines are predominantly Grenache, and Château Rayas eschews all other permitted varieties to make a 100 per cent Grenache wine.

Well-made Grenache-based wines tend to have enough body and character to be enjoyable with or without food. Hearty beef and lamb dishes, especially stews made with Côtes-du-Rhône as an ingredient, seem to bring out the delightful spiciness in Grenache. The most powerful versions of Châteauneuf-du-Pape stand up well to steak au poivre and other powerfully seasoned dishes, whereas tamer bottlings match well with goose, duck and the like – not summer food, and not summer wine. In hot weather, try pairing a rosé-style Grenache with a salad or simple picnic fare.

Gamay

Main growing region: Beaujolais (France)
Aromas and flavours: Strawberries, cherries, bubble gum and banana
Acidity: Moderate
Tannin: Low
Body: Light
Major mixing partners: None

The granite soil of the Beaujolais, the south-ernmost subregion of Burgundy, brings out the best qualities of the Gamay grape. The red wine of Beaujolais is fresh, light and fruity, and it is enjoyed all over the world. The lively fruit flavours – strawberry and rasp-berry – show well in the absence of substan-tial tannin. These qualities lend themselves well to carbonic maceration (fermentation in the complete absence of oxygen). This process protects the delicate fruit compo-nents and readies the wine for early release.

Beaujolais Nouveau, the first release of the wine, reaches the market on the third Thursday in November, immediately fol-lowing the harvest. Once eagerly awaited by the drinking public, the shine has gone off Beaujolais Nouveau in recent years, as quality has often failed to shine.

The Gamay grape reaches its summit of quality in the '*cru* Beaujolais' wines. These are red wines produced from Gamay grapes grown within the ten townships regarded as superior to the rest of the subregion: Moulin-à-Vent, Brouilly, Côte de Brouilly, Fleurie, Chiroubles, Morgon, Chénas, Juliénas, St-Amour and Régnié. Taken together, these townships comprise the heart of the Beaujolais subregion. It has been observed that these wines, unlike other wines from Beaujolais, can benefit from two or three years of ageing.

With its pleasant balance of fruit over tannin, a Gamay-based wine can take a slight chilling and may be offered with just about any food, from poached salmon to barbecued pork ribs. These wines, with their overt fruiti-ness, are also enjoyable alone.

Georges Duboeuf is the king of Beaujolais wines. The quality and pricing of these wines are more than fair. Louis Jadot is another reliable bottler of Beaujolais. This firm bottles all manner of wine from this sub-region – Beaujolais Nouveau, Beaujolais-Villages and all of the *crus*.

Tempranillo

Main growing region: Rioja (Spain)
Aromas and flavours: Strawberries, leathter, tobacco, vanilla and coconut
Acidity: Low to moderate
Tannin: Low to moderate
Body: Medium
Major mixing partner: Grenache/Garnacha (Rioja)

While Tempranillo is rarely labelled as such, it's Spain's most important grape variety, and is at the heart of that country's most famous wine, Rioja. It is also grown in Portugal, where it is known as Tinta Roriz. Tempranillo-based wines range from the very inexpensive to fabulously expensive, world-class red wine. The inexpensive versions often display the body of Pinot Noir without the flashy fruit. The subtle strawberry fruit of Temranillo is often well masked by tobacco flavours and oakiness. Grenache (Garnacha) is the minority blending partner in Rioja, and it adds some fruitiness to the wine. The greatest versions of Rioja cost as much as any great wine, and show a depth and length of flavours that justify their price.

As a light- to medium-bodied red with modest acidity, red Rioja matches well with grilled fish, well-seasoned vegetable dishes, and pasta, and also goes well with chicken and red meats. As such, Rioja might accurately be called a fool-proof red wine.

Rioja is a good place for the neophyte to start in his or her exploration of red wine.

Good Tempranillo in Ascending Order of Price

1. Marques de Griñon (Rioja, Spain)
2. Muga Reserva Seleccion Especial (Rioja, Spain)

Chardonnay

Main growing regions: Burgundy (France), California (USA), Australia, South Africa, Chile and New Zealand
Aromas and flavours: Varies greatly by region and degree of oak; melon, grapefruit, pineapple, toast, butter, vanilla and nuts
Acidity: Moderate to high
Body: Light to moderate
Body: Light to moderate
Major mixing partner: Sevignon Blanc (Australia)

The wine-drinking public is so accustomed to saying, 'I'll have a Chardonnay!' that it is worth a reminder that Chardonnay is the name of a white wine grape variety. In fact, Chardonnay is the most popular and most versatile white grape in the world.

Chardonnay grapes are used to make the austere, bone-dry wines of France's Chablis subregion; they are truly great seafood wines. Chardonnay is a crucial component of Champagne, and is the sole grape in a particular Champagne labelled Blanc de Blancs. Chardonnay makes the great white Burgundies from France – the most expensive dry white wines in the world.

It also makes good – sometimes great – white wines in the New World. Grown in warmer climates, the wines are fruity and sometimes syrupy; high in alcohol and often framed in oak, although winemakers have, of late, become more judicious in their use of oak Finally, Chardonnay blends well with other grapes, especially with Semillon, with which it is commonly blended in Australia.

What makes Chardonnay so versatile? Perhaps Chardonnay has little indigenous character of its own, and instead displays the best characteristics of the soil and climate in which it is grown, like a lawyer who can argue any side of an issue. However, in all of its incarnations Chardonnay does display a propensity for both glycerine and acid, whose interplay results in the most velvety, sensually delightful texture of all white wines. So, under all its trappings, Chardonnay is mostly about texture. That is what one looks for in even simple Chardonnays. Unlike the red-wine kingpin Cabernet Sauvignon, Chardonnays can be of high quality in the £5–8 price range.

So what does Chardonnay taste like? It depends on whom you ask. It is difficult to define a standard of varietal correctness in a grape variety with so many personalities. However, some generalizations about Chardonnay can be made.

The astringent flavour imparted by oak barrels marries well with Chardonnay in different regions. So well, in fact, that it can be difficult to separate in one's mind the flavour of the grape and the flavour of the oak. If you want to taste a pure, unoaked Chardonnay, look for a Chablis or a New World version, which will usually be labelled 'unwooded' or 'unoaked'.

Far to the south of Chablis in France is the Burgundy subregion of Côte de Beaune, where Chardonnay grapes become the world's greatest Chardonnay wines. Corton-Charlemagne, Meursault and the various Montrachet vineyards produce beautifully structured Chardonnays, that are brilliant and clean, with acidity, mouth-filling body and aromas of toast, nuts, butter and a variety of subtle fruits. When ripened in the sunshine, the fruit aroma becomes even more apparent.

Napa Valley, the first California appellation to excel with Chardonnay, tends to produce high-glycerine, well-oaked versions with ample fruit – apple and pear aromas intermingled with oak is a frequent observation. Drive over the Mayacamas mountain range into Sonoma Valley and you will find a more tropical element in Chardonnay, usually pineapple. The Santa Barbara growing area, far south of Napa/Sonoma, tends to bottle an even riper

Chardonnay. The fruit impression there is even more tropical, and the acidity profile is quite soft. For yet more fruit flavour, you must go to Australia.

The grape-growing climate in Australia is unique to wine-producing countries. The Hunter Valley in southeastern Australia experiences intense sunshine. This would normally over-ripen wine grapes, but the ripening effect of the sun in this region is greatly tempered by cool breezes. This combination of plentiful sunlight and refreshing air brings grapes to a full ripeness slowly, so as to develop the most intense flavours imaginable in Chardonnay. Suggestions of pineapple, coconut and bananas spring forth from this deep-golden wine. These wines used to lack the necessary acidity, but innovative winemaking techniques seem to have solved this problem.

Because Chardonnay has such a range of styles, one needs to consider the type of Chardonnay when trying to find the right wine for a particular meal. Chablis is the driest, most acidic interpretation, and belongs with seafood, especially shellfish and delicate white fish like Dover sole. The rounder white Burgundies from the Côte de Beaune are also seafood wines but can accompany meats such as chicken and veal. Seafood doesn't match so well with fruitier Chardonnays such as those from California and Australia.

If you insist on a fruity Chardonnay with your fish, Californian-style cuisine comes into play. The tasty ingredients used – generous additions of fresh herbs and chili peppers, and wood grilling – can transform a delicate piece of fish into a jam session of loud flavours. A big wine is called for; California Chardonnay is ideal. In fact, big Chardonnays like these can stand up to many dishes not normally paired with white wine – even grilled meats!

Finally, if you want to drink Chardonnay without food, any of the Australian, South African and Chilean versions, with their generous fruit and mild acidity, make an excellent choice.

Good Chardonnay in Ascending Order of Price

1. Inycon Chardonnay (Sicily, Italy)
2. Alamos Chardonnay (Argentina)
3. Danie de Wet Unoaked Chardonnay (South Africa)
4. Wente Chardonnay (South Africa)
5. Domaine Vessigaud Mâcon-Fuissé (Burgundy, France)
6. Catena Chardonnay (Argentina)
7. Concha y Toro Amelia Chardonnay (Chile)
8. Verget Premier Cru Fourchaume, Chablis (Burgundy, France)
9. Domaine Leflaive Clavoillon, Puligny Montrachet (Burgundy, France)

Sauvignon Blanc

Main growing regions: Bordeaux and Loire (France), South Africa, New Zealand,
Chile and Australia
Aromas and flavours: Cut grass, nettles, asparagus, passion fruit, guava
and gooseberries
Acidity: High
Body: Medium
Major mixing partner: Semillon (Bordeaux)

In comparison to Chardonnay, it may take a little more wine knowledge to appreciate a great Sauvignon Blanc. That is because the hallmark of quality Sauvignon Blanc – bright, crisp acidity – is not as sensually pleasing as the seductive texture of good Chardonnay. Yet this high acidity makes for a great pairing with seafood – Sancerre from the Loire, Bordeaux's white wines, and varietal Sauvignon Blanc from New Zealand, South Africa, Chile and even California are perfect with fish. When Sauvignon Blanc is grown in cool climates, 'grassy' and 'herbaceous' are common descriptions, as is the rather less elegant 'cat's pee on a gooseberry bush'. Sauvignon Blanc from warmer areas often tends towards aromas of tropical fruits, particularly passion fruit, guava and pineapple.

In recent years, the New Zealand version of Sauvignon Blanc has become just as much of a benchmark as those made in the grape's traditional French heartland of the Loire. The Kiwi versions are often quite elegant and racy, but tend to have more fruit than their Old World cousins.

An alternative vinification style of Sauvignon Blanc yields a richer wine. 'Fumé Blanc' is the name for a style created in California in the 1960s by Robert Mondavi. Styled after the legendary Pouilly Fumé of the Loire region in France, Fumé Blanc has a richer, fuller style. Whereas the Sauvignon Blancs are excellent with seafood, the more substantial Fumé Blanc may be paired with a wider variety of dishes, including chicken, veal and pasta.

There are a few world-class wines made from Sauvignon Blanc that earn this variety its place beside the other white noble grapes, Riesling and Chardonnay. Château Haut-Brion blanc of Graves is universally regarded as the finest of its type and an equal to the great white Burgundies. Close on its heels is Domaine de Chevalier, also from Graves. Sauvignon Blanc is blended with a lesser amount of Semillon in most Graves whites. This formula is reversed in the dessert wines from neighbouring Sauternes.

In spite of its legitimate claim to nobility, Sauvignon Blanc might well have an inferiority complex. The public hasn't taken to this variety like it has to Chardonnay. Some winemakers have even employed a heavy-handed oaking to make Sauvignon Blanc seem more like Chardonnay. Fortunately, low demand has kept the prices down somewhat. Try serving a good Sauvignon Blanc with an uncomplicated seafood dish without telling your guests what they are drinking. You will look very wine-smart.

Good Sauvignon Blanc in Ascending Order of Price

1. Lurton Sauvignon Blanc (Loire, France)
2. Oracle Sauvignon Blanc (South Africa)
3. Gooseberry Patch Sauvignon Blanc (Loire, France)
4. Veramonte Sauvignon Blanc (Chile)
5. Oyster Bay Sauvignon Blanc (New Zealand)
6. Stella Bella Sauvignon Blanc (Western Australia)
7. Villa Maria Cellar Selection Sauvignon Blanc (New Zealand)
8. Didier Dagenau Pouilly-Fumé Silex (Loire, France)

Riesling

Main growing regions: Germany, Austria, Alsace (France), Australia
and New Zealand
Aromas and flavours: Apricots, citrus, flowers, apples and honey (in sweet wines)
Acidity: Moderate to high
Body: Light; medium to heavy for dessert wines
Major mixing partners: None

Just as Pinot Noir rivals Cabernet Sauvignon for preeminence among noble red varieties, the Riesling grape has a following who regard it as superior to Chardonnay. Like Pinot Noir, Riesling has not traveled as well as its rival. Both Pinot Noir and Riesling turn shy in warmer areas and require a cooler climate in order to perform well.

Whereas the demand for quality Pinot Noir has motivated New World winemakers to seek out promising vineyards for it, Riesling has never been in high demand in the UK. Our anti-Riesling sentiments probably stem from the fact that the grape is tainted with its association with the over-sweetened, low-cost German wines that were so popular a decade or two ago. Things have changed, though, and there are now a lot of very good German Rieslings on the market for a very reasonable price.

Perhaps if Riesling had been widely planted in France it would have found its niche in French gastronomy and secured its immortality. However, only in the Alsace region of France is Riesling permitted to grow in French soil.

Riesling's alleged sweetness has also kept it out of the fast lane in today's wine market. Riesling grapes can make sweet wine. Their prominent acidity provides the perfect balance for late-harvest sweetness, and they can produce the sweetest dessert wines in the world. However, some excellent Rieslings, notably those from Alsace, can be nearly bone-dry. The aroma of well-made Riesling is flowery as well as fruity. Riesling *smells* sweeter than Chardonnay.

Riesling has long been the basis for the finest wines of Germany. The steep slopes along the Rhine and Mosel rivers retain warmth and incubate the Riesling to full ripeness in the otherwise chilly climate. In fact, some German winemakers wait to pick the last of their berries until late autumn or even the depths of winter to make dessert wines. To attain the necessary sweetness and become a good dessert wine in such a northerly climate is a victory over nature.

Although the Semillon-based dessert wines from Sauternes, France ,are equally noteworthy as world-class dessert wines, these wines need some acidic Sauvignon

Blanc blended in to balance the flaccid sweetness of *Botrytis*-affected Semillon. Sweet Riesling need not be blended.

Some of the best values in the wine world today are the German Rieslings designated QbA and labeled 'Riesling'. The superior QmP white wines from Germany are by definition made from Riesling unless labelled otherwise.

There have been some notable successes with Riesling in the New World, particularly in New Zealand and Australia's Clare Valley and Adelaide Hills. The wines tend to be bone-dry, with a delicious streak of lime cordial acidity. Some producers in the USA have also been successful with the variety, although little of the wine makes it over here. In Canada, winemakers use the grapes to produce a sumptuously sweet ice wine.Be wary of imitations!

Several lowly grape varieties, including Olasz Riesling and Welschriesling, are deceptively named and have nothing to do with the real thing. Look for wines labelled 'Riesling'. In addition, don't be afraid of trying out an older bottle. Rieslings have demonstrated a capacity to improve with age, much more so than Chardonnays. This is especially true of Alsace, Austrian and German Riesling.

Good Riesling in Ascending Order of Price

1. Reichsrat von Buhl Riesling Spätlese Trocken (Pfalz, Germany)
2. Leasingham Bin 7 Riesling (South Australia)
3. Felton Road Dry Riesling (New Zealand)
4. Trimbach Riesling (Alsace, France)
5. JJ Prum Wehlener Sonnenhur Spätlese (Mosel-saar-Ruwer, Germany)

Chenin Blanc

Main growing regions: Loire (France) and South Africa
Aromas and flavours: Quinces, apples, peardrops, barley sugar and honey
when sweet
Acidity: Moderate to very high
Body: Light to medium
Major mixing partner: Chardonnay

Chenin Blanc is widely grown around the world and has several distinct personalities. In the Loire Valley of northwestern France, where it has been cultivated for over 1,000 years, Chenin Blanc is responsible for the acidic white wines of Anjou and Touraine. The best known of these is Vouvray, which itself can take several forms.

Vouvray, whose name comes from the village in Touraine where it is produced, is probably the most weather-sensitive table wine in the world. Whereas winemakers elsewhere usually attempt to produce a somewhat consistent style from vintage to vintage, Vouvray is made in very different styles depending on the weather. A pleasant, sunny summer brings the Chenin Blanc grapes in Vouvray to full ripeness. In such years demi-sec (half-dry) wine is usually produced. These wines have a pleasant level of residual sugar, but they are dry enough to enjoy with dinner. Chenin Blanc's inherent bracing acidity provides ample balance to the sweetness in demi-sec wines. These wines match well with a variety of light dishes.

A cold and rainy summer is unwelcome in any vineyard. Rather than gnash their teeth, though, the winemakers of Vouvray respond by making Vouvray sec. This dry version of Chenin Blanc is *very* acidic. Such wine is nearly impossible to drink without food, and even then is difficult to match with anything other than shellfish.

Vouvray sec does have a following, however, among connoisseurs who prize naked acidity. On the other end of the sweetness spectrum is Quarts de Chaume, a melony, honeyed dessert wine made from *Botrytis*-affected Chenin Blanc from Anjou in the Loire Valley.

These sweet wines are said to live indefinitely in the bottle, as do the sweeter versions of the Vouvray demi-sec.

High acidity is the backbone of well-made sparkling wine, and the naturally acidic Chenin Blanc grape is used to make high-quality sparkling wine in the Loire region. Semi-sparkling wine labelled 'Vouvray Mousseux' can be found, and the great Champagne firm of Taittinger produces its Bouvet Brut from Chenin Blanc in the Loire. These sparkling wines, though not as complex as true Champagne, are often as well made and offer excellent value.

Chenin Blanc has travelled abroad with success. It was brought to South Africa in the 1600s by Dutch settlers and is widely grown there under the name of Steen. Chenin Blanc is sometimes blended with Chardonnay in New Zealand, Australia and the USA.

In general, Chenin Blanc–based wines match well with summer foods. Because of their high acidity, restrained fruit and balance, well-made versions can be a welcome respite from your usual white wine. These wines have a natural affinity with sweet shellfish like sea scallops, but are also enjoyable with anything light, such as pasta, fish and chicken.

Good Chenin Blanc in Ascending Order of Price

1. Peter Lehmann Chenin Blanc (South Australia)
2. Marks & Spencer Domaine de la Pouvraie, Vouvray (Loire, France)
3. Ken Forrester FM Chenin Blanc (South Africa)

Pinot Blanc

Main growing regions: Burgundy (France), Alsace (France) and Italy
Aromas and flavours: Can be somewhat subdued: almonds and apples
Acidity: Moderate to high
Body: Medium to full
Major mixing partner: Chardonnay (Burgundy)

Also known as Pinot Bianco in Italy, Pinot Blanc is known for its simple, full-bodied, clean structure and forward acidity. It is used (in combination with other grapes) for some premium sparkling wines in California. Not widely produced in the New World, Pinot Blanc can be a good value among Alsace wines. Because it usually makes a relatively uncomplicated wine, Pinot Blanc is enjoyable with a wide variety of dishes and does not require particularly careful matching.

Originally cultivated in ancient Burgundy, Pinot Blanc has long been cultivated side by side with Chardonnay. Indeed, some mutations of Pinot Blanc are capable of producing a Chardonnay-like wine. But for the most part, Pinot Blanc makes a rather nondescript wine with weak aroma – good with food and somewhat boring without. Although we encourage occasional daring and uninformed purchases in the wine shop, for Pinot Blanc we suggest you start with our recommended bottles.

Good Pinot Blanc in Ascending Order of Price

1. Paul Zinck Pinot Blanc (Alsace, France)
2. Marks & Spencer Pinot Blanc, Turckheim (Alsace, France)

Semillon

Main growing regions: Bordeaux (France), Australia and California (USA)
Aromas and flavours: Citrus, honey, lime and sweet marmalade
Acidity: Low to medium
Body: Full
Major mixing partners: Chardonnay (Australia) and Sauvignon Blanc (Bordeaux)

The Semillon grape rarely stands alone as a varietal. It is often blended in the Graves subregion of Bordeaux, France, with Sauvignon Blanc. Its silky richness complements the acidity of the Sauvignon Blanc. In Australia Semillon is used in Semillon/Chardonnay blends. These wines are pleasant and relatively inexpensive.

Semillon is the main variety in Sauternes, the dessert wine–producing subregion of Bordeaux. These wines also have Sauvignon Blanc mixed in to give them a little acidity.

Good and affordable dessert Semillon, in its pure form, is produced in Australia.

Its signature characteristics are low acidity and thick body, and its aromas and flavours of figs, honey and lemon are restrained. This set of qualities does not add up to an exceptional table wine, but good, inexpensive varietal Semillon is available. However, Semillon's propensity for richness and its susceptibility to 'noble rot' make it a useful grape variety, albeit one with limited applications.

Good Semillon in Ascending Order of Price

1. Basedow Semillon (South Australia)
2. Henschke Louis Semillon (South Australia)

Viognier

Main growing regions: Rhône and Languedoc (France), California (USA), Chile, Australia and South Africa
Aromas and flavours: Apricots, peaches and flowers
Acidity: Low to medium
Body: Medium to full
Major mixing partners: Marsanne, Rousanne and Rolle in France, Syrah and Côte Rôtie (France

The increasingly popular Viognier grape has been producing some fine wines in France's upper Rhône for quite some time now. As a straightforward New World varietal, however, its popularity is fairly recent. Its apricot/floral/peach flavours are a refreshing alternative to the repetitive oak-and-fruit flavours of big New World Chardonnays. In fact, Viognier's biggest asset may be its vastly different flavour structure compared to Chardonnay, making it a good choice for those seeking an alternative to Chardonnay.

The northern Rhône valley of Condrieu is the home turf for Viognier. The smallest recognized appellation in France is Château Grillet, a single estate within Condrieu. The Viognier grape approaches world-class status at this tiny property: A bottle of Château Grillet fetches £80 or more, and is said to age well *forever* in the bottle. Less expensive but certainly noteworthy versions of Viognier come from the surrounding Condrieu vineyards.

At its best, Viognier has aromas and flavours of peach, apricot and flowers, although it is not as overtly flowery as Riesling. With the aromas and flavours of

The Vitis Vinifera Family (most notable members)

Red-, Purple- or Black-Skinned Grapes (Red Wine):
Cabernet Sauvignon, Gamay, Grenache, Merlot, Nebbiolo, Petite Sirah, Pinot Noir, Sangiovese, Syrah, Tempranillo, Zinfandel

Green-Skinned Grapes (White Wine):
Chardonnay, Chenin Blanc, Gewürztraminer, Pinot Blanc, Pinot Grigio, Riesling, Sauvignon Blanc, Semillon, Viognier

these particular fruit, Viognier is a natural match with pork, which has an affinity for both. However, if you substitute Viognier for Chardonnay in any food-wine pairing, you won't be disappointed.

Good Viognier doesn't usually come cheap. For bargains, look for varietal Viognier from big French producers. Inexpensive *vin de pays* varietal Viognier has caught on in the French countryside, at least for export. These 'budget wines' are often good value in terms of quality, particularly when compared with similarly priced Chardonnay.

Good Viognier in Ascending Order of Price

1. Yalumba Y Viognier (South Australia)
2. Anakena Viognier (Chile)
3. Guigal Condrieu (Rhône, France)
4. Château Grillet (Rhône, France)

Pinot Grigio/Pinot Gris

Main growing regions: Italy, Alsace (France) and New Zealand
Aromas and flavours: Smoke, spice, apples and pears; can be bland
Acidity: Medium (generally higher in Europe)
Body: Medium
Major mixing partners: None

A close relative of Pinot Blanc, Pinot Grigio has recently become a very popular varietal wine from Italy. In Friuli and Aldo Adige, two northern regions of Italy, Pinot Grigio can produce a well-structured and acidic match for seafood, with somewhat muddled aromas. In warmer climates, however, the acidity level can be undesirably low. Pinot Gris is a relatively recent visitor to the New World. Many of these wines have yet to succeed in making wines comparable those in northern Italy, although New Zealand's versions are very promising indeed.

Alsatian soil brings out the best in several white varieties, and Pinot Grigio, known there as Tokay Pinot Gris, is one of them. This pink-skinned variety is not very strong-willed and is a perfect vehicle for the

Alsace *terroir* – rich, minerally soil flavours mingle with the substantial acidity.

Because it doesn't have particularly prominent fruit flavours, Pinot Grigio is relatively easy to match with a variety of food. The drier, more acidic versions are excellent with shellfish and other seafoods, whereas the fuller-bodied versions can be used to accompany chicken and pasta dishes well.

Good Pinot Grigio/Pinot Gris in Ascending Order of Price

1. Cave de Ribeauvillé Pinot Gris (Alsace, France)
2. Rolly-Gassmann Tokay Pinot Gris Rottleibel de Rorschwihr (Alsace, France)

Gewürztraminer

Main growing regions: Germany and Alsace (France)
Aromas and flavours: Lychee, rose petal and spice
Acidity: Low to medium
Body: Full
Major mixing partners: None

A mouthful, literally, Gewürztraminer (gah-VERTS-truh-MEEN-er) can be as difficult to enjoy as it is to pronounce. Rich, pungent, spicy flavours with fruit notes of lychee and grapefruit rind make for a difficult food-wine pairing. As such, Gewürztraminer is often suggested with spicy Asian food – an awkward blind date at best. Regional tradition in Alsace matches Gewürztraminer with sausage and ham. Because of its low acidity and bold flavours, Gewürztraminer can be enjoyable all by itself, without food.

Good Gewürztraminer in Ascending Order of Price

1. Undurraga Gewurztraminer (Chile)
2. Paul Zinck Gewurztraminer (Alsace, France)
3. Domaine Zind-Humbrecht Gewürztraminer Grand Cru Rangen Clos St Urbain (Alsace, France)

Alternatively, a simple, creamy cheese provides a good background for the complex, full personality of this grape.

Gewürztraminer is a pink-skinned clone of the much older Traminer vine that probably originated in northern Italy. The 'Gewürz-' is German for 'spicy' or 'pungent' and reflects the powerful aromas of Gewürztraminer wines. It is the least subtle of all the well-known *vinifera* grapes.

Although it grows best in Alsace (France), it plays second fiddle there to the Riesling grape. Its share of vineyard space in Germany has been on the decline in recent years, again being out-muscled by the Riesling grape. The many New World versions of this quirky variety tend to lack the complexity of their European counterparts, but can be both enjoyable and generally affordable.

Other Grapes

There are, of course, thousands of other members of the *Vitis vinifera* family, but most of are unknown to wine drinkers and wine-shop shelves. Vines grow all over the world, but relatively few varieties are used for the commercial production of wine. The well-known wine grapes are famous because they produce good or balanced wine, and to grow them requires little-to-reasonable effort.

While we've looked in reasonable depth at some of the key varieties, there are a number of other grapes you should know about, either because of their regional importance or because they are major components in particular blends. Don't be tempted to dismiss these grapes as meaning-less. A number of the famous wines of Italy, France and Spain have some minor grapes blended in for the sole purpose of making the wine better. Different countries have dif-ferent laws concerning the legal percentages of these grapes in the wine. A grape variety that accounts for 5–25 per cent of wine, depending on the country, doesn't need to be credited. Of course, most European wines don't even credit the star grape on the wine label. It is to be hoped that all this secrecy will be eliminated someday.

RED GRAPES

Barbera (Piedmont, Italy) A light red that is higher in acidity than tannins, Barbera has long been Piedmont's workhorse wine. The very best versions have plenty of fruit and make great mealtime wines.

Cabernet Franc (Bordeaux and Loire, France, and, to a lesser extent, the New World) A close cousin of Cabernet Sauvignon, Cabernet Franc is a lighter, less tannic version of its relative. Its aromas are often more herba-ceous, or even floral. In Bordeaux, it is usually part of the blend of red grapes although, unusually, it makes up two-thirds of the blend of Château Cheval Blanc, a famous first growth property in St-Emilion.

Carmenère (Chile, originally from Bordeaux, France) For many years after it was first planted in the country, this grape was mis-taken by the Chileans for Merlot. The confusion has now been resolved and Carmenère, now practically extinct in its native Bordeaux homeland, is becoming established in its new home. It makes pow-erful, spicy wines with low acidity, fairly high tannins and a velvety texture.

Carignan (Rhône and Languedoc, France) For many years the most planted grape in France, Carignan fell out of favour a while back. The problem was that, if not checked, it grows rampant, producing tannic, tough wines with a pretty coarse flavour. Producers are now beginning to realize that, if kept under control and harvested from old vines,

Carignan can make an interesting wine with bold flavours. It's still usually used, however, as part of a blend of the typically southern grapes Syrah, Grenache and Mourvèdre.

Malbec (Argentina, originally from Bordeaux, France, still also grown in Cahors, France) The Malbec grape makes big, meaty red wine wherever it is grown. With its big tannins, it's made itself pretty much at home in Argentina, where it makes a perfect match for gaucho-style steaks. The best Malbec wines can have a silky richness.

Mourvèdre (Rhône and Languedoc, France, and Spain, where it is known as Monastrell)

Mourvèdre can add a herby, meaty note and high alcohol to a blend. It rarely makes successful varietal wine by itself.

Zinfandel (California, USA, also known as Primitivo in its native southern Italy) Zinfandel is a grape that thrives in heat and sunshine, so it is equally at home in southern Italy and northern California. The best examples are rich, almost jammy black fruit bombs, often with high alcohol. In the States, Zinfandel is also used to make an uncomplicated, rather sweet rosé misleadingly known as White Zinfandel.

Some Good Blends Worth Looking For:

Red

The Wolftrap (South Africa)
Fairview SMV (South Africa)
Fitou Les Douze (Languedoc, France
Alter Ego de Palmer (Bordeaux, France)
Le Cigare Volant (California, USA)
Château Haut-Brion (Bordeaux, France)

White

Malambo Chenin Blanc/Chardonnay (Argentina)
Torres Viña Esmerelda (Spain)
D'Arenberg The Hermit Crab (South Australia)
Mas Jullien Blanc (Languedoc, France)
Domaine de Chevalier Blanc (Bordeaux, France)

WHITE GRAPES

Albariño (Spain, Portugal) An aromatic white grape that makes wines with pronounced peach and lemon aromas, Albariño has l ong been popular in Spain and Portugal, where it is used to make the famous Vinho Verde wines.

Grüner Veltliner (Austria) These spicy, white-pepper-scented wines are never made outside the grape's native Austria, and can be difficult to track down in the UK. This is a shame, as good examples make great food wines and can handle serious bottle age.

Furmint (Hungary) If you're a sucker for Hungary's sweet Tokaji wines, you're already a Furmint fan. If not, you've a treat in store when you take your first sip. This is a grape that never travels far from home.

Marsanne (Rhône Valley, Languedoc and Roussillon, France, Victoria, Australia, the USA) Roussanne's classic blending partner in the Rhône, Marsanne can be found in the white wines of the Languedoc and Roussillon. On its own, it can lack a bit of acidity and have a slightly weird marzipan aroma.

Muscat (France, Australia, Chile, Italy) Although Muscat can make some attractive, light-bodied wines, it comes into its own as a sweet grape, making wines in a range of styles from quaffers like the slightly fizzy Moscato d'Asti to rich, syrupy fortified versions in the New World. Oddly enough, it's the only grape that makes a wine that smells like, well, grapes.

Roussanne (Rhône Valley, Languedoc and Roussillon, France, Victoria, Australia, the USA) By itself, Roussanne is full-bodied and fragrant, with floral notes and a nice, zingy acidity. Most often, however, it is blended with its partner Roussanne.

BLENDS

While all of the major grapes we've written about here are used to make what's known as varietal wines, most of them are also used to make blended wines. To most of us, the use of the word 'blended' sounds slightly derogatory. But, unlike whisky, wine is not necessarily at its best when unblended. In fact, many of the world's most famous wines – particularly those from the Old World – are blends.

For instance, top-class Bordeaux is usually a blend of Cabernet Sauvignon and Merlot, often with some Cabernet Franc and/or Petit Verdot. The Rhône's Châteauneuf-du-Pâpe can contain up to 13 different kinds of grapes; while even apparently white Champagne usually contains two black grape varieties (Pinot Noir and Pinot Meunier) as well as Chardonnay. Some apparently red wines have white grapes mixed into the blend, too – foremost among these is Chianti, which contains the white grapes Trebbiano and Malvasia along with the dominant Sangiovese and lesser (red) partner Canaiolo. The Northern Rhône's Côte Rôtie wines also usually feature a dash of Viognier to give a bit of a lift to the spicy, peppery Syrah.

Until recently, the New World has majored in varietal wines, even if some of them actually contain a splash of something other than the grape named on the label (see table page 47 for information of minimum percentages). There have always been blends – for instance, Australians often mix Shiraz and Cabernet Sauvignon together – but, by and large, these have been simple wines intended for easy drinking.

These days, though, New World winemakers, keen to add that extra dimension to their wines, are increasingly turning their attention to creating blends. Some of these are solidly grounded in Old World tradition – the USA's Meritage wines, for example, are based on Bordeaux blends. Others are playing fast and loose with the historical rules, sometimes achieving unexpected success, but often, apparently, only to prove the point that 'if it ain't broke, don't fix it'. One particular 'experiment', the so-called Cape Blend of South African wines (a mix of Bordeaux varieties and Pinotage, a cross between Pinot Noir and Cinsault), looks set to be a bit of a hit – once the country's winemakers can actually agree on a legal definition of a Cape Blend.

For consumers, the main problem with Old World blends is the same as with varietals: by law, winemakers aren't allowed to put the grape varieties on the label. This means that it's down to you to know that a wine from the Margaux subregion of Bordeaux contains a mix of Cabernet Sauvignon and Merlot grapes, or that a wine from the appellation of Fitou in the Languedoc will be made up of a Syrah-dominated blend of Grenache, Mourvèdre and Carignan. If you don't fancy swotting up before you buy a bottle, try and find a wine shop with knowledgeable staff and tell them what kind of varietal wines you enjoy – they will usually be able to help you make your way through the maze of blends.

CHAPTER 5

SPECIAL OCCASION
WINES

Champagne and Sparkling Wine

'Come, for I am drinking stars!'

So said cellarmaster Dom Pérignon, according to legend, when he tasted the first Champagne. The bubbles in Champagne and sparkling wines set them apart from all other wines, lending a sense of frivolity and joyousness not otherwise associated with wine-drinking. Champagne has long been virtually a requirement for celebrations such as New Year's Eve, sports victories and weddings. People who normally do not drink wine nonetheless enjoy Champagne at such occasions. It remains for consumers to discover that Champagne and sparkling wines are not just for celebrations they can

be as well made, affordable and appropriate with good food as any other wine.

Sparkling wine of any kind starts out plain, bubble-less wine (white or pink). It is then put in a bottle or barrel with yeast and sugar for a second fermentation, which produces a little more alcohol (1 per cent of volume) and a lot of carbon dioxide (bubbles). The alcohol kills the yeast, which is eventually removed with great care so as not to lose the carbonation.

The result is white wine or rosé enhanced by natural carbonation and the complex flavours developed during the second fermentation. If the second fermentation occurred in the same bottle in which it is sold, then it was made via the Champagne method, or *méthode champenoise* as it is known in France, where it was supposedly invented by the blind monk named Dom Pérignon. This is the best, but most labour-intensive, way of making sparkling wine.

The best sparkling wines in the world, according to the French and many other people, come from Champagne, a wine-producing region in northern France. Only sparkling wines produced in this region via the Champagne method are denoted as Champagne. Therefore, the only true Champagne comes from Champagne, France.

Champagne has become to sparkling wines what Kleenex is to facial tissues in terms of name use and recognition. Much to the fury of the French, some cheap sparkling wines made in some New World countries can legally call themselves champagne (with a small 'c') in those countries. The French

have long jealously guarded this place-name. The treaty of Versailles specifically forbade the Germans from appropriating the name, and the EEC nations honour the French label law.

Sparkling wine should be served well-chilled, so that the carbonation will last longer and feel smoother. However, those who are drinking very expensive Champagne will want to serve it at a slightly warmer temperature so that they may, at least theoretically, taste why they paid so much for a bottle of sparkling wine.

For somewhere between £5 and £7 you can pick up a bottle of Cava, Spanish sparkling wine. For a few pounds more, you're into New World sparkling territory. £8 will score you a pretty reasonable bottle, over £10 and you're heading into quality country. We consider New World sparkling wine to be very good value; it is often fruitier and less dry than French versions.

The driest of Champagnes and sparkling wines often contain a high proportion of Chardonnay, and are appropriate with any light seafood dish. Pale bubbly (that is not Rosé bubbly) is rarely *incorrect* with any dish. Historically this has been an easy way out of the food-wine matching game for many a host.

SWEET SPARKLING WINE

People who don't enjoy dry table wines often do enjoy two types of wine – sweet and sparkling. Sweet sparkling wine offers a way to double their wine-drinking pleasure. The sweetness usually comes from a high amount of added sugar –

Champagne & Sparkling Wines Buying Guide

Sparkling
  Jacob's Creek Sparkling Chardonnay/Pinot Noir (Australia)
  Brown Brothers Sparkling Pinot Noir & Chardonnay (Australia)
  Montana Lindauer Rosé (New Zealand)
  Cloudy Bay Pelorus (New Zealand)
  Nyetimber Classic Cuvée Brut (England)
  Graham Beck Sparkling Brut NV (South Africa)

Champagne & Sparkling Wines Buying Guide

Champagne
H Blin (Vintage)
Jacquart (Vintage)
R de Ruinart Brut (NV)
Billecart-Salmon Rosé (NV)
Bollinger Grande Année (Vintage)
Krug (Vintage)

almost all sparkling wines have at least some sugar added after the dead yeast is removed. Sweet sparkling wine, usually labeled demi-sec, is usually drunk without food, although it matches well with simple creamy cheeses and many desserts.

PINK CHAMPAGNE/ BRUT ROSÉ

The better sparkling wines, including Champagne, are usually made from both green-skinned grapes (Chardonnay) and black-skinned grapes (Pinot Noit and Pinot Meunier). If pigment from the black-skinned grapes is permitted to lend colour to the wine, the result is pink-coloured sparkling wine, also called brut rosé.

There is a broad price spectrum of pink-hued bubbly, from the £5 bottle of pink Cava from bulk producers in Spain to exquisite and rare French versions that can cost over £150.

Dessert Wine

Dessert wine is a very sweet wine, often white, with a rich golden colour. It can be made in several ways. In many cases, the residual sugar the residual sugar in these sweet wines is the result of the 'noble rot', the *Botrytis cinerea* fungus on grapes left on the vine to become over-ripe. This 'affliction' draws water from the grapes and adds complex flavours. The resulting crop of grapes has a high concentration of sugar, not all of which converts to alcohol during fermentation. Other types of dessert wines are made from over-ripe grapes that are simply very high in sugar content.

Because the grape juice used to make dessert wines has so much sugar, the fermentation process can potentially produce a high level of alcohol. The high sugar content also helps preserve the wine, so it can improve in the bottle for many years. Unlike most dry white wines, these wines can last for several days after being opened. They are best served at around 10°C (50°F).

If you are interested in trying a dessert wine, you probably should start with a half bottle. Two people together are very unlikely to drink a half bottle

Botrytis Cinerea (Noble Rot)

In certain regions, grapes are allowed to stay on the vine after they are ripe to contract a fungus called *botrytis cinerea*. Unlike *Phylloxera*, this condition is desirable and controllable. What this fungus does is cause the grapes to dehydrate (lose water), thus concentrating the juice and sugar. This affliction, often referred to as the Noble Rot, yields an extremely thick and sugar-laden juice for the winemaker to work with. The grapes are apt to pick up some complex flavours that complement the sweetness. These sweet white-wine juices are turned into thick sweet wines called dessert wines.

In France these dessert wines come from the small but famous area of Sauternes. Like most wines in France, these wines are named after the region in which they are made. Germany's most coveted wines are dessert wines from *botrytis*-infected grapes from vineyards of the Rhine and Mosel.

These are not the only two countries that use *botrytis*, but they are the sources of the very best dessert wines in the world. California, Austria, Hungary and Australia also produce dessert wines made from grapes afflicted with the Noble Rot.

in a sitting. In fact, if you are just experimenting, you can probably stretch a half bottle to four people.

These wines are sometimes better served alone as dessert, rather than as an accompaniment to dessert. They are often too sweet to match with dessert food. Ironically, they are often served as an appetizer!

Good Dessert Wines

1. Cranswick Estate Botrytis (NSW, Australia)
2. Andrew Quady Elysium Black Muscat (California, USA)
3. Château Filhot, Sauternes (Bordeaux, France)
4. Tokaji Aszu 5 Puttonyos (Hungary)
5. Château de Fesles Bonnezaux (Loire, France)
6. Bott-Geyl Tokay Pinot Gris Grand Cru Sonnenglanz Vendanges Tardives (Alsace, France)
7. Château d'Yquem, Sauternes (Bordeaux, France)
12. Château d'Yquem Sauternes (Bordeaux, France) $250

Fortified Wine

There are four primary types of fortified wines: Port, Sherry, Madeira and Marsala. The popular drinking wines are Port and Sherry. The Madeira and Marsala are better known for being cooking wines, but there are good bottles of each for drinking. 'Fortified' refers to the addition of alcohol in the production process. The wine's alcohol content is boosted from 10–14 per cent up to 18–20 per cent by adding grape brandy that is usually made from the same grape as the original wine.

When brandy is added after fermentation, the fortified wine is dry (has no residual sugar). If added before fermentation is complete, the fortified wine is sweet because the extra alcohol stops the yeast from converting the sugars. Fortified wine runs the gamut from bone-dry Fino Sherry to rich, sweet Port and Madeira. All four of these fortified wines have lengthy stories, as do most things in the wine world.

PORT

Port, or Porto, comes from Portugal. The name, however, comes not from the country but from the city of Oporto at the mouth of the Douro River. As the most commonly available red fortified wine, it has natural appeal among red wine lovers who prize Port's capacity to improve with age in the bottle for many decades.

Port is sold in several different styles – Vintage, Tawny and Ruby are the principal versions. Vintage Port, the most expensive of these, is also the easiest to produce – as long as nature co-operates; Tawny Port, so named for its brownish cast, is the result of long barrel-ageing; and Ruby Port, named for its bright, unoxidized colour, is an inexpensive style that is perfect for neophytes and fine cooking.

Port is made from several different red varieties that grow to extreme ripeness in Portugal's hot Duro valley. The dark-coloured 'Tintas' – Tinta Cao, Tinta Barroca and Tinta Roriz (Spain's Tempranillo) – are blended with Touriga Francesa and Touriga Nacional in various proportions. A white Port is produced, although it is not nearly as prized as the red versions. All (red) Port, then, starts out as 'musts' from these varieties, which are allowed to ferment half-way to dryness before the addition of brandy. Since half of the natural sugar remains unfermented, the resulting fortified wine is sweet. It then begins its life in 'Port pipes' (138-gallon storage casks).

Vintage Port

After two years in storage a vintage may be 'declared' by agreement of a majority of the Port producers. This means that the Port from that particular vintage is deemed to be of sufficient quality to justify offering it as top-of-the-line Vintage Port. Vintage Port is then bottled and is best aged for at least a decade. Because Vintage Port ages in the bottle, often for several decades, it inevitably deposits a substantial amount of sediment in the bottle.

Vintage Port has always been quite popular in Britain, and 'match made in heaven' is Vintage Port and a wedge of Stilton. The pungent saltiness of the cheese complements beautifully the sweet richness of Vintage Port.

Tawny Port

Unlike Vintage Port, which is transferred to bottles in its youth, Tawny Port may remain in the cask for 10, 20 or even 30 years. 'Tawny' refers to the pale-brown hue of these fortified wines after so long in the cask, where oxidation occurs more readily than in the bottle. With the high alcohol guarding against the formation of vinegar, the oxidation in this case improves the flavour over time. The fruit flavours of youth evolve into mellower, more subtle flavours, and the Port becomes seemingly less sweet.

Tawny Port requires far more blending skills then does vintage Port. Unless labelled 'Port of the Vintage' (another form of Tawny Port), most Tawny's are blends of ports from several different years chosen for their complementary characteristics.

Ruby Port

Ruby Port, named for its bright crimson colour, is a blend of young, lesser lots of Port. Again the blender's art is of importance – lesser lots (casks) of Port may be skillfully blended to produce an inexpensive and delicious Ruby Port.

The forthright flavours of Ruby Port make it a perfect choice for recipes that call for Port – the flavours of Ruby Port endure the cooking process far better than will the other types. Ruby Port is a perfect introduction to Port as you begin to explore fortified wines.

SHERRY

Like the other types of fortified wine, Sherry owes its popularity to the British. In fact, the name 'Sherry' is an Anglicization of 'Jerez', the port city on the coast of Spain from which Sherry is shipped.

Sherry is made by fortifying dry white wine made from the Palomino grape grown in southern Spain. Sherry is not as well respected as Port in the UK, probably because it's seen as being something sweet and sticky that your aged auntie drags out of the liqueur cabinet every year at Christmas. As a result, quality Sherry is often overlooked and underpriced. And yet quality Sherry can be an ideal substitute for a variety of hard drinks:

- Serve a well-chilled fino Sherry in place of a martini;
- Offer a dark, dry Oloroso Sherry (at room temperature) after dinner instead of Cognac;
- Replace sweet liqueur with a glass of PX Sherry.

Whereas Port, particularly vintage Port, is perceived as closely akin to fine wine by consumers, quality Sherry is regarded as a manufactured product by many people, more like liquor than wine. Indeed, the ageing, fortification and blending processes for Sherry are far more involved than those for Vintage Port.

How Sherry Is Made

All Sherry begins its life in the warm, dry vineyards of southern Spain. Here the Palomino grape, a variety of little use apart from Sherry production, is made into dry, still wine. This wine, called *mosto*, is initially fortified with brandy to an alcohol level of 15 per cent and permitted to age in the presence of air. While contact with air would destroy most wines at this stage, the partially fortified *mosto* thrives on it. In most (but not all) of these huge barrels, a cushion of spongy yeast, called *flor*, develops on the surface of the wine.

In barrels with ample flor development, the wine beneath the layer of yeast is protected from oxidation and remains pale in colour. The *flor* yeast also imparts flavour on the wine and further concentrates the alcoholic content. Sherry from these barrels is generally called 'fino' and may become one of the three paler types of Sherry—Fino itself, Manzauilla or Amontillado.

The barrels that develop little or no *flor* yeast yield 'oloroso' Sherry, which is finished as one of the darker styles – dry Oloroso itself, sweet Amoroso or very sweet cream Sherry. An especially rare type of Sherry is Palo Cortado, an Oloroso that develops *flor* yeast late in its life and can combine the finest qualities of both Finos and Olorosos.

Because the alcohol in Fino Sherries is concentrated by the *flor* yeast, these types of Sherry are given additional fortification only as required by importers worldwide. In Spain, Fino Sherry is often not additionally fortified and can be found at 16 per cent alcohol. As such, this type of Sherry will not survive indefinitely in an opened bottle.

The darker Oloroso Sherries usually receive a second fortification that raises the alcoholic strength to 18–20 per cent. Because of this, Olorosos can live for a long time in the bottle after it is opened.

The blending process used in Sherry production, called 'solera', is unique. Barrels of young Sherry are connected to older barrels in such a manner that Sherries from different years are blended; this is why these are no vintage sherries. You may, however, find an expensive Sherry with a year on the label. This is usually the vintage year of the oldest Sherry in the solera blend and may be over 100 years old.

Types of Sherry

The Fino Family

Manzanilla – This is a pale, dry, fino Sherry that comes from the coastal town of Sanlúcar de Barrameda. Because it matures in casks stored near the sea, it acquires a tangy salty flavour from the coastal air. Serve it with *tapas*.

Fino – Fino is both the general name of the unfinished *flor* Sherries and the name of one of the finished products within that group. This Sherry is pale, dry and best served chilled as an apéritif in the hot summer.

Amontillado – This style of Sherry is most notable for its nut-like flavour and aroma. These characteristics, along with a light brown colour, can develop when a fino-type Sherry ages. Like the other fino types, Amontillado is a before-dinner drink, though better served at room temperature. While the paler fino types are most enjoyable in the hot summer, Amontillado is more an autumn apéritif with its richer flavours.

The Oloroso Family

Oloroso – There is a popular perception that darker Sherries are, by definition, sweeter – not so. Oloroso Sherry itself is, in its natural state, quite dry. (Like Fino Sherry, Oloroso Sherry is both the name of a category of sherries – those unaffected by *flor* – and the name of one of the finished products in this category. Good Oloroso is dry, richly flavoured and full-bodied, and is medium-brown in colour.

PX Sherry – A super-sweet, syrupy wine made from a grape known as Pedro Ximenez (pronounced Him-er-nez). Although you can drink it by itself – or, rather, sip it slowly, it is very sweet – PX is absolutely delicious when poured over vanilla ice cream as a sauce

Cream—The sweetest of Sherries, if not the darkest, is Cream Sherry, first developed in Bristol. The widespread success of Harvey's Bristol Cream notwithstanding, Cream Sherry (even Harvey's!) can be an enjoyable after-dinner drink.

MADEIRA AND MARSALA

Whereas Port and Sherry are generally enjoyed as beverages, Madeira and Marsala are more commonly used for cooking. If you find that you enjoy Sherry and Port, you might want to experiment with these.

Madeira

Madeira is a small Portuguese-governed island in the Atlantic Ocean off the north-west coast of Africa that produces fortified wines named after the island. The most common of these wines are used for cooking, but the better ones are consumed as an apéritif. Madeira is unusual in that it is heated during production, a technique that was discovered to improve the taste of the wine during the long sea voyages of the 1600s.

Light brown in colour, Maderia can be sweet or dry. The four primary types of Madeira are Sercial, Verdelho, Bual and Malmsey. If you don't see one of these four names on the bottle, you are getting a lesser Madeira. If you are going to venture into the world of Madeira wines, compare a pale Sercial to a dark Malmsey and figure out what style you like. The best Madeira is often aged for many decades, and is a rare treat.

'Malmsey' is a British corruption of 'Malvasia', and all Madeira labelled 'Malmsey' is, in fact, made from Malvasia grapes. Plan on spending around £10 for your first Sercial Madeira.

Marsala

Named for the town on the western tip of Sicily, Marsala is a brown-coloured fortified wine made from the green-skinned Catarratto grape, a local variety. After harvesting, the grapes are dried prior to fermentation, which raises the sugar level. After fortification, Marsala is often sweetened and darkened with grape juice syrup. Barrel-aging mellows its flavours.

Of all the fortified wines, Marsala is the least distinctive as a beverage and is best kept in the kitchen. Marsala comes in two styles, dry and sweet. Both are used for cooking.

FORTIFIED WINES WORTH TRYING

1. *Very Dry Fino Sherry.* Recommended producer is Tio Pepé (Spain). Serve chilled, with appetizers.
2. *Amontillado Sherry.* Recommended producer is Savory & James (Spain). Drink it alone or with snacks. It tastes like nuts and smells like an autumn forest.
3. *Vintage Port.* Recommended producers are Smith-Woodhouse, Dow's Croft, and Quinta do Noval. These can be very expensive, often £40 or more.
4. *Tawny Port.* Recommended producer is Taylor-Fladgate.
5. *Bual Madeira.* Recommended producer is Cossart's (Madeira). Sweet, but not too sweet. Good for cooking and as a before-dinner drink.
6. *Malmsey Madeira.* Recommended producer is Cossart's (Madeira). Sweet, rich, and nutty (just like a favourite uncle). Good as an after-dinner drink.
7. *Dry or Sweet Marsala.* Recommended producer is Florio (Sicily). Often used for cooking.
8. *Croft Late.* Bottle vintage Tawny Port. Reminiscent of a great Vintage Port, only much cheaper.

Note: There are many price points for fortified wines from the same producers.

10 Lesser Known Treasures

1. MOSCATO D'ASTI (ITALIAN WHITE)

There's nothing like it. It tastes like Italian wedding cake. It has a slight fizz, is low in alcohol (5.5 per cent), and is pleasantly sweet. Enjoy it with fruit, fried rice or Italian wedding cake. *Price:* £5–10

2. GERMAN RIESLING

Most Rieslings are less sweet than you think and are a great match with spicy Asian foods. Look for the German word *trocken* on the label, which means dry. Beware of *halb-trocken*, which means half dry, unless you are interested in a sweeter wine. *Price:* £4–8

3. VIN DE PAYS D'OC (FRANCE)

These varietal wines are among the best bargains to be had on the supermarket shelves. A dynamic attitude to winemaking has changed this region, once famed for producing dilute plonk, into a powerhouse of wine production with a competitive edge. The wines themselves are great alone, without food, but slip down a treat with dinner. *Price*: £4–7

4. NEW ZEALAND PINOT NOIR

These light, delicate reds resemble good French Pinot Noirs that sell for much more. *Price:* £9–12

5. ARGENTINA MALBEC

In the past few years, Argentinian wine-makers have really got to grips with this red grape. These days they're using it to produce wines that are often soft and fruity, but with enough structure to be taken seriously. And, thanks to Argentina's disastrous economy, they're a real bargain. *Price*: £4–8

6. SOUTHERN ITALIAN WINES

A decade or so of investment in the vineyards of southern Italy – places like Puglia and Sicily – has paid off, big-time. Although you may never have heard of half the grape varieties, at these kinds of prices it's worth taking a punt. *Price*: £4–6

7. NEW WORLD SPARKLING WINES

You'll get a lot of bang from your buck by directing your attention New World-wards. California, Australia, New Zealand, South Africa and Argentina all make thoroughly respectable – sometimes even really exciting – fizz for less than half the price of the French originals. *Price*: £5–12

8. WHITES FROM ALSACE

Riesling vines are at their best in the Alsatian soil, yet are overlooked by wine drinkers scrambling for Chardonnay. Here is a chance to enjoy very high quality wines at bargain prices. *Price*: £6–14

9. PORT

This is a good way to bring the hard liquor and wine drinkers together. It's good wine with a kick. Serving Port is a cost effective, fun way to be a bit less pedestrian in this era of mass brands and fast foods. A great half bottle or a good full-size bottle go for the same money. *Price*: £7–25

10. PORTUGUESE REDS

Dry Portuguese reds are a bit of a bargain, thanks to low demand for non-Port wines from the country, and a general lack of interest. You may not know the grape varieties, and it may be a bit of a hit-or-miss proposition, but it's worth trying a few of the mid-priced reds. You may hit the jackpot. *Price*: £5–10

WHITES
at a glance...

	CHEAP	BETTER	GREAT	OFF DRY	DRY	WITH FOOD	WITHOUT FOOD
Chardonnay	🍷	🍷	🍷🍷		🍷	🍷	🍷
Riesling	🍷	🍷	🍷🍷	🍷	🍷	🍷	🍷
Sauvignon Blanc	🍷	🍷	🍷		🍷	🍷	
Chenin Blanc	🍷	🍷		🍷	🍷	🍷	
Pinot Blanc		🍷			🍷	🍷	
Pinot Grigio (Gris)	🍷	🍷			🍷	🍷	
Gewürztraminer			🍷	🍷			
Semillon		🍷	🍷	🍷		🍷	

Cheap: Under £6   *Better:* £6–15   *Great:* £30 and up   🍷🍷 Extrodinary performance within category

WHITES AT A GLANCE

The authors have assigned a 🍷 to almost all of the wine grapes in the *Better* category. In this price range we feel that personal preference is the strongest variable in the equation. A 'double' 🍷🍷 means 'especially so'.

White wine generally isn't as complex as red wine. This is why we have so few in the *Without Food* category. On the flip side, it tends to be acidic (in a good way), which gives it a thirst-quenching quality. That is why whites go so well with food.

Gewürztraminer is often recommended as a good complement to Chinese food, but the authors prefer a simple Riesling. Most Gewürztraminers are a little too quirky to be matched up with food. Drink them without food or, if you must, with simple food that doesn't require careful matching, like bread or cheese.

REDS AT A GLANCE

The authors have assigned a 🍷 to almost all of the wine grapes in the *Better* category. In this price range we feel that personal preference is the strongest variable in the equation. Cabernet Sauvignon, more than any other grape, benefits from ageing. Additionally, it makes (arguably) the best red wines in the world. So although we have given it a 🍷 in the £6–15 category, you shouldn't expect greatness in those bottles. Usually the Cabs are very

REDS
at a glance...

	CHEAP	BETTER	GREAT		WITH FOOD	WITHOUT FOOD
Cabernet Sauvignon		🍷	🍷🍷		🍷	🍷
Merlot		🍷			🍷	🍷
Gamay	🍷🍷	🍷				🍷
Pinot Noir		🍷	🍷🍷			🍷
Syrah (Shiraz)	🍷🍷	🍷	🍷		🍷	
Grenache	🍷	🍷			🍷	🍷
Nebbiolo	🍷	🍷	🍷🍷		🍷	🍷
Sangiovese	🍷	🍷	🍷		🍷	🍷
Zinfandel	🍷	🍷			🍷	🍷
Tempranillo	🍷	🍷	🍷		🍷	

Cheap: Under £6   *Better:* £6–15   *Great:* £30 and up

🍷🍷 Extrodinary performance within category

forward, with perhaps too much tannin for some people. You may want to look at the Aussie Cab/Shiraz blends in this price range. However, if you like a strongly flavored wine, then you shouldn't hesitate to try some straight Cabernet.

There are good wine values in all price ranges for almost all varietals. This chart is meant to be a general guide of what to look for. It reflects general quality and quantity of wines available at the various price levels.

The right £5 Syrah can be a very eye-opening experience for a wine novice or a person on a budget. It will have a boldness and complexity that imitates the qualities found in many higher priced wines. *Beware:* if you don't like tannin, some Syrah/Shirazes are apt to be too tannic for your tastes.

If you just want a cheap red that tastes good, Gamay-based Beaujolais from France is the way to go.

Tempranillo is grown almost exclusively in Spain and is the principal grape of the red wines from the Rioja region of that country. Riojas are light bodied and very compatible with food.

CHAPTER 6

WINE AROUND THE WORLD

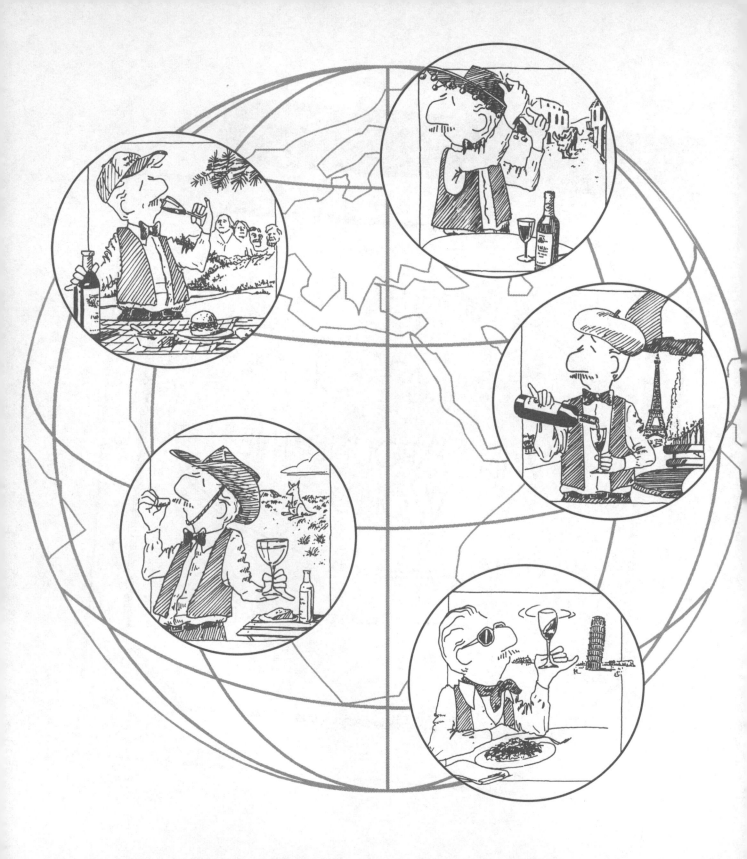

France

France is to wine what Microsoft is to personal-computer software.

As Julius Caesar concluded 2,000 years ago, France is a pretty good place to grow wine grapes. Through trial and error, after centuries of careful cultivation and meticulous record-keeping, particularly by the Church, the French learned how to make very good wine. Indeed, it is not far-fetched to say that they have defined good wine. The wineries in California, South America and Australia strive to produce wine that will compare favourably with French wines. These New-World regions may have succeeded in producing beautiful wines that often exceed their French counterparts in sheer power, but never in finesse.

It is generally accepted among wine experts that France produces many 'best-of types':

The best Champagnes are the finest sparkling wines in the world.

Alsace Gewürztraminer is the best version of this quirky wine.

The Pauillac and Margaux districts of Bordeaux produce the finest Cabernet Sauvignon–based wines in the world.

Merlot best displays its qualities in the Bordeaux subregions of Saint-Emilion and Pomerol.

The *grand cru* vineyards of the Côte de Beaune produce the finest Chardonnays.

The most refined Sauvignon Blanc–based wines are produced in Sancerre and the Graves subregion of Bordeaux.

Chenin Blanc is in its glory along the Loire River.

Sauternes, from the town of the same name, is widely acclaimed as the world's finest dessert wine.

The prototype Pinot Noir comes from the vineyards of Côte de Nuits in Burgundy.

For a simple, acidic shellfish wine, Muscadet is without equal.

Finally, the dry rosé wines of Provence are considered to be the best of their type.

The only gap in the spectrum of French appellation wines is a selection of fruity, low-acid wines that go best without food. This might well be by design, as the French rarely drink wine without food, nor do they often enjoy food without wine. Also, the cool climates of France are not conducive to achieving the degree of ripeness required for rich, fruity wines. The Gamay-based wines from southern Burgundy are a notable exception to this rule.

Although it is widely accepted that France produces the best wines in the world, it does not have a monopoly on good, inexpensive wines. The French section in the wine shop might offer a £30 bargain, but £5 bargains are more difficult to find. Recently,

French producers have begun to respond to the consumer's desire for inexpensive variety-labelled wines. In addition to the usual suspects – Chardonnay, Merlot, Cabernet Sauvignon – one may find Viognier, Syrah, and others at prices below £7.

While most of these wines are simple food wines, they can represent good value. These wines are usually labelled, in accordance with French law, as country wine *(vin de pays)*. It is difficult to find better Merlot anywhere in the world for under £5 than those from the Languedoc region.

Other wines worth finding in the £5–7 range are Côtes-du-Rhône reds; white Bordeaux; and Saint-Véran, a simple white Burgundy made from Chardonnay.

Except for the *vins de pays*, French wines are usually labelled by geographical region (i.e., Bordeaux) rather than grape variety. This reflects the French view that soil is of supreme importance in producing quality wines. Except for the inexpensive *vin de pays* country wine varietals, only the wines from the Alsace region are labelled by variety.

In order to understand the degrees of specificity of French wine labelling, think of an archery target. The outer circle is all of France; the next-largest circle is a region of France such as Bordeaux; the next circle is in the district of, say, Médoc; within that is the commune name, say, Pauillac; finally, the bull's eye –

the individual producer, a château or domaine. The better (and often the more expensive) the wine, the more specific is the indicated source of the wine.

Just as French society is hierarchical, sometimes ridiculously so, so is her classification of her beloved wines. A general understanding of the classification of French wine is vital to your wine knowledge, since France long ago invented the wines that the rest of the world imitates.

Label Law from the top down:

Appellation d'origine contrôlée (AOC or AC): the most widely applied standard used on French wine labels. It indicates that the wine meets the legal standards (per French wine law) for the area indicated. The more specific the area of origin, the higher the standards.

Vins délimités de qualité supérieure (VDQS): a second set of standards for wines in areas not covered by AOC law. Although a notch down in quality, VDQS is still a reliable government guarantee of quality.

Vins de pays: 'country' wines from outlying areas. Most varietal wines (the name of the grape is on the bottle) come under this heading.

Think of France as seven major regions, each with its own system of organization and classification: Bordeaux, Burgundy (Bourgogne), Rhône, Loire, Alsace, Champagne and Languedoc.

BORDEAUX

Bordeaux, an industrial city in southwestern France, is the centre of the world's most famous wine region. Several types of wine are produced here:

Dry white wines: Blends of Sauvignon Blanc and Semillon.

Sweet dessert wines: Blends of Sauvignon Blanc, Semillon and Muscadelle afflicted with *Botrytis cinerea* (Noble Rot), a grape mould that concentrates the natural sugars.

Medium-bodied red wines: Blends of Cabernet Sauvignon, Merlot, Cabernet Franc and Petit Verdot. Some subregions produce

wine made primarily from Cabernet Sauvignon, whereas the Merlot grape is dominant in other areas. Here are the most important subregions of Bordeaux and the wines they produce:

Sauternes – sweet dessert wines
Pomerol – Merlot-dominant reds
Saint-Emilion – Merlot-dominant reds
Entre-Deux-Mers – light, simple whites
Graves – fine dry whites, Cabernet
   Sauvignon–based reds
Médoc – Cabernet Sauvignon–
   based reds

The Médoc, a subregion of Bordeaux, is a relatively large area and contains six 'communes' (wine-producing areas, kind of like small towns) that are entitled to their own appellation:

Saint-Estèphe
Saint-Julien
Margaux
Pauillac
Moulis
Listrac

Satellites
The outlying regions of Bordeaux, known as the 'satellite communes', are often good sources of well-made, reasonably priced wines. These are made in a similar style to those in the major communes, but are often simpler, fruitier and cheaper. Look out for names like Côtes de Castillon, Côtes de Bourg, Côtes de Blaye and Lalande-de-Pomerol.

FRANCE LABEL – BORDEAUX

CHATEAU PICHON LONGUEVILLE COMTESSE DE LALANDE: The name of the château where the wine was produced.

PAUILLAC: The appellation of origin, Pauillac is a commune (or village) within the Médoc subregion of Bordeaux.

1988: Vintage.

GRAND CRU CLASSE: Means that this wine was classified in the 1855 classification of Médoc red wines. The label fails to mention that this château is a second growth, or *Deuxieme cru.*

MIS EN BOUTEILLE AU CHATEAU: 'Put in the bottle at the château.' This is a château-bottled wine, as opposed to a shipper-bottled wine, and is often an indication of quality.

You will find on the market a great number of châteaux-bottled Bordeaux wines. A château, in this context, is literally a piece of land, rather than a fairytale castle. In anticipation of an agricultural exposition in 1855, the local government in Bordeaux asked representatives of the wine trade to rate the red wines of Médoc according to price history. Those wines that over time had fetched the highest prices were given the highest ranking, and so on down. The highest ranking, *premier cru* ('first growth'), includes only five (originally four) châteaux, one of which (Château Haut-Brion) is actually from neighbouring Graves but was included because of its record of excellence. The other four are Château Margaux in the commune of Margaux, and Châteaux Lafite, Mouton-Rothschild and Latour, all in Pauillac. The classified growths of Médoc are ranked first growth, second, third, fourth and fifth. Below this level are the *cru bourgeois* wines and the *petits châteaux* wines.

The sweet dessert wines of Sauternes were classified at the time of those of Médoc. Other subregions of Bordeaux have since adopted some form of classification. Although such quality classifications may become outdated and no longer reflect reality, they can be a self-fulfilling prophecy – a *premier cru* is expected to be expensive and excellent; therefore, the winemaker can afford to make such a wine, knowing that the market will accept the price.

BURGUNDY (BOURGOGNE)

Burgundy produces three general types of wine. There are others, but these are the most important.:

1. Light, velvety red wine made from Pinot Noir
2. Light, fruity red wine made from Gamay
3. Dry white wine made from Chardonnay

Travelling from north to south through the heart of France, you pass through the subregions of Burgundy in sequence:

Chablis – very dry whites
Côte de Nuits – full-bodied Pinot Noir reds, a few whites
Côte de Beaune – lighter Pinot Noir, excellent Chardonnay
Côte Chalonnaise – less expensive Pinot Noir and Chardonnay
Mâcon – Chardonnay whites, including the famous Pouilly-Fuissé
Beaujolais – Gamay reds

The Chablis vineyards are ranked (in descending order of quality) as Chablis Grand Cru, Chablis Premier Cru, Chablis and Petit Chablis.

The red and white vineyards of the Côte de Nuits and Côte de Beaune (together known as the Côte d'Or) are ranked either Grand Cru, Premier Cru or no rank at all.

The famous villages of the Côte de Nuits are Nuits-Saint-Georges; Gevrey-Chambertin; Vosne-Romanée; Morey-Saint-Denis; and Chambolle-Musigny. These villages are all famous for their red wines, some of which are fabulously expensive.

Famous villages of the Côte de Beaune (by wine type) are:

Reds
Pernand-Vergelesses
Savigny-lès-Beaune
Volnay
Pommard
Beaune
Meursault
Chassagne-Montrachet
Aloxe-Corton

Whites
Puligny-Montrachet
Chassagne-Montrachet
Meursault
Beaune
Aloxe-Corton

Beaujolais may be labelled as Beaujolais, Beaujolais Supérieur (which is 1 per cent higher in alcohol than simple Beaujolais), Beaujolais-Villages, or *cru* Beaujolais with a village name. Moulin-á-Vent, Brouilly and St-Amour are the best known of the *crus*. There are ten such *cru* villages entitled to use their own names. *Cru* Beaujolais is the best of the Beaujolais, but it usually costs less than £10.

RHÔNE
Earthy and gutsy wines, both red and white, are produced along the Rhône River, south of the Burgundy region. The wines of the Rhône are (mercifully) without a ranking system.

Northern Rhône Reds: Big, Syrah-based reds worthy of ageing for at least a few years.
Côte Rôtie
Hermitage/Crozes-Hermitage
Cornas
St. Joseph

Northern Rhône Whites: Substantial whites made from Viognier or a blend of Marsanne and Roussane.
Condrieu
Hermitage/Crozes-Hermitage

Southern Rhône Reds: Grenache-based blends: With Syrah, Cinsault, Mouvèdre and other grapes.
Côtes-du-Rhône
Gigondas
Châteauneuf-du-Pape

Southern Rhône Whites: Not so common, these big wines are made from Marsanne and Roussane, and are an interesting alternative to Chardonnay.
Côtes-du-Rhône Blanc
Châteauneuf-du-Pape Blanc

Southern Rhône Rosé: Tavel, a dry rosé made primarily from Grenache, is considered by many wine buffs to be the finest rosé in the world.

LOIRE
The vineyards along the largest river in France yield a variety of refreshing (mostly white) wines. Here are the most important ones:

Muscadet – a perfect shellfish wine made from the grape of the same name.

FRANCE LABEL – BURGUNDY

MEURSAULT-PERRIERES: Meursault is a commune in the Côte de Beaume subregion of Burgundy; Perrières is a vineyard ranked *premier cru* (second to *grand cru* in the Burgundy hierarchy).

PREMIER CRU: Second to *grand cru* in the Burgundy hierarchy.

Meursault-Perrières

PREMIER CRU

APPELLATION MEURSAULT 1ᵉʳ CRU CONTROLÉE

Louis Latour

MIS EN BOUTEILLE PAR LOUIS LATOUR

NÉGOCIANT A BEAUNE (COTE-D'OR), FRANCE

LOUIS LATOUR: Producer/shipper (négociant).

MIS EN BOUTEILLE PAR LOUIS LATOUR: Put in the bottle by the négociant, as opposed to domaine- or château-bottled.

Vouvray – made from the Chenin Blanc grape, Vouvray may be bone-dry (sec), delightfully off dry (demi-sec) or sparkling.

Rosé d'Anjou – an off-dry rosé made mostly from Cabernet Sauvignon and Cabernet Franc.

Pouilly Fumé – straight Sauvignon Blanc in a rich, heady style.

Sancerre – unblended Sauvignon Blanc in a style more acidic than Pouilly Fumé.

Reds – light-bodied, aromatic red wines are made from Pinot Noir or Cabernet Franc grapes'

Sweet wines – some of the most unctuous sweet wines in the world are made in the Loire from the Chenin Blanc grape.

ALSACE

Historically, the geographical area of Alsace has belonged to whoever won the most recent war between France and Germany. As such, it is currently part of France but not without considerable German influence in her wines. Late harvest sweet wines are produced in Alsace, as well as dry ones.

In this region there is a tradition of varietal labelling: no 'cutting' is allowed. If a grape is named, then the content of it must be 100 per cent. The term *grand cru* may appear on an Alsace label as an indication that the wine has a minimum alcohol content of 10 or 11 per cent (depending on the grape) and meets some perfunctory yield requirements. The varieties used are:

Riesling
Gewürztraminer
Pinot Gris (Tokay Pinot Gris)
Muscat
Pinot Blanc
A small amount of Pinot Noir (the only red, often used for rosé)

CHAMPAGNE

In order to qualify for the Champagne appellation (according to French *and* EEC law), a sparkling wine must (1) be produced in the Champagne district, (2) be produced from the Chardonnay, Pinot Noir and/or Pinot Meunier (red) grapes grown there, and (3) get its bubbles via the *méthode champenoise* (Champagne method.)

The Champagne method is an expensive and labour-intensive means of naturally carbonating a wine. First, wine is made from local grapes. This is no easy feat; the vineyards of Champagne lie so far north that ripeness is an issue in many years. After clarification and a measure of ageing, the wine is put into thick Champagne bottles, along with enough yeast and sugar to initiate a second fermentation. It is this second fermentation in the tightly sealed bottle that puts the bubbles in the bubbly – the carbon dioxide cannot escape, so it is dissolved in the wine. The hard work is in removing the dead yeast. After ageing the wine with the dead yeast – sometimes for many years, as this adds character to the Champagne – the dead yeast is coaxed into the neck of the bottle by gradually tilting the bottle a little bit each day until it is inverted. The dead yeast is then carefully removed. At this time, the bottle is topped up and adjusted for sweetness with the addition of a mixture of wine and sugar syrup known as the *dosage*. The degree of sweetness appears on the label as:

Extra Brut – less than 6g sugar/litre
Brut – less than 15g sugar/litre
Extra Dry – 12–20g sugar/litre
Demi-Sec – 17–35g sugar/litre
Rich or doux – more than 50g
  sugar/litre

Some other Champagne terms are:

Blanc de Blancs – made only from white grapes, i.e., Chardonnay.
Brut Rosé – pink-coloured Champagne. The colour comes from the red skins of Pinot Noir and/or Pinot Meunier skins.
Blanc de Noirs – pale sparkling wine from dark-skinned grapes.
Tête de Cuvée – a super-premium Champagne, usually vintage dated.
Vintage – in contrast to the far more common practice of blending wines from different years, vintage Champagne is made from wine from a single harvest. Although most *tête de cuvées* are vintage-dated, a year on the bottle doesn't mean that it is superior to a non-vintage bottle.

THE LANGUEDOC

Once the source of a vast lake of watery plonk, the Languedoc is now becoming well known as a source of both easy-to-drink, varietally labelled vin de pays and increasingly well-made appellation wines. There are a dozen or so of these appellations. The ones you find most frequently come from Fitou, Minervois, Faugères and the Coteaux du Languedoc.

The red wines tend to be made from a blend of grapes that may include any or all of the following: Syrah, Grenache, Carignan and Mourvèdre. They vary in style between concentrated, velvety Syrah-based wines to slightly more tannic versions that often contain a higher proportion of Grenache or Carignan. The latter are said to smell of the garrigue, the herby scrub that covers the local mountains.

Rosés tend towards the dry end of the scale and are often great value. The whites are fruity and round. They contain an eclectic mix of grapes, but tend to major in oddities like Grenache Blanc, Rolle and our old Rhône friends Marsanne and Roussanne.

Italy

Italian wine is a tough nut to crack. Although the wines of the New World can be explained in relationship to their French counterparts, the wines of Italy seldom can. The land we now call Italy has been making wine for four thousand years; however, it was not politically unified within her present borders until the mid-1800s. This land of diverse climates, cultures, and even languages produces a baffling variety of wines.

The wines of Italy rival those of France in variety and, in some cases, quality. Like France, Italy also labels her wines according to geographical origin rather than grape variety (of course, as with France, there are exceptions). Italy is divided politically into 20 regions (18 mainland, plus Sicily and Sardinia). The regions of Tuscany, Piedmont and Veneto produce the majority of the quality Italian wine found in wine shops. Northern Italy is becoming a good source of dry, aromatic whites, while southern Italy is increasingly exciting. Down in the heat of Puglia, Sardinia and Sicily, a whole range of exotic red grapes with names like Negroamaro, Aglianico and Primitivo (the USA's Zinfandel) thrive. Whatever your price range, and wherever you buy your wine, it should be easy to get your hands on a really classy bottle of Italian wine. Even if you're not quite sure what you're getting, it's worth a try – experimenting is half the fun.

The Italian government has officially recognized the traditional wines of Italy (as well as some newcomers) with a system similar to that of France:

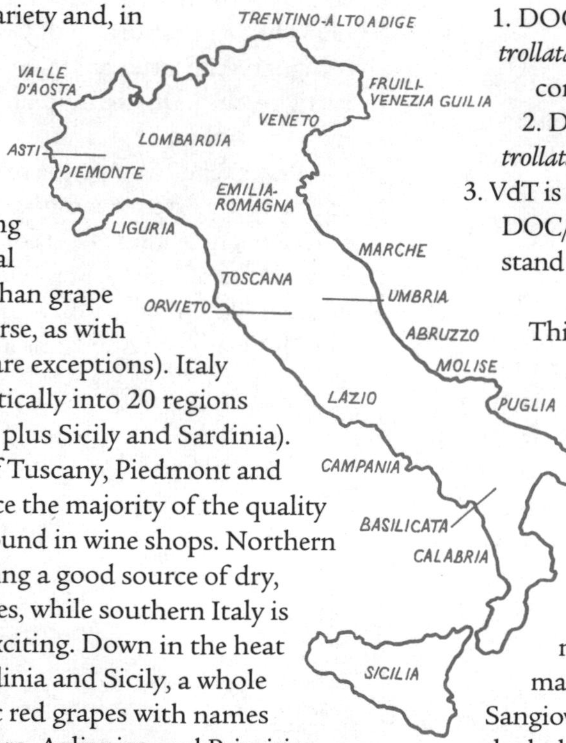

1. DOCG (*denominazione di origine controllata e garantita*) is the highest status conferred on Italian wines.
2. DOC (*denominazione di origine controllata*) is the next highest level.
3. VdT is a general category for non-DOC/DOCG wines. These initials stand for *vino da tavola*, or table wine.

This system recognizes traditionally outstanding wines and establishes the geographic origin, grape variety or varieties to be used, minimum alcohol content and ageing requirements. For example, Chianti Classico is a recognized DOCG wine. It must be made from (primarily) the Sangiovese grape, have a minimum alcohol content of 12 per cent and

Map labels: TRENTINO-ALTO ADIGE, VALLE D'AOSTA, FRUILI-VENEZIA GUILIA, VENETO, LOMBARDIA, ASTI, PIEMONTE, EMILIA-ROMAGNA, LIGURIA, MARCHE, TOSCANA, ORVIETO, UMBRIA, ABRUZZO, MOLISE, LAZIO, PUGLIA, CAMPANIA, BASILICATA, CALABRIA, SICILIA

ITALY LABEL

CONTERNO: Producer.

BAROLO RISERVA: Type of wine – specific grape variety (Nebbiolo), region of origin, and method of production all assured by DOCG designation.

DENOMINAZIONE DI ORIGINE CONTROLLATA E GARANTITA (DOCG): This designation means that *Barolo Riserva* is recognized by the Italian government as a traditional wine-type and that this wine meets the standards set forth for this wine-type grape variety, maximum yield, minimum alcohol, ageing requirements, etc.

MONFORTINO: A proprietary name used by this producer for its blend of Barolo from several top vineyards. In place of this name you might find a vineyard name on similar bottles.

Although the year is not shown here, it appears on a separate, smaller label on the bottleneck.

come from a particular zone in central Tuscany. With a higher alcohol content (12.5 per cent) and three years' ageing prior to release, it may be called 'Chianti Classico Riserva'. DOC/DOCG status is a guarantee as to where and how the wine is produced; it is not a guarantee as to how it will taste.

The DOC/DOCG laws do not cover all the good or great wines of Italy. Some of the most expensive wines from Tuscany are the 'super-Tuscans', delicious and ageworthy, often blends of Sangiovese and Cabernet Sauvignon. Also of considerable importance is the production of inexpensive varietal wines: Chardonnay, Pinot Grigio, Cabernet Sauvignon, Merlot, and Sangiovese.

The major red grape of the Piedmont region is Nebbiolo. If you encounter an Italian wine with a label written in Italian, Piedmont may be denoted as Piemonte. Barolo and Barbaresco are the two most famous Nebbiolo wines from Piedmont. They aren't cheap, but if you like red wine, they are worth the money. Barbera, another Piedmont red grape, makes everyday wine.

Italy produces a lot of very good red and white wine, some varietally labelled. Find a wine merchant you trust and ask for a tour of Italian wines. The following is a comprehensive table of major Italian wine types, not individual wines. Chianti, for example, is a type of wine.

MAJOR ITALIAN WINE TYPES

COLOUR	TYPE OF WINE	REGION	GRAPE VARIETIES
Red	Barolo	Piedmont	Nebbiolo
Red	Barbaresco	Piedmont	Nebbiolo
Red	Valpolicella	Veneto	Corvina, Rondinella and Molinara
Red	Amarone	Veneto	Corvina, Rondinella and Molinara
Red	Barbera d'Asti	Piedmont	Barbera
Red	Chianti	Tuscany	mostly Sangiovese
Red	Brunello di Montalcino	Tuscany	Brunello (a grape closely related to Sangiovese)
Red	Piave Merlot	Veneto	Merlot
Red	Morellino di Scansano	Tuscany	mostly Sangiovese
Red	Taurasi	Campania	Aglianico and Piedirosso
Red	Salice Salentino	Puglia	Negro Amaro
White	Soave	Veneto	Garganega and Trebbiano
White	Gavi	Piedmont	Cortese
White	Orvieto	Umbria	Trebbiano, Verdello and Grechetto
White	Greco di Tufo	Campania	Greco and Coda di Volpe

United States

The American wine industry began in several different places and exists today in a surprising number of states. The most important for the UK market, however, are California and, to a lesser extent, Washington (the northwestern state, not the city) and Oregon.

California wines are widely available, but bargains are getting harder to find. This is because the California wine industry has become so profit-driven that few wines remain underpriced for long. Having said that, there are still more than a few bottles priced around the £4-7 mark on the supermarket shelves. These will usually be varietal wines – look for Zinfandel, an American speciality. This juicy grape ripens well in California, producing wines with high alcohol and jammy dark berry fruit. The other main grapes grown in California are Cabernet Sauvignon and Merlot, which are often used to make 'Meritage' wines, based on Bordeaux blends; Pinot Noir; Chardonnay; Viognier, Syrah and Sauvignon Blanc.

The superstar winemakers at the 'boutique' wineries, many of which are based in Napa Valley, have repeatedly demonstrated their ability to produce world-class wines. These wines compare favourably with their French counterparts in power, if not in finesse.

The key areas to remember include Napa Valley, home to California's most prestigious wines – and wineries. Napa is known for both its powerful, punchy Cabernet Sauvignon and its heady, high-alcohol Chardonnays. Pinot Noir

tends to be grown in the cooler areas of Carneros and Santa Barbara. The Central Valley is home to many of the bigger branded wines.

Washington, way to the north of California, up by the Canadian border, enjoys a longer ripening season than the southern state. This allows its grapes to ripen more slowly, allowing them to develop full and complex flavours. Although the state produces some fine Syrahs, Rieslings and Viogniers, you're more likely to find Chardonnay, Cabernet Sauvignon, Merlot and Meritage wines in the UK. Oregon, sandwiched between the two states,

excels in cool-climate-loving grapes like Pinot Noir and Pinot Gris. They can be tricky to find, but if you track a bottle down it's well worth a shot.

Like most wines from the New World countries, those from America must indicate a specific grape variety on their label. But watch out, that doesn't necessarily mean that it only contains that particular grape (see page xxx [again, Ian, this was the table that got shifted early on in the book]). Many inexpensive bottles of premium varietals such as Chardonnay and Merlot are often 'stretched' with less expensive grapes.

UNITED STATES LABEL

KATHERINE'S VINEYARD: All of the grapes came from this vineyard.

ESTATE BOTTLED: This means that the grapes were grown by the producer.

1995: Vintage year.

CAMBRIA: Producer.

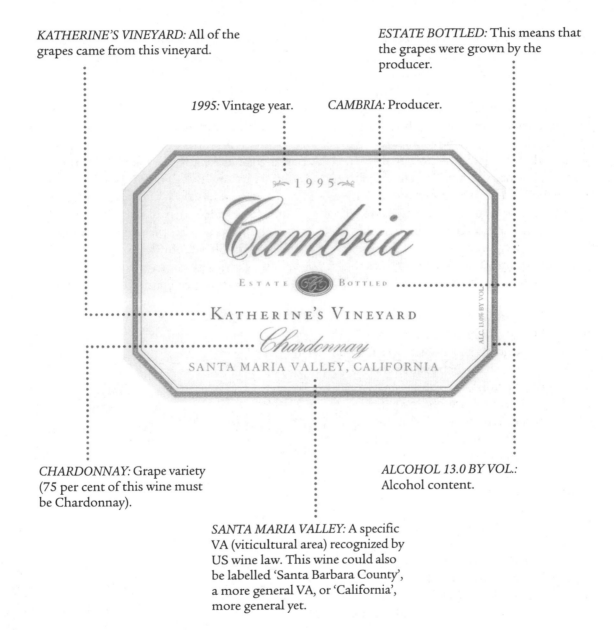

CHARDONNAY: Grape variety (75 per cent of this wine must be Chardonnay).

ALCOHOL 13.0 BY VOL.: Alcohol content.

SANTA MARIA VALLEY: A specific VA (viticultural area) recognized by US wine law. This wine could also be labelled 'Santa Barbara County', a more general VA, or 'California', more general yet.

Australia

Australia has been making wine since soon after the first shipload of British settlers arrived in 1788. Geographically isolated, Australia developed her own sophisticated winemaking technology largely independent of that developed in Europe. This factor, along with a combination of intense sunshine and cool breezes, helps to make Australian wines unique. Therefore, a varietal with which you have become familiar, such as Chardonnay or Shiraz (Syrah), will often display different characteristics in Australia.

Blending of premium varietals is common in Australia. One often finds the Chardonnay grape blended with Semillon, and Cabernet Sauvignon blended with Shiraz. This practice pre-dates the wine boom of the 1970s, when varietal wines became so popular. The Aussies knew, as did the Europeans, that when grape varieties are skilfully blended, the whole can be much more than the sum of the parts.

Many different styles of wine are produced in Australia. Dry whites are often made from Chardonnay or a blend of Chardonnay and Semillon. In addition, other white grapes, such as Riesling, Sauvignon Blanc and Viognier are now far more widely planted than a decade ago and are starting to make some classy wines.

Australian Chardonnays used to be made in a heavily oaked style. As well as loads of vanilla oak, these wines were often over-ripe, with excessive tropical fruit and flabby acidity. This tendency has been corrected, by and large, and a lot of Aussie winemakers are even experimenting with unoaked Chardonnays. Aussie Riesling has a growing number of fans, who love its crisp, clean acidity and lime and lemon cordial flavours. These make great food wines and are a great alternative for members of the ABC (Anything But Chardonnay) club.

Australia has always been a welcoming home for a wide variety of red grapes, and is well equipped to meet the surging worldwide demand for Shiraz. Shiraz is made in a variety of styles to suit a variety of different pockets. You can get a pleasant, basic fruity version for around £5 – more complex ver-

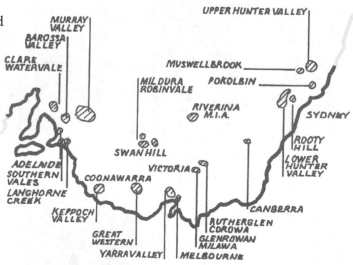

AUSTRALIA LABEL

SHIRAZ CABERNET: Grape varieties used – because neither grape comprises 85 per cent of the wine, the wine does not qualify for varietal labelling, and both varieties' proportions are given.

SOUTH EASTERN AUSTRALIA: Region of origin.

LINDEMANS: Producer.

CAWARRA HOMESTEAD: Property where produced.

CAWARRA
HOMESTEAD

1993
SOUTH EASTERN AUSTRALIA

SHIRAZ
CABERNET

58% SHIRAZ · 42% CABERNET SAUVIGNON

58% SHIRAZ, 42% CABERNET SAUVIGNON: The blend of grape varieties used.

RED WINE PRODUCT OF AUSTRALIA
PRODUCED AND BOTTLED BY   1.5L   VIN ROUGE PRODUIT D'AUSTRALIE
PRODUIT ET MIS EN BOUTEILLE PAR
LINDEMANS WINES, EDEY ROAD, KARADOC, AUSTRALIA 3496 12.5% alc./vol.

sions will set you back up to £25 or £30. In fact, Australia's most iconic wine, a Shiraz known as Penfolds' Grange, costs closer to £100 a bottle. Because of the warm climate in which Shiraz is produce, the wine shows both fresh and dried fruit flavours. Such fruit makes Shiraz both a perfect fireplace wine and a worth match for powerful spices. You'll also find Cabernet Sauvignons, an increasing number of Rhône-style wines, Pinot Noirs and Cabernet-Shiraz blends.

At the lower end of the price range, around the £5 mark, Australian wines are heavily branded and are often sold on promotion in the supermarkets. While these wines are a bargain in sheer price terms, it's worth spending a little more to discover what the Australians really can do.

Germany

Germany is a country that produces a lot of quality white wine and hardly any red wine of note. The reds that are produced are rarely exported. Germany earns its place among the elite wine-producing countries of the world because of the white wines it produces from the Riesling grape. The overall annual wine output of Germany is small compared to France, nor are the Germans big wine drinkers either.

While Chardonnay-based wines are far more familiar to the general public, Rieslings, especially those from Germany, are just as good. So when people think of German wines, they usually think of Riesling. But Germany has other wines of distinction as well.

German wine has not played a significant part in the recent UK wine boom. This is partly because German wines have a reputation for being too sweet. While many of the branded German wines in the supermarkets are overly sweet, most of these are Liebraumilch rather than Riesling. Liebfraumilch is a blend of grapes usually dominated by Müller-Thurgau, with a minimum legal sugar level of 18g/litre.

True German Riesling, on the other hand, is often made in a dryer style – and the sugar in the sweet ones is usually balanced by high acidity, making the wine pleasant and refreshing to drink rather than overly sweet.

Those in the know are often German wine enthusiasts and believe these Rieslings to be among the foremost of the wine world's hidden treasures. Thanks to their lack of general popularity, however, many of these wines are on the market for bargain basement prices and are well worth experimenting with.

When people look at the indecipherable German wine labels on today's wines, many wonder if they are looking at a Liebfraumilch-type wine. Perhaps if people understood the labels on the bottles, they would be more willing to experiment with German wines.

Here is some help.

Like other European Union countries, Germany has a government-regulated wine rating system. The levels are:

Tafelwein: Lowest level wine.
Qualitätswein bestimmte Anbaugebiete (QbA): Middle-quality wine
Qualitätswein mit Prädikat (QmP): Highest quality wine

QbA indicates quality wine from a quality region. Unless the label indicates that the wine is a Riesling, then it is made from another variety or, more likely, varieties. Other common German varieties are Sylvaner, Müller-Thurgau (a cross between Riesling and Sylvaner) and Gewürztraminer.

QmP is the designation of highest quality, and QmP wine labels offer more information about the wine. The *Prädikat*, or levels of distinction, indicate the sugar level at harvest. Because Germany's vineyards are so far north, it is difficult to get the grapes to ripen, hence grape sugars are highly prized. Chaptalization, the addition of sugars to increase the alcohol content via fermentation, is not allowed in QmP wines.

These *Prädikat*, or distinctions, are as follows:

Kabinett – normal, fully ripe grapes (9.5 per cent minimum potential alcohol).
Spätlese – 'late-harvested' grapes, which may produce slightly sweet wine.
Auslese – individually selected, very ripe bunches used to make sweet wine.
Beerenauslese – individually selected, very ripe grapes ('berries') used to make very sweet dessert wine.
Trockenbeerenauslese – individually selected, *Botrytis*-afflicted grapes used to make the sweetest, most expensive German dessert wines.

Look for the word *trocken* on your German wine label as well; this means dry. *Halbtrocken* means half-dry.

GERMANY LABEL – QBA

MOSEL-SAAR-RUWER: Quality region of origin.

RIESLING: Grape variety.

SCMITT SOHNE: Producer.

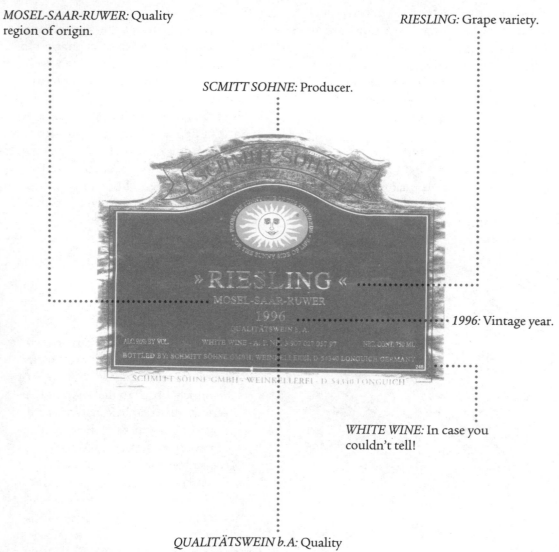

1996: Vintage year.

WHITE WINE: In case you couldn't tell!

QUALITÄTSWEIN b.A: Quality level designation.

GERMANY LABEL – QMP

1991er: Year of harvest; the 'er' suffix is a charming Germanism still used on fine wines.

WILLI HAAG: Producer.

BRAUNEBERGER JUFFER: This means that the grapes are primarily from the *Juffer* vineyard in the village of *Brauneberg.*

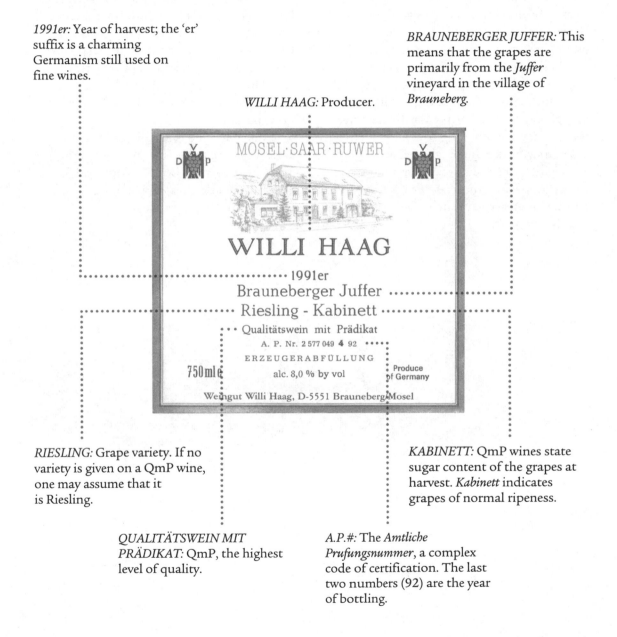

RIESLING: Grape variety. If no variety is given on a QmP wine, one may assume that it is Riesling.

KABINETT: QmP wines state sugar content of the grapes at harvest. *Kabinett* indicates grapes of normal ripeness.

QUALITÄTSWEIN MIT PRÄDIKAT: QmP, the highest level of quality.

A.P.#: The *Amtliche Prufungsnummer*, a complex code of certification. The last two numbers (92) are the year of bottling.

In addition, the term *eiswein* may be used in conduction with the *prädikat* if the grapes are crushed after a naturally occurring freeze. By pressing the grapes while frozen, the sugars, acids and other qualities of the grapes become concentrated. All QmP wines are Riesling unless otherwise indicated on the label, the opposite of QbA labelling.

QmP Kabinett and Spätlese wines are as complex and delicious as Chardonnays in the £5–15 price range. A growing trend in German wine is varietal-labelled Riesling QbA wines. At £4–8, these wines represent a very good value and match well with Asian cuisine because their touch of sweetness puts out the spicy fire.

Of the many wine-producing areas in Germany, the two most outstanding are the Mosel-Saar-Ruwer region (along the Mosel River and its two tributaries), and the three contiguous regions along the Rhine River – Rheingau, Rheinhessen and the Pfalz. The Riesling grape is the top grape in both areas. Fine Mosel Reisling tends to have mineral and citrus notes, with the classic Riesling floral bouquet.

Rhine Riesling is usually richer, with apricot-like fruit. These rival areas distinguish themselves by bottle colour – bright green for Mosel wines, brown for Rhines.

Spain

The Spanish wine industry is as old as that of France. The similarities between their wines, however, are few, although there was once a rich exchange of wine information between the two countries. When *phylloxera* invaded the French vineyards, many French winemakers fled their country – and a number ended up in the Rioja region. Here they taught the locals how to raise the quality of the wines made from the local grapes, the primary one being Tempranillo.

At one stage, Spanish wine was practically synonymous with Rioja. The red Rioja is a well-known value, with many of them selling at £7–10. These days, however, prices are spiralling, and a really good bottle can set you back £15 or more. There are four grades of Rioja, *joven*, *crianza*, *reserva* and *gran reserva*. Although there is a link to quality in the ranking (the better the vintage, the more likely the top grapes are to be made into gran reserva wines), the actual definition of these terms has more to do with how long the wines have been aged before they're sold. *Joven* wines are unoaked, while *gran reservas* will have spent at least two years in oak barrels and then been matured in bottle for an additional three years before going on the market.

White Rioja does not enjoy the same quality and reputation as the red. It is made from the local Viura grape. However, some are good: dry and oaky are two adjectives that come to mind for these wines.

In recent years, you're likely to find wine from all over. Some of these will be made from traditional Spanish grapes, but you're just as likely to find wines made from Merlot and Cabernet Sauvignon.

Spanish sparkling wines, known as Cavas, are usually good value for money. Whenever you are looking to buy a Spanish sparkling wine, look for *méthode champenoise* and 'brut' on the label.

It may be Sherry for which Spain's wine industry is most famous. The word 'sherry' is an Anglicized version of Jerez, the port city from which Sherry is shipped worldwide.

SPAIN LABEL

BERBERANA: Producer.

1988: Vintage year.

RESERVA: Indicates that wine has received additional barrel age – at least three years in barrel and bottle.

RIOJA-Denominacion de Origen Calificada: Rioja is the region, and *Denominacion de Origen Calificada* is the Spanish equivalent of the French AOC or the Italian DOCG designation.

Portugal

Wine grapes have been cultivated in Portugal since the days of the Roman Empire. Extensive trade with England during the Renaissance led to the development and widespread distribution of Portugal's famous fortified wines, Port and Madeira. However, apart from inexpensive Portuguese Rosés (Mateus and Lancers), the table wines of Portugal remain a mystery to most of us. One of the few exceptions has been Vida Nova, a property in the Algarve owned by Sir Cliff Richard. Each vintage made so far has sold out within weeks of hitting the shelves. Most Portuguese producers, however, aren't in such a position.

There has been no equivalent of neighbouring Spain's Rioja in Portugal – no region that has become world famous for inexpensive, high-quality wine. Portuguese winemakers have also refrained from widespread production of the popular grape varieties like Chardonnay and Merlot, which probably would grab an instant market share. Instead, Portuguese winemakers plant varieties barely known outside of Portugal.

Finally, the wines of Portugal aren't fruity enough for the typical British wine drinker, so the wines of Portugal occupy very little space in British wine shops.

But it is for these very reasons that you should give wines from Portugal a try. The wines are different and their producers feel compelled to resist the market forces, which have 'Americanized' winemaking all over the world. They are also cheap. A couple of purchases of inexpensive Portuguese wines made from that country's mysterious grape varieties may allow you to uncover an off-beat gem at a very good price. These producers generally follow the European winemaking tradition of producing lighter food wines.

Portugal is divided into several wine-producing regions for table wine production:

Entre Minho e Douro
Douro
Tras os Montes
Beira Alta
Dão
Agueda
Estramadura
Algarve
Alentejo

Portuguese wine labels will generally give you the name of the region, the predominant grape

PORTUGAL LABEL

PERIQUITA: The name of
a grape variety, co-opted as
a brand-name.

VINHO REGIONAL TERRAS:
Region of origin.

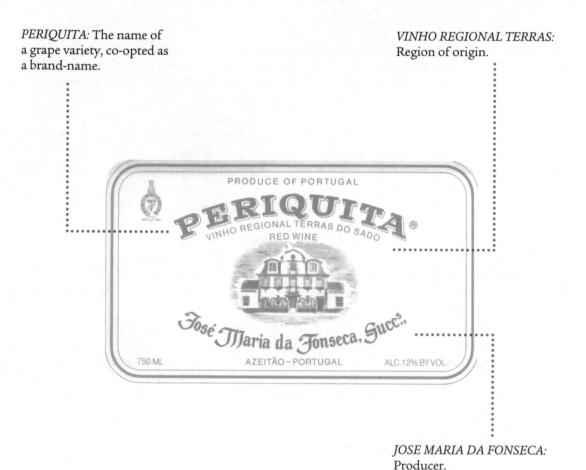

JOSE MARIA DA FONSECA:
Producer.

The vintage year appears on a bottleneck label.

variety, and the colour of the wine. *Tinto* indicates a red wine and *branco* means white..

Vinho Verde, which means young wine, is a designation used only for young, acid wine, perhaps *fizzy* from a malolactic fermentation in the bottle. This wine is from the Entre Minho e Douro region.

'Garrafeira' means matured wine, as do 'Maduro' and 'Reserva'.

Some of the grape varieties you are apt to encounter are:

Albariño (red)
Tinta Roriz (red)
Touriga Francesa (red)
Touriga Nacional (red)
Esgana Cao (white)
Verdelho (white)
Arinto (white)

Chile

This 5,000km-long nation along the Pacific Coast of South America has rapidly become one of the most important sources of inexpensive varietal wines in the world. The popular varietals – Chardonnay, Sauvignon Blanc, Merlot and Cabernet Sauvignon grapes – have a very loyal following among British consumers looking for something drinkable for £5. Better Chilean wines, costing £7-12, are often excellent value for those wanting to treat themselves to something special.

The Chileans are increasingly keen on alternatives to their traditional grapes, and their Syrahs and Pinot Noirs are increasingly sought after. Another grape worth looking for on the label is Carmenère.

Red grapes are at their best in the north and centre of the country, while whites thrive in the cooler climates further south, although some very nice whites are grown in the Casablanca Valley. Strenuous attempts are being made by Chile to be a growing wine power. It is hoped that it won't outgrow its well-earned reputation for bargain wines.

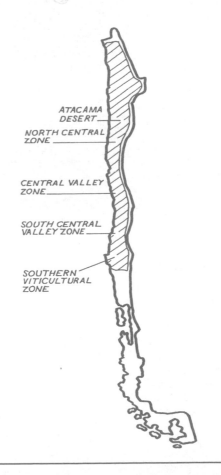

ATACAMA DESERT

NORTH CENTRAL ZONE

CENTRAL VALLEY ZONE

SOUTH CENTRAL VALLEY ZONE

SOUTHERN VITICULTURAL ZONE

CHILE LABEL

120 SANTA RITA: Brand
name/producer.

1989: Vintage year. Keep in
mind that Southern
Hemisphere wines are picked in
the *spring* of the vintage year,
rather than in the *autumn*.

MERLOT: Grape variety.
Chile has yet to make its mark
with anything other than
varietal wines.

South Africa

Fine wine has been produced in South Africa since the 1600s. However, because of politics, South Africa was unable to benefit from the wine boom of the 1980s. These days, though, it's politically correct to support the South African industry – a lot of work has been put into improving the quality of the wines and into making them great value for money.

South Africa first came to prominence for its white wines. Chenin Blanc (known locally as Steen, although this is seldom seen on bottles these days), Chardonnay and Sauvignon Blanc all do well here. The best of these wines are light and crisp, with contrasting elements of fruit and minerals.

The reds are equally interesting. Elegant Cabernet Sauvignon and Merlot are both grown here, and are sometimes bottled varietally and sometimes blended, Bordeaux-style. Shiraz is also produced with some success, as are other southern French grapes. Perhaps the most intriguing of the South African grapes, though, is Pinotage, a cross between Pinot Noir and Cinsault, another Rhône grape.

Whether red or white, the £6–9 wines are fairly priced. Once you step up in price, and you need not pay more than around £10–15, you stand a good chance of getting great wine for your money.

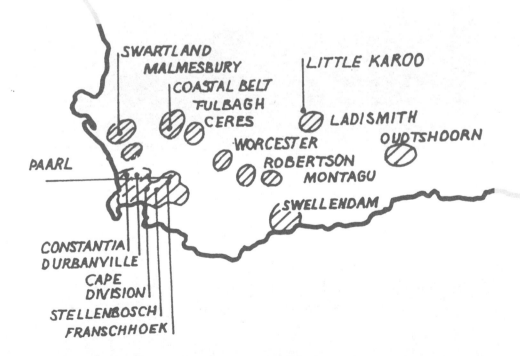

SOUTH AFRICA LABEL

CABERNET SAUVIGNON:
Grape variety.

W.O.: May also be written out as 'wine of origin'. Indicates that the coastal region is the officially recognized region in which this wine was made.

SPRINGBOK: Producer.

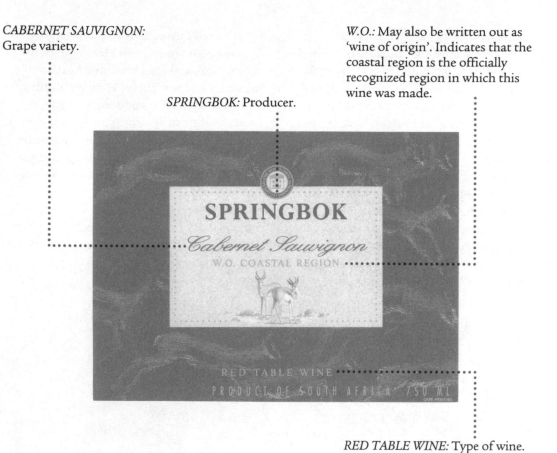

RED TABLE WINE: Type of wine.

If the vintage date does not appear on the label itself, it will be on the bottleneck label or the back label.

Others

NEW ZEALAND

New Zealand may only produce a small percentage of the world's wine, but it bats well above its weight when it comes to quality. Its version of Sauvignon Blanc has become just as much of a benchmark for the grape as its historical home in France's Loire Valley. While its flavours are fruitier – often tropical fruits like passion fruit and guava – than French versions, which tend towards green, herbaceous aromas, it still has that razor-sharp acidity that makes it so refreshing.

Chardonnay is another white variety that thrives in the southern islands, while aromatic grapes like Riesling and Pinot Gris are being grown with increasing commercial and critical success.

Reds can do well here, too, although areas that really do justice to grapes like Cabernet Sauvignon and Merlot are few and far between. Some years ripen better than others. A better bet, by far, are New Zealand's Pinot Noirs, which can rival Burgundian versions for their finesse and complexity, often at a fraction of the price.

Given that cool-climate varietals thrive in New Zealand, it's not surprising to discover that there are some pretty classy sparkling wines made here. And, at around £10 a bottle, they're often a good-value substitute for the real thing.

ARGENTINA

With the collapse of the Argentine economy a few years back, Argentinian wines became even better value than they had been previously. This is a country that makes a lot of wine, and much of it is sold off pretty cheap, when you consider the quality of what's in the bottle. Although the usual range of Cabernet Sauvignon/Merlot/Chardonnay grapes are grown in Argentina, its strong point lies in a range of well-made, slightly offbeat varietal wines.

Malbec, which produces extremely tannic, inky-dark wines in its native south-western France, turns into something far more supple and silky when grown in Argentina – although it's still full-bodied enough to go with a gaucho-style rare steak. When it comes to whites, Argentina does well with the aromatic, peach-scented Torrontes grape, and makes some very nice Chenin Blanc, to boot.

EASTERN EUROPE

Back during the Soviet era, Eastern Europe's winemakers didn't really need to worry about making commercially popular wines. They had a captive Soviet-Bloc audience that, frankly, didn't take much satisfying. As long as a wine contained alcohol, it could be as tainted, sweet or oxidized as possible, and no one would really care.

With the fall of the Berlin Wall in the late 1980s, this cosy little world came crashing down around the ears of the more laissez-faire of the co-operatives. Those more savvy in the ways of the world realized that their winemaking techniques needed to be revolutionized before their wines could compete on the open market.

While there's still an awful lot of catching up to do, most of the Eastern European wines in the shops these days are well made, often providing great value for money, as they're seldom priced above £5. In particular, look for dry white wines from Hungary and Bulgarian reds in this range.

You'll also find one of Hungary's treasures, the sweet wine known as Tokaji (pronounced tock-aye), on the supermarket shelves. If you're into sweet, honey-and-apricot-scented dessert wines, don't hesitate to try some. The sweetness is measured in a scale of puttonyos, from 1–6. The higher up the scale the numbers go, the sweeter (and more prestigious, therefore more expensive) the wine.

OTHERS

Although we've now visited some of the most important winemaking countries in the world, it's important not to forget that wine is made almost everywhere the climate permits (with the exception of the most rigorously Muslim countries, of course). As more winemakers go in search of the best places in their native countries to grow grapes, don't be surprised to see wines from some surprising places make it into the shops in the next few years.

Among the countries that are beginning to develop an export market, it's worth checking out wines from:

Greece
Although most of us think of retsina when it comes to Greek wine, there's been an upsurge of interest in producing more conventional styles of wine, from dry whites and reds to super-luscious sweeties. The key challenge to anyone wanting to explore these is the names of the indigenous grapes. Anyone for Agiorgitiko or Mavrodaphne?

Lebanon
Although Lebanon isn't a large-scale wine-producing country, the efforts of Château Musar's Serge Hochar have caught the attention of the wine world. The (red) wines are available in the high street, and at around £8–12 are worth buying for more than mere curiosity value.

Uruguay
Uruguay is starting to make waves with its Tannat, another red grape variety from southwest France.

Canada
Let's face it, the Canadian climate isn't going to make it one of the top winemaking countries in the world. Having said that, it's a great source of divinely decadent ice wines, whose grapes are picked in mid-winter, when below-zero temperatures have concentrated their sugars.

Austria

If you think the Germans have been dealt a rough hand, the situation in Austria is even worse. Still tainted by an anti-freeze scandal that happened some 20 years ago, the country's winemakers are struggling to sell their wines in the UK. This is a pity, because Austria's elegant white wines are great matches for a wide range of foods.

The UK

Unless our climate changes drastically, the UK is unlikely to produce top-quality red wines. The sparkling wines produced on the chalk soils of Kent and Sussex, however, can, in good years, rival Champagne in finesse.

THE LUNATIC FRINGE

There are some wines on the market that are so out of whack with the mainstream that they deserve special mention. Such wines can be a welcome change of pace.

Retsina

Well known to tourists who've visited the Greek islands, Retsina is a white or rosé wine flavoured with pine pitch. This seemingly peculiar practice has ancient historical roots. The earliest winemakers, including the Greeks, often treated clay vessels with pine pitch in order to store wine, and the flavour of pine pitch became accepted over time as a fundamental component of wine.

When glass bottles came into use, pine pitch became unnecessary for storage, but its use continued as a flavouring agent. If this sounds weird, remember that oak evolved as a flavour component in a nearly identical manner. Not coincidentally, this wine goes well with Greek food.

Vouvray Sec

The winemakers of Vouvray, located in the Loire region of France, defer to the weather when it comes to winemaking style. In warm, sunny seasons they make the delightfully off-dry white Vouvray demi-sec. After cold and rainy growing seasons, these winemakers turn their grapes into Vouvray sec, which can be the world's most acidic wine. In its driest manifestations, this wine can be excruciatingly tart.

Connoisseurs tend to develop an appreciation for highly acidic white wines, so Vouvray sec has a following. If you want to experience this 'acid trip', do not think of drinking Vouvray sec without food. Raw shellfish matches well with these sharp wines. Creamy cheeses also go well, providing a pleasing contrast in textures with the wine's acidity.

Rioja Gran Reserva

The finest red wines of the Rioja region in Spain are traditionally aged for up to ten years in oak barrels. Not especially fruity to begin with, Rioja becomes even less so with barrel age. The flavour of oak dominates the wine. Quality Rioja is not thrown out of balance by this flavor component, rather, Rioja Gran Reserva is a very dry, oaky, medium-to-light-bodied red wine with subtle and complex flavours – of which fruit, often strawberry, is a minor component. This wine is especially good with lamb.

Australian Chardonnay

The term 'fruit-driven Chardonnay' applies to many of the Australian versions of this versatile grape. The combination of intense sunlight and cool breezes in Australian vineyards can bring Chardonnay to its fullest possible state of ripeness. Acidity usually diminishes with such full ripeness, making way for a spectrum of obscenely rich fruit flavours – banana, pineapple, peach, coconut, papaya and fig.

The boldest Australian Chardonnays are high in alcohol, generously treated with oak, and display enough rip-roaring fruit to make your average California Chardonnay seem like spring water. Wine this fruity is very satisfying without food, and somewhat difficult to match with most dishes. Pacific Rim cuisine and seafood that has a natural

affinity for fruit, such as shrimp, lobster, swordfish and shark, do pretty well alongside these massive white wines.

Black Muscat

This funky, sweet raisin juice is as delicious as it is weird. Black Muscat is unlike any other wine grape. More often used for eating than for winemaking, it nonetheless yields a sweet and spicy wine when grown to full ripeness in California.

It is difficult to imagine this wine with food. Black Muscat is a perfect 'fireplace wine' and makes a good low-alcohol alternative to Port. One California version to look for comes from Andrew Quady.

Old Vine Reds

Grapevines first produce useful grapes in their fifth year and reliably yield grapes for another 15 or so. Middle age then sets in, and the yields diminish. It is a common practice for volume-oriented growers to uproot and replace when their grape production begins to tail off. Some growers, however, maintain vines that are many decades old and are richly rewarded (in quality) for doing so. Although old vines yield relatively few grapes, 'old vine' wines usually have more complex, concentrated flavours than wines of the same variety from younger vines.

'Old Vine' Zinfandel is fairly common in California. Its grapes offer up peppery, concentrated wines and make a cost-effective alternative to high-priced California Cabernet Sauvignon wines. You can also find some French red Burgundies with a 'Vielles Vignes' (old vines) designation on the label.

Alsace Gewürztraminer

As the true personality of this quirky grape is laid bare on the therapy couch of Alsatian soil, we learn that Gewürztraminer is the Chris Eubank of *vitis vinifera*. Its in-your-face aromas and unsubtle flavors of lychee, rose petal and grapefruit rind overwhelm the senses and make it the most easily recognizable variety of wine. Cheese and crackers, and other bland foods, do well with it, but in general, it is difficult to match with food. Notable exceptions are German sausage and sauerkraut, which have a regional affinity with Gewürztraminer.

Some well-known Alsatian producers are Domaine Zind Humbrecht, Zimbach, Domaine Weinbach and Hugel.

CHAPTER 7

BUYING WINE

Retail Wine Shopping

Unless you set out for the wine shop with a specific bottle of wine in mind, you will have to make a buying decision based on limited information. Your goal is to bring home a wine you will like, at a price you feel comfortable with. In the end you may end up with a bottle you've had in the past, because this was the most informed selection you could make.

Although every wine shop is unique, it is possible to make some useful generalizations that might help you decide which shop you should shop. There are big shops; there are little shops; and there are shops in between. In most cases, the big shops can take advantage of huge-quantity discounts at the wholesale level. The bigger the shop or chain, the bigger the discounts it is apt to receive. However, this doesn't necessarily mean big shops are better for all of the people all of the time.

The second variable is expertise. 'Wine anoraks' cost more money to employ than unskilled assistants. The greater the level of expertise in a shop, the higher the labour cost. Wine shops (of any size) with excellent service generally cannot afford to offer much of their stock at rock-bottom prices.

So we have two variables—size and expertise. Every shop is different, but we can get some sense of the retail wine-buying experience from these hypothetical shop types:

Specialist merchants
Small shop with expertise
Small shop without expertise
Big shop with expertise
Big shop/supermarket without expertise
Supermarket with expertise

SPECIALIST MERCHANTS

The British have a long-standing tradition of importing fine wine from around the world. Thanks to this fact, some of our specialist wine merchants have been in business for, quite literally, centuries. But you don't need to come from an aristocratic family to take advantage of their wine-buying expertise.

The people who work there don't tend to stand on ceremony, and are keen to share their knowledge with anyone who's interested in buying good wine. These companies have built up their contacts with the world's top winemakers, and so are often the best place to go if you're looking to buy fine wines. Many of them are specialists, so if you develop a real taste for German Riesling or Californian Cabernet, it makes sense to track down the best supplier.

These merchants often sell premium wines made in limited quantities. This means they can sell out of in-demand wines very quickly. If you've set your heart on buying something particular, get in as quick as you can – especially if you know there's not going to be much of it around.

Another potential downside to buying from a specialist merchant like this is that you have to buy by the case (although some allow mixed cases). So, unless you've got an empty cellar and some serious cash to spend, a specialist merchant may not be the retailer of choice for the wine novice.

SMALL SHOP WITH EXPERTISE

This shop might well be a hobby, or at least a labour of love, for a semi-retired big shot from the wine industry or for a corporate fast-track dropout. Chances are that there won't be a bad bottle of wine in the shop. The proprietor has probably tasted and personally selected them all. Need advice?

This is the best place to get it. Shops like this do well in university towns, because university professors like to soak up all the free wine information available and talk wine with their colleagues.

The downside to such a place is that a staple item such as Jacob's Creek Cabernet Sauvignon Chardonnay will be far more expensive in this type of shop than in any other. This boutique has far less purchasing power than the big shops and doesn't make it on volume.

SMALL SHOP WITHOUT EXPERTISE

The wines in shops like this are often limited to huge brands such as Gallo, Jacob's Creek,

Is the Wine Bottle in Good Shape?

When you buy a bottle of wine, you don't want to buy damaged goods. Since there are no tyres to kick, you need to use other tests.

1. Is the bottle filled up? This used to be more of an issue in the less industrial days of wine bottling. See how high the wine is in the neck of the wine bottle compared to other bottles. There is no need to pay the same for less.

2. Feel the cork through the plastic wrapper on the top of the bottle. The cork shouldn't feel pushed in or out. The top of the cork should be close to flush with the top of the bottle. Cork movement can be

indicative of a bad cork or a wine that has been exposed to temperature extremes.

3. Hold the bottle up to the light. Is it clear or murky? Only in an older wine is it OK to see sediment. Wine from the same 'batch' should be the same colour. If you can't work out which color is the right colour, buy a different wine.

Before you buy wine at a shop, you should be convinced that the shop is kept at cool temperatures 24 hours a day. You also don't want to buy wines that are shopd in a place where they get a lot of light or are exposed to a radiator.

Hardy's and the like. And why not? With all the money such wineries invest in advertising, plus their name recognition, these wines sell themselves. The prices aren't cheap, but they may be cheap for a shop this size. The selection is usually going to be disappointing at such a shop.

However, some of these shops may have had some expertise at one time. Sometimes such expertise is asked to leave in order to keep the shop from going bankrupt from its excellent and costly wine inventory that doesn't move fast enough. This means that a bargain, buried in the bargain bin, could be a real treasure that the remaining staff did not know enough to mark up as it aged. Browse in this type of shop very carefully the first time you go there.

The small shop without expertise might be a convenience shop. Here you are looking for something you know is drinkable. Such wines seem to taste great when purchased in the middle of nowhere five minutes before closing.

BIG SHOP WITH EXPERTISE

At first glance, this type of shop might look like a discount shop, since the 20-case floor stacks are evidence of considerable purchasing power. Upon further inspection you see a lot of wines from remote regions of the world, maybe even from Lebanon or Austria. There may also be a small army of neatly dressed assistants helping customers and offering expertise. Here you have a high labour cost, and at least part of the inventory isn't jumping off the shelves.

This big shop with expertise is a good place to find wines that you can't find anywhere else, such as:

Older wines, particularly red Bordeaux and Port
Hard-to-find Champagne, such as Blanc de Noirs or Brut Rosé
A good selection of Alsace and German wines
Wines from countries that don't export much wine
An expensive wine that no one has heard of
The perfect gift for a knowledgeable wine buff

BIG SHOP/SUPERMARKET WITHOUT EXPERTISE

This shop has truly strong purchasing power. They buy single brands by the lorry-load, and their wholesalers jump whenever anyone from such a shop calls to place an order. Such a shop can buy for less and afford a lesser markup on their inventory (30–40 per cent, rather than 50–60 per cent), because of the volume of business they do. Some of the wines at such a shop sell at prices below what the smaller shops pay *wholesale* for the same wines. The wine-buying public flocks to these shops to take advantage of the great prices and good selection.

Big shops without expertise might not have as esoteric a selection as the big shops with expertise, but if you are looking for popular wine driven by national advertising (such as Moët et Chandon White Star Champagne, Jacob's Creek Shiraz, Arniston bay and Blossom Hill), this is where you should be going, especially if you are going to be buying in bulk.

SUPERMARKETS WITH EXPERTISE

Some supermarkets make a special effort to make their wine selections a bit more interesting than the average. Some stock an esoteric range of wines in addition to the discounted, heavily hyped brands. Others have specially trained wine managers in the department, who help shoppers find the right wine at the right price, and encourage them to experiment with the unusual.

If you have a supermarket like this near you, take advantage of what's on offer. Because of their purchasing power, wine in these shops is often relatively cheaper than it is elsewhere. You'll also often find these shops have stocks of wines that are available in limited quantities. So, if you develop an enthusiasm for a particular style of wine, the chances are you'll be able to explore it in greater depth.

MAKING A DECISION

Unless you are in a shop with expertise, how can you get information about the wines? Can you trust the little 'shelf talkers' taped to the racks? Probably not, since they are

likely to be composed by the wholesaler or the wineries themselves. These are hardly objective sources of information. A shelf talker in a shop with expertise may be pointing to a wine worth buying, when written by someone from the shop. (You may see the shop logo on the card.) It is quite likely that the shop bought a lot of a good wine, and they want to move the wine and make you a satisfied customer.

Assuming you can't get any good information from a shop worker or display, here are some good tips:

Know a Grape: If you like Sauvignon Blanc but can't find your favourite bottle, you may want to try a bottle from a different producer.

Know a Region: If the Cabernet you like is from Coonawarra, Australia, try a different Cabernet from that same region. Climate and soil, *terroir*, play a big part in winemaking.

Know a Producer: If you like Pride Mountain Merlot, you may like Pride Mountain Cabernet Sauvignon, since the two wines are made by the same person, or at least with the same philosophy.

If you have enough interest in wine to have made it this far into the book, then you owe it to yourself to attend a free wine tasting, which is often held at wine shops. Certainly, tasting a wine without having first to buy it is a worthwhile opportunity.

Cheap Wine

Everybody needs cheap wine at some point in their lives. Maybe you're saving your money to buy something more significant than wine; maybe you're making Sangria, for which good fruit juice is a better investment than good wine; or maybe you're hosting an art exhibition opening. Whatever the reason, you want to get a lot for a little.

It is foolish to spend a lot on wine for such occasions as a barbecue or picnic, just as it is also foolish to bring a lesser wine to a dinner table where very good food is being served. Rosés are considered to be a good choice for informal occasions (and not so good a choice for semi-formal and formal meals).

As you learn about wine, and your £4-a-bottle palette becomes an £8-a-bottle palette, it becomes very difficult to slum it. Why? Because you know what your cheaper wines are missing. Yet money is a reality that most of us can't afford to ignore all the time. You need to search for a £4 wine that reminds you of an £8 bottle, or one that simply tastes really good; both are out there.

If you are having a cocktail party, you should serve both a red and a white wine. Chilean wine is your cheapest option for a low-cost varietal wine (as opposed to a generic box wine). Australia may be the best

choice for an extra pound or two per bottle, assuming you want to spend the money. The Australians like to blend grapes at the low end of the price spectrum, and the result is usually better than the sum of the parts. They have two winning formulas, one red and one white. The red blend is the Shiraz/Cabernet Sauvignon blend. The white blend is the Semillon/Chardonnay blend.

The Shiraz/Cabernet wines tend to be blended at about a 50/50 ratio, whereas whites tend to be around 70/30 Semillon. Both are great values and will impress anyone who understands wine at your party.

Another good cocktail party red/white pairing is Spanish Rioja – red and white. Rioja is less fruity than the Australian wines. This makes it better with food, for some people's tastes, but you may find it lacking if you aren't serving nibbles.

When you go to a wine shop, choosing a bottle for under £5 can be very tricky. In this range you run the risk of buying a wine you don't like at all. Although the choices we listed above are usually safe, you will probably be confronted with more than one of each type of wine in that price range. Fortunately, it is in the wine merchant's interest to give you good advice. It will make you more likely to return to his shop for wine, and more likely to want to drink more wine in the future.

If you are making a wine drink such as Sangria, you are probably going to make a lot of it. Sangria has juice, spirits, sugar and other ingredients, so you won't be able to tell good from bad wine. You need box wine, and lots of it. Don't buy the cheapest one in the shop, though. Try and find a name you recognize and trust.

If you are having a reception and you want to serve cheap wine, but box wine just isn't good enough, you have some tough choices. Box whites are often easier to enjoy than box reds. You could spend more money on your red wines, or, if you have access to some clean, empty carafes or even old wine bottles, you could be a little inventive. If you have patience and a couple of empty bottles or containers, you can mix yourself a lot of 'starving artist' wine. We have found that if you take some decent box wine and add to it the right bottle of £7–8 wine, the box wine gets much better. We have found that a 750ml bottle can perk up a magnum (1500ml) of lesser wine.

Cheese makes almost all wines taste better, and this is especially true for cheap wine. So if you are serving wine at your reception, make sure you have cheese and crackers, not Smarties and pretzels.

Vintage 1992
TYRRELL'S WINES
NIL MAGNUM NISI BONUM
LONG FLAT RED
South Eastern Australia Table Wine - Alcohol 12.5% by Volume
Produced by Tyrrell's Vineyards Pty Ltd
Pokolbin, Hunter Valley, Australia
PRODUCT OF AUSTRALIA
750 ml

The Safest Wines to Buy

Although this book attempts to demystify wine, there are way too many wine-buying options and wine-making parameters to make buying wine too easy. Even if you find a wine you like, when stock of that vintage runs out you may be searching for a new wine. Many wines taste different from vintage to vintage.

If you buy wines with labels printed in English and the grape variety or varieties in the wine are denoted, you will at least know a few things about your potential purchase, like what on earth you're buying. Not only will you have some idea of what you are buying, but after you drink the wine you can look at the bottle and know what type of wine you just did or didn't enjoy.

Because Australia and Chile have good grape-growing weather most years, and wine from both places is labelled in nothing but English, buying wines from these two is the best place for wine beginners to start. But don't get the impression these wines are better than wines from other regions.

If you are buying box wines, they are going to be the same every year. These wines get a bad deal from wine snobs. If you need a lot of wine, these large commercial wines are an excellent choice. But chances are, if you are reading this book, you want your tastes to be able to branch out into less familiar territory.

Australian or Chilean wines may be the safest red-wine bet around. These wines tend to be accessible without being overly simple. The white wines from Australia, especially the blends of Semillon and Chardonnay, tend to be crowd-pleasers. Straight Chardonnay is a fairly safe bet, although some versions could be considered too fruity for the dinner table.

Again, since the wine's grape variety or varieties are printed on the label, it will be easy to reproduce a positive wine experience, even if you can't find the same bottle the next time you buy wine in a shop or order it in a restaurant. Both Chile and Australia export a lot of good, easy-to-drink, inexpensive red and white wines, and keeps things easy for consumers, since they don't seem to export many bad bottles.

Chardonnays from large New World producers that sell in the £7–10 range are a very safe bet. Chardonnay is an easy grape to grow in the New World climate. The big producers have the formula down pat. They grow some Chardonnay grapes; they buy some other Chardonnay grapes from other vineyards; they have a goal – their Chardonnay formula; and they always reach that goal.

Beaujolais is an easy red wine to buy. Although the label doesn't say so, all of this wine comes from the Gamay grape. Unless the wine comes from one of the 10 crus, it is meant to be consumed within a few months, so you won't have to worry that the wine you are buying is too young. Basic Beaujolais is made in a light, simple, fruity, good-with-food style. Best of all, they are relatively cheap. Good ones can be had for under £7. The very best crus Beaujolais usually sell for less than £12.

Pinot Gris (or Pinot Grigio, as it is called in Italy) is a white wine that is very easy to drink and to match with food. Powerfully spiced foods can overwhelm this somewhat timid wine, but it goes well with a wide variety of pastas, seafood and lighter chicken dishes.

Another good way to get a good wine is by sticking with producers whose wines are generally good and widely available. This may be the best way to venture into European wines. Reliable European producers include Louis Latour (France), Ruffino (Italy) and Montecillo (Spain).

Consistently Good Red Wines (£7 and under)

Merlot – Dulong (France)
Cabernet Sauvignon – Santa Rita (Chile)
Beaujolais-Villages – Louis Jadot (France)
Shiraz – Hardy's Nottage Hill (Australia)
Rioja – Bodegas Monticillo (Spain)
Zinfandel – Rosenblum (California, USA)
Shiraz – Lindemans Bin 50 (Australia)
Cabernet Sauvignon – Dunnewood (California, USA)
Chianti – Castello di Quercetto (Italy)

Risky Wine Purchases

What can go wrong when you buy a bottle of wine?

You can buy wine that is just plain awful. Some wines, like some films, just shouldn't have been made. This is one of the best reasons for keeping a couple of auxiliary bottles around the house at all times.

Other wines may deserve to have been made, but like some movies, you just don't like them. If you have no idea what you like and/or have no idea what you are buying, you may end up with a good wine that you happen not to like.

If you are buying wine to be consumed with a meal, you can get into trouble with the 'right wine at the wrong time' syndrome. The concept of buying *the* right wine is a silly one. When painting your house, you may look at a hundred colour samples and pick *the* right one, but the wine-buying scenario is very different. There is a good chance you have never tasted the wine you are thinking of buying. If you have, you may not have had it with the food you are planning on serving. Even if you have had the identical wine with the dish you are planning on cooking, the ingredients in the food you are making can vary. Onions can vary in intensity, as can garlic and lemon juice. Not all medium-rare steaks are cooked alike.

However, our concern is wrong wines. If you are selecting a wine for four people to enjoy with dinner, you really only have one objective – pleasing everyone. If you are selecting a wine for your own enjoyment, you have a much easier task and no one to apologize to if your wine choice doesn't work out.

So, what is the most likely scenario for buying a bad wine? Wines that are inexpensive or that have a label that boasts of a popular grape variety can often be bad wines. If a bottle of Chardonnay or Cabernet Sauvignon were of high quality, it wouldn't sell for £4. You are much better off trying a nonvarietal wine or a 'lesser' variety at the low end of the price spectrum.

Some wines are quirky. Gewürztraminer is a white-wine grape grown in Germany and Alsace (France), and elsewhere it produces white wines that are frequently too sweet for many. Even for people who like some Gewürztraminers, many are apt to be too sweet. Any wine that is noticeably off-dry is risky unless you, and anyone else expected to drink the wine, have had it before and enjoyed it. Gewürztraminer is an interesting grape variety worth exploring, but you probably should do some scouting before buying some for others to drink.

Zinfandel has a lot of fruit and a lot of body. Some of these wines are too overpowering for many people. However, once you get to know a Zinfandel or two you like, you will find it matches well with a variety of hearty meals.

Now, if you have an idea of what wine grape varieties you like, buying a European wine can be difficult without a pocket guide or knowledgeable salesperson to guide you. If you find you like New World Pinot Noir and are thinking of trying a French Pinot, you won't usually find the words 'Pinot Noir' on the bottles of French wines you see at the shop. You need to develop an understanding of the cross-relationship between New World varietals and French wine regions. Cheat sheets are allowed.

If you are buying wine for people other than yourself, especially wine to be consumed with meals, don't be daring. Stick with the rules, unless you know that your group doesn't like red or white wine.

Older wines are difficult to buy. Some wines fade when they are aged too long; other older wines are still too young. You may see a 15-year-old bottle of wine that could easily be five years too young or five years too old.

Consistently Good White Wines (£7 and under)

Sauvignon Blanc – Kronendaal (South Africa)
Chardonnay – Monterey (California)
Saint-Véran – Louis Latour (France) (it's Chardonnay!)
Chardonnay – Meridien (California, USA)
Semillon/Chardonnay – Penfolds Koonunga Hill (Australia)
Pinot Grigio – Mezza Corona (Italy)
Riesling – Bernkasteler Kurfurstlay Kabinett (Germany)
Riesling – Schmitt Soehne (Germany)
Muscadet – Marcel Martin (France)

Buying Wine for the Non-connoisseur

If you are buying wine for a person who has only a casual interest in wine, chances are that person is going to drink the wine with a meal. Your goal is to buy a wine that is easy to like.

If you are buying wine for someone who likes white wine and who likes things that are familiar, then a New World Chardonnay is a good choice. The wine is probably going to taste good, assuming you don't look for the cheapest Chardonnay in the shop. Also, there is nothing more familiar to the casual white-wine drinker than "Chardonnay." If there is a knowledgeable salesperson in the shop, ask for a bottle that isn't too acidic or oaky; an £8 Chardonnay from the New World is a very safe bet.

If you want to give something a little less conventional in the white-wine area, an Italian Pinot Grigio costing aroind £7 is a good choice for a lighter white wine. These wines are excellent with food. The Semillon/Chardonnay blends from Australia are also usually very good and fairly priced at around £6. You could also track down a bottle of wine from your home state. The majority of states have a commercial wine industry that produces accessible wines, although they tend to be a couple of dollars overpriced.

When it comes to red wine, there is no sure thing equivalent to the Chardonnays. If you are trying to buy a red wine for a person who wants something familiar, you might try a Chianti from Italy, which matches very well with food. Chianti, thanks in part to the American jug wine named Chianti, has a lot of name recognition. Although decent £5 bottles are out there, you may want to improve your odds of getting a good bottle and spend £7.

If you want to buy a red wine for someone adventurous, your choices are vast.

Although it sounds ridiculous, you could buy a red wine with an interesting or funny label and/or name. There are a lot of bottles for $10 and under to choose from in this category. If you buy a nonvarietal table wine, you are probably going to end up with a middle-of-the-road safe wine. If the person to whom you are giving the wine really doesn't know one grape from another, packaging may be the thing to look for.

If you are interested in spending upwards of £12 for a red, an Australian Shiraz may be your best option.

Buying Wine for the Connoisseur

If you are going to buy wine as a gift for a connoisseur, and you are not a connoisseur, you have a couple of good options. If the gift is for someone who takes pride in his or her roots, try to buy a good bottle from the homeland. (Let's hope that the homeland isn't France or Italy.) Good bottles of wine are produced in many countries around the world. Good wines from Israel, New Zealand, Chile and Switzerland, to name a few, are definitely out there. South Africa is not the only country in Africa that produces wine – Morocco, Algeria, and even Egypt make wine.

Such purchases may require some research, but a knowledgeable wine sales-person, or possibly the Internet, can point you in the right direction. A £12–20 bottle is apt be good, and spending any more for a wine of unknown quality is foolish.

Another approach is to buy a 'best-of type' with a reasonable price tag. The best wines from the famous regions of the world are going to cost you a couple of hundred pounds. However, the best wines from Chile, New Zealand or the underappreciated Alsace region of France will cost you far less. For example, £18 will buy you an excellent Riesling from Alsace. The premium French *cru* Beaujolais wines won't kill you financially. These wines are especially good for people who live in warm climates or who entertain a lot.

Buying a magnum (double-sized bottle) of good wine is another offbeat but sensible idea. The wine itself may not wow the connoisseur, but these bottles look impressive at any dinner table. Expect to spend £25–40 for a magnum that is capable of impressing a wine connoisseur.

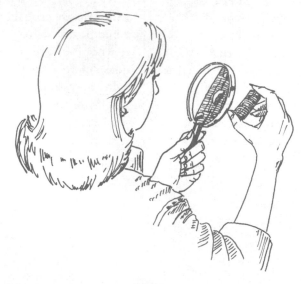

Wine for People Who Don't Like Wine

What qualities in wine do some people find objectionable? Three, usually – acidity, tannin and alcohol.

Wine is the most acidic beverage we consume. The acids in wine are balanced in part by its fruit and sugar. In dry wines, those with little or no residual sugar, the acidity can be overwhelming for a non-wine person. Acidic wines are often described as 'food wines', mainly because they can be best appreciated with food already in your mouth. Starchy foods, such as bread, rice or pasta, provide balance to the acidity.

So, the answer is to find wines low in acidity. Most New World rosés fit into this category, as do Australian Chardonnays. French Beaujolais (made from Gamay grapes) is the red wine that is most likely to be acceptable to a person who doesn't like the acidity of wine.

For those who dislike the strong taste of alcohol, there are two wonderful types of wine to enjoy. Moscato d'Asti is a low-alcohol, slightly sparkling wine from Northern Italy. At 5.5 per cent alcohol, half that of normal wine, its subtle floral components shine through. Only slightly higher in alcohol is late-harvest, somewhat sweet German Riesling, which can be exquisitely rich (and a somewhat expensive gift for someone who claims not to like wine).

Red Wine for People Who Don't Like Red Wine

Don't waste big money on red wine for someone who claims to hate it. There are many people who enjoy white wine who, after tasting a few reds, give up on the genre. Cheaper red wines tend to be more offensive than cheaper whites. Since most people start off drinking inexpensive wine, it makes sense that a lot of them write off red wine during their formative wine-drinking years.

Look for low-tannin wines. Beaujolais, from the southern Burgundy region of France, is a fruity, crowd-pleasing, gulping wine. This Gamay-based wine may be the strongest argument against red-wine prejudice. Australian blends of Cabernet Sauvignon and Shiraz show enough raisiny fruit to put the tannin in its place for under £8. For another £3–5, Australian Shiraz, thick with unctuous fruit and sp[ice, converts many a red-wine sceptic. Rioja from Spain is another option.

If tannin isn't the problem, then maybe it's a yearning for fruit. Californian and Chilean Pinot Noir is the fruitiest incarnation of the varietal. Zinfandel is also very fruity, but it may be too tannic to convince someone that red wine deserves another chance. If you choose a Pinot Noir, look for the rich and fruity Pinots that come from the New World, particularly those from the Carneros and Santa Barbara regions. French Pinot Noir, and those from the New World tend to be more austere as they have less ripe fruit flavour.

White Wine for People Who Don't Like White Wine

This one is difficult. If they say they don't like white wine, then they probably don't like typically oaky New World Chardonnay. White wine that is served chilled and that lacks tannin is generally a less complicated beverage, which, for many red-wine drinkers, translates into boring. Imagine trying to convince someone who thinks fishing is boring that it isn't.

There are many directions to take:

1. Try good French Chardonnay – white Burgundy is less fruity and more acidic (in a good, thirst-quenching way) than most New World Chardonnay.

2. Go weird with Viognier, the Rhône white with a personality so different from Chardonnay as to be unrecognizable to a Chardonnay drinker. Viognier is growing in popularity with New World winemakers.

3. Gewürztraminer, the Chris Eubank of white grapes, is certainly worth a shot.

4. Best of all options may be a decent French Alsace or German Riesling. Less pungent than Gewürztraminer, Riesling is more flowery than fruity – again, different enough from Chardonnay that it is worth a try.

Experimentation

Like any pursuit, the study of wine requires experimentation: finding out what is what, and what your likes and dislikes are. However, since you can't do computer simulations in your research, and your research costs money and would take a lot of time to do correctly, you will probably need to make some compromises in your research techniques.

If wine is a new interest, your first goal is probably to find one wine you like. Do you like red better than white, or vice versa? Most people have a preference. Let's say you think you like red wine better. Now what?

Unfortunately, money is the first issue that you need to address. How much are you willing to spend on a bottle of wine? If you have a friend or spouse with whom you are going to do your experimenting, that saves money. It also saves time, as you can go through bottles twice as fast. If you can get a group of four people together, you can tackle two to four bottles at a time. Remember, each of you can bring some leftover wine home. You can then report to each other on which leftover improved the next day and which didn't.

Another way to save research time and money is to go to a wine tasting. A lot of wine shops hold tastings, and at such a tasting, you may have the chance to sample a few wines, after which you may want to buy a bottle of a wine you liked. It is a good idea to patronize such a shop. Developing a relationship with a knowledgeable wine salesperson is a very good idea for any wine drinker, regardless of how much one knows about wine or spends on a bottle. These people taste a lot of wines you haven't tasted and can save you from many mediocre wines.

Anyway, let's assume you are willing to spend £5 on a bottle. Now what?

First, you need to realize that you won't be able to taste all types of wine for £5. Pinot Noir, whether it comes from New Zealand or France, doesn't come that cheap. If you find a bottle, you probably won't want to drink it. It is difficult, but not impossible, to purchase a Rioja for that price. Chianti from Italy, made from the Sangiovese grape, can be found for £5. You can try some good Syrah from Australia, South Africa or France. Spanish wines made from Tempranillo elsewhere in Spain are very affordable; at £5 you will find yourself a level or two up from the bottom. Chile also produces a wide variety of wines at bargain prices.

Decide on a grape variety, rather than region, to study. Try at least three different wines from a single grape variety before drawing any definitive conclusions about your preference. Wines from any grape can be made in many different styles. If you have a wine person who can help you select a diverse grouping of good wines within a variety, your experiments will be more enjoyable and your findings more accurate.

For £3–5 you can find wines you like, but it can be difficult to get to grips with the true nature of the grape varieties at this level because the quality just isn't there. At this price level, you should be looking for the nonvarietal gems that most shops offer.

Your experimentation with wine may last a week or a lifetime. Along the way you should be able to come up with at least one grape variety you consistently enjoy. If you are buying a wine from a grape variety you usually like, chances are good that you are buying a wine you are going to enjoy.

No matter what your price range is, it is easy to go through streaks of bad luck buying wine. Not that the wines will necessarily taste bad, but you will find them to be disappointing, which often translates to boring. When this happens, it may be time to return to an old favourite.

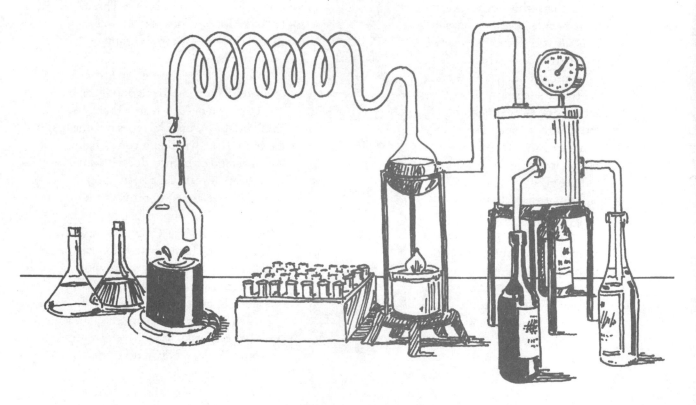

Keeping Track of What You Like

If you drink wine, you want to remember whether or not you liked it. This allows you to repeat a good wine experience and avoid a bad one. If you are like most people, including the know-it-alls who wrote this book, you think you can remember what you liked and didn't like without writing anything down. This system doesn't work. If you write one sentence about each wine you try, you will learn what your preferences are and avoid unnecessary disappointments. This is a good use for your home computer.

If *grape* equaled *wine*, then record keeping probably wouldn't be necessary. However, the equation is *grape + grape quality + soil + climate + winemaker + oak = wine*.

What happens to a lot of people is that they drink a bottle of a certain type of wine that they like, such as an Australian Shiraz, then think they have found *the* red wine for them. They may, over time, come to realize that they really only like one Australian Shiraz out of every three or four they try. Without record keeping, it may take a while to work this out. Worst of all, it is easy to forget which ones you actually liked. The Australian Shiraz you like may actually be crafted in a style that is more common in France's Syrahs, less fruity and more tannic.

By keeping track of the wines you consume, you will discover what wines you need to try. If you have had ten New World Chardonnays and never had a white wine from Italy, then you owe it to yourself to try an Italian Pinot Grigio.

If you have a wine that is really good and you want to remember what it is when you go to the wine shop the next time, then you need to make sure that information is with you when you go. This means you want your short list of favourite wines to be in your wallet at all times, just like your driver's license. If you carry an address book with you at all times, you could write your wine list there. You could use the space for *Q* names to write your white wines and the *X*'s to write your favourite red wines, or you could keep one list and record the red wines you like in red ink.

Don't add a wine to your special list until you've had it twice. For every wine you like twice, there will be five wines that you like a lot more the first time you drink them. This phenomenon seems to happen quite a bit to new wine drinkers.

The Wine Journal

We have included a sample of a wine-tasting journal. This journal includes a place to stick the label from the bottle. Removing a wine label isn't that difficult. First, empty the contents of the bottle. Then, fill up a large kettle or pot with hot water, add a small amount of soap and the empty wine bottle. Let the bottle soak for several hours (or overnight). In the morning, the label will peel off. If this method only yields partial success, a butter knife is a good tool for getting the rest of the label off the bottle.

You will then need to let the label dry. It is best if you let it dry on a surface that touches only a small portion of the label, like a dish rack. This will help keep the label from adhering to another surface. It the label does get stuck, water will take it right off the surface, but your label will be wet again.

NAME OF WINE _____

VINTAGE YEAR _____

VINTNER _____

REGION AND COUNTRY _____

PRICE _____

WHERE TASTED _____

FOOD SERVED WITH _____

_____

COLOUR _____

AROMA _____

TASTE _____

COMMENTS _____

_____

_____

Place label here.

NAME OF WINE _____

VINTAGE YEAR _____

VINTNER _____

REGION AND COUNTRY _____

PRICE _____

WHERE TASTED _____

FOOD SERVED WITH _____

_____

COLOUR _____

AROMA _____

TASTE _____

COMMENTS _____

_____

_____

Place label here.

NAME OF WINE _____

VINTAGE YEAR _____

VINTNER _____

REGION AND COUNTRY _____

PRICE _____

WHERE TASTED _____

FOOD SERVED WITH _____

_____

COLOUR _____

AROMA _____

TASTE _____

COMMENTS _____

_____

_____

Place label here.

NAME OF WINE _____

VINTAGE YEAR _____

VINTNER _____

REGION AND COUNTRY _____

PRICE _____

WHERE TASTED _____

FOOD SERVED WITH _____

_____

COLOUR _____

AROMA _____

TASTE _____

COMMENTS _____

_____

_____

Place label here.

NAME OF WINE _____

VINTAGE YEAR _____

VINTNER _____

REGION AND COUNTRY _____

PRICE _____

WHERE TASTED _____

FOOD SERVED WITH _____

_____

COLOUR _____

AROMA _____

TASTE _____

COMMENTS _____

_____

_____

Place label here.

NAME OF WINE _____

VINTAGE YEAR _____

VINTNER _____

REGION AND COUNTRY _____

PRICE _____

WHERE TASTED _____

FOOD SERVED WITH _____

_____

COLOUR _____

AROMA _____

TASTE _____

COMMENTS _____

_____

_____

Place label here.

NAME OF WINE _____

VINTAGE YEAR _____

VINTNER _____

REGION AND COUNTRY _____

PRICE _____

WHERE TASTED _____

FOOD SERVED WITH _____

_____

COLOUR _____

AROMA _____

TASTE _____

COMMENTS _____

_____

_____

Place label here.

NAME OF WINE _____

VINTAGE YEAR _____

VINTNER _____

REGION AND COUNTRY _____

PRICE _____

WHERE TASTED _____

FOOD SERVED WITH _____

_____

COLOUR _____

AROMA _____

TASTE _____

COMMENTS _____

_____

_____

Place label here.

NAME OF WINE _____

VINTAGE YEAR _____

VINTNER _____

REGION AND COUNTRY _____

PRICE _____

WHERE TASTED _____

FOOD SERVED WITH _____

_____

COLOUR _____

AROMA _____

TASTE _____

COMMENTS _____

_____

_____

Place label here.

NAME OF WINE _____

VINTAGE YEAR _____

VINTNER _____

REGION AND COUNTRY _____

PRICE _____

WHERE TASTED _____

FOOD SERVED WITH _____

_____

COLOUR _____

AROMA _____

TASTE _____

COMMENTS _____

_____

_____

Place label here.

NAME OF WINE _____

VINTAGE YEAR _____

VINTNER _____

REGION AND COUNTRY _____

PRICE _____

WHERE TASTED _____

FOOD SERVED WITH _____

_____

COLOUR _____

AROMA _____

TASTE _____

COMMENTS _____

_____

_____

Place label here.

NAME OF WINE _____

VINTAGE YEAR _____

VINTNER _____

REGION AND COUNTRY _____

PRICE _____

WHERE TASTED _____

FOOD SERVED WITH _____

_____

COLOUR _____

AROMA _____

TASTE _____

COMMENTS _____

_____

_____

Place label here.

NAME OF WINE _____

VINTAGE YEAR _____

VINTNER _____

REGION AND COUNTRY _____

PRICE _____

WHERE TASTED _____

FOOD SERVED WITH _____

_____

COLOUR _____

AROMA _____

TASTE _____

COMMENTS _____

_____

_____

Place label here.

Wine Tasting (Rather than Wine Drinking)

Drinking wine is easy; tasting wine requires following a fairly standard set of procedures.

Professional tasters prefer a daylit, odour-free room with white walls and table-tops to allow for optimum viewing of a wine's colour without anything visually stimulating enough to distract one from the wine. Normal people enjoy tasting wine with friends at a dinner table, and don't worry about the distractions of food smells and other niceties.

No matter where you conduct your tasting, make sure your wines are served at the right temperature. This is critical! Wines served too cold can't really be tasted. Those served too warm will seem out of balance. By this we mean a warm white wine may seem too sweet, while a warm red wine is apt to taste too acidic or alcoholic.

Because different people come to a tasting with different tasting experiences, they will describe the same wine differently, even if it is registering the same in each person's brain. If one person usually drinks Cabernet Sauvignon and another usually drinks a softer wine like Merlot, then they are apt to differ in opinion on whether a particular wine is tannic. So it's an inexact science, but an enjoyable one.

Remember that tasting is not a test – your subjective response is more important than any 'right answers'. The bottom line is: Wine that tastes good to you is good wine.

Below is the basic six-step process of wine tasting.

1. *Look at a Wine:* Judging a wine's colour allows you to make some assessment about how old a wine is and how heavy a wine might feel in your mouth. Young red wines are close to purple in colour. In time, they pass through red toward brown. White wines start off in various shades of clear and head towards a straw colour.

   Different wines have different colours. Cabernet Sauvignon is darker by nature than Sangiovese. Also, the riper the harvested grape, the more colour it adds to a wine.

   Judging density of colour is where the strong light source and white background come in to play. Clear, clean glasses are also essential. Thickness of colour usually indicates a richness, fruitiness and/or heaviness. Thickness is best judged toward the edges of the wine as it sits in the glass. Glasses are tipped to a 45° angle to create a large edge of wine against the side of the glass. This means you don't want your glass much more than a quarter full during a critical tasting. The proper way to hold any wine glass is by the stem. This will keep smudges off the bowl so you can see your wine better and not influence its temperature with the warmth of your hand.

2. *Swirl the wine in the glass:* Swirling will help expose a wine to more oxygen, which could be a goal of the taster eager to taste a wine right out of the bottle, but is usually done to release aromas. Swirling is another reason to conservatively fill your wine glass. The tears of wine that slowly run down the side of the bowl after the swirling stops will evaporate quickly and release concentrated aromas.

     The easiest way to swirl a glass full of wine is to leave the base of the glass on the table. If you swirl your glass somewhat vigorously, you will create an invisible tornado of aromas that lift up and out of your wine glass.

3. *Smell the wine:* This is where all hell can break loose. Cries of "tar', 'elderberries', 'coconut', 'coffee', 'tobacco' and so on, are apt to be uttered at a tasting. This may be the most difficult aspect of a tasting for the novice to swallow. The best way to smell a wine is to stick your nose into the glass. There is no getting around this. If you aren't in a social setting that will support this type of behaviour, at least bring the glass very close to your nose. Sticking your nose into the glass right after you swirl it will allow you to catch the updraft of the little tornado of aroma you have created. It

Wine Tips for People on a Date (Even If It's with Your Spouse or Mum)

1. Red wine can temporarily stain your teeth, although it brushes off easily.

2. If you have plans to do something after dinner, you should consider drinking lower-alcohol wine. There is a big difference between 11 per cent and 14 per cent. German white wines are usually low in alcohol.

3. No box wines or screwcaps, unless you are looking to end a relationship.

4. Don't overspend, as it can intimidate the other person and make you appear to be pompous and/or insecure.

5. Always ask the other person if they would like more wine before pouring it straight into their glass.

6. When pouring wine, always pour yours last.

7. Don't feel the need to finish the bottle.

will take you a while before you believe your nose. When you walk near a coffee shop and you smell something that reminds you of what coffee smells like, you conclude you are smelling coffee. When you stick your nose into a wine glass, you may have a difficult time convincing yourself that you are indeed smelling a wine aroma. Our olfactory sense is our strongest sense and it has the best memory, but most of us don't use it very much in our daily lives.

4. *Taste It:* Finally, the moment even a neophyte can understand. You may not taste everything the wine veteran claims to taste, but if you listen to what more experienced wine drinkers say about a wine, your mind and your mouth will begin to sense what they are talking about. With time, you will be able to experience and understand the many flavours of wine, as well as its important components such as acidity and tannin.

It is important to let the wine linger in your mouth for at least ten seconds; otherwise, you aren't really tasting it. It's important to roll the wine around your mouth with your tongue, exposing it to as much of your mouth as possible. Serious tasters will open their lips a bit and inhale into their mouths while wine rests on the tongue. This encourages vapourization, which releases aroma and flavour.

5. *Swallow or Spit:* If you are at a dinner table, you are probably not going to be spitting out your experiments. However, if you go to a tasting where you sample a lot of wine, you are going to want to spit out most of the wines you try. Of course it is easier to judge a wine's aftertaste, known as its 'finish', when you swallow it, rather than spitting it into a bucket.

6. *Make a Note – Written or Mental:* If you are at a serious tasting, most people will be making written notes on the wines they are tasting. If you are at a dinner table or friend's living room, you might not want to pull out a notebook, but you should make a permanent mental note of a wine you really like. Then, back at home, write your notes in this book.

Buying Wine in a Restaurant

The more you learn about wine, the more painfully aware you become of the prices of wine in restaurants. If you enjoy going to restaurants and want to enjoy wine when you are there, consider the following:

If nobody bought wine, there would be fewer restaurants

Most restaurants need wine sales to survive. If you like a particular restaurant, your wine purchases will help keep it there.

You can send it back

... within reason. If a wine has gone bad, has suffered from a spoiled cork (commonly referred to as 'corked'), has turned sour or smells rotten, any restaurant should gladly take it back. If a wine waiter has enthusiastically recommended a wine and you don't like it, you should be allowed to return it. But, if you simply don't like a wine, step back a bit. Do others at your table agree? Have you tasted it without food? If so, taste it with a well-chewed piece of bread in your mouth. Wine is meant to be tasted with food. Might it need to breathe? If you aren't sure, ask the waiter to pour some wine into a glass, and let it breathe for a few minutes. If you still just don't like it, a good restaurant will probably try to keep you happy, especially if you are a regular customer. It is best not to make a habit of this practice. By the way, most wines sent back in restaurants go back to the supplier, thus relieving the restaurant of the cost. The exception to this is older wine.

Older wine

Let's say you order a 20-year-old Bordeaux. This wine may have been in the restaurant's cellar for 15 years. For £80 a bottle you have a right to expect good, solid wine. However, can you send it back if, while showing no flaws, it fails to provide the expected religious experience? Probably, but you should consider that the price of older wine often reflects its scarcity rather than its intrinsic value. You pay a premium for the opportunity to enjoy wine on your 20th anniversary from, say, the year of your marriage. So, be thoughtful about returning such wines – the restaurant will probably have to eat the cost of the bottle (which, when they bought it, might have been surprisingly little money).

How Wines Go Bad

Red wine. If the fruit vanishes and the colour fades, it's too old. A brown colour or a vinegary taste indicates improper storage.

White wine. If it's brown or tastes burnt, it is too old or was improperly shopd.

Either wine can be 'corked' – when the cork is contaminated by a chemical known as TCA, causing the wine to smell mouldy, a bit like a damp cellar.

Sparkling wine. No fizz indicates improper storage or a wine that is too old.

Wine by the Glass Is Usually a Rip-Off

The mark-up on bottles of wine is far less than the markup on mixed drinks. Many customers now order a glass of wine in place of that initial cocktail, so smart restaurant operators make sure that they make the same money on that drink and mark up wine by the glass accordingly. A better value is premium wine by the glass, a category in which the markup is more in line with the wine programme than with the martini programme. These premium wines by the glass are a convenient service for those who can't agree on a bottle or don't want to drink that much.

Know the Price Structure

In a retail shop, you can calculate the price of wines very easily. In most cases the wine costs about 50 per cent over wholesale. After a few shopping trips, you will know what the most commonly sold wines in your area cost on the wholesale level.

Good restaurants often mark up more expensive wines at a lower percentage than their inexpensive choices. This encourages customers to 'trade up' for better value.

Know Your Comfort Level

Everyone who buys wine develops a price point in their mind beyond which they are not comfortable, for fear that they will not appreciate a wine's value. This point becomes more important the more you learn about wine.

Enjoying Wine with Your Dinner

Just as at home, in a restaurant you have some control over the enjoyment of your wine. Is this white too cold? Let it warm up on the table and in the glass, and taste the hidden flavours as they emerge. Is the red too warm? Your waiter should cool it for you in ice water for five minutes or so. Your waiter should be pouring it for you – in proper glassware, never more than half full – though it's OK to pour it yourself. Don't drink it all before the food arrives (unless you're planning to buy another bottle).

The Wine Ritual

You ordered the wine, and you are shown the label. Is it the right year? If you ordered a 'reserve', make sure it is not a lesser bottling from the same producer. So far, so good. Tell the waiter to keep the cork, unless you collect corks; it is of no use to you once you have verified that it hasn't rotted during its years in the bottle. Do taste the wine while the server is there. Any problem should be addressed immediately. Your waiter should then pour wine for everyone at the table.

The Bottom Line

If you enjoy drinking wine with dinner, it may make more sense to go out for dinner less often and then indulge yourself on those occasions. Or, you may prefer to go out for dinner as often as possible and order only a glass of wine, rather than incurring the expense of a whole bottle.

*Wines for People with Too Much Money**

'Let's start with a toast, dear...'
>Louis Roederer Cristal 1996 Champagne is about £125 a bottle.

'Care for Chardonnay?'
>Le Montrachet 1998 from Domaine de la Romanée-Conti costs a breath-taking £1,180 a bottle.

'How about Merlot...'
>A bottle of Château Le Pin 1998, from Pomerol (in Bordeaux), will set you back around £700.

'... or maybe an elegant little Burgundy?'
>A bottle of 1999 La Tâche, from the Domaine de la Romanée-Conti, Burgundy's most prestigious property, will cost you about £450,

'At least California is still a bargain...'
>One of the most expensive California Cabernet Sauvignons is Caymus Special Selection, which will only cost about £80

'The wife here has a sweet tooth...'
>A half-bottle of Château d'Yquem, the most famous sweet Sauternes in the world, comes in at about £155.

These prices are for NEW wines. You can pay tens of thousands of pounds for older wines. Get the idea? Wine is like anything else – cars, watches, clothes.... You are limited only by your budget and your sanity.

>* Prices listed are retail and subject to availability.

CHAPTER 8

WINE AND FOOD

Food and wine have always been a great combination at the dinner table. Meals featuring wine have come to symbolize good times. Here is a partial list of reasons, past and present, why people enjoy wine and food together:

1. Few beverage options existed when wine became part of food culture centuries ago.
2. Pure drinking water has not always been widely available.
3. With its high acidity and other properties, wine assists in the digestion of food.
4. Certain wines are so delicious with certain foods that they seem made for each other, enhancing each other and your enjoyment.
5. When a meal is served as a celebration or holiday feast, the alcohol in wine raises everyone's spirits.
6. When an intimate meal is enjoyed by a couple, wine seems to enhance the intimacy.
7. Water is boring.
8. If you don't drink anything when you eat, the food might get stuck.

You can probably think of other good reasons for matching wine with food. Of course, just as you can enjoy food without wine, you can enjoy many wines without food. Sweet wines, wines naturally low in alcohol, and low-acid wines are easy to enjoy alone. Rich, chewy wines may have too much flavour for your taste at the dinner table. If you like such wines, you'll want to drink them at other times. Drinking a favourite wine alone is always a pleasure without food.

Matching Food and Wine

Since food and wine are so enjoyable together, it should be a fairly simple matter to match them. Unfortunately, it is doubtful that any dining ritual has caused more needless anxiety than that of choosing the 'correct' wine for dinner. What a shame! We're talking about two very enjoyable things – good food and good wine. Unless you make a fundamental error and choose a pairing that results in an unpleasant chemical reaction in your mouth, an error that is 100 per cent avoidable, you can't go wrong. With a little effort and thought, you can pair wine and food so that they make each other taste better!

Many people are familiar with the old, well-established rule of food/wine pairing – 'White wine with fish, red wine with meat'. While this rule is not as valid as it once was (we'll show you why), the reasoning behind it is sound and deserves examination.

Think of a nice, fresh fillet of sole, neatly grilled. Most of us who enjoy fish would welcome a squeeze of fresh lemon on it. Why? The acid in the lemon 'cuts' the intrinsic fish flavour without overpowering it. Thus white wine, with its more apparent acidity and less powerful flavours, would be more appropriate for sole than red wine.

Imagine roast beef with delicious gravy made from onions and pan sauce. The assertive flavour of the gravy matches in magnitude the flavour of the beef, as would a rich red wine. Just as onion gravy would overwhelm the fillet of sole, so would most red wines. And just as a squeeze of lemon would be lost on the roast beef, so too would most white wines. If only it were that simple.

Chef August Escoffier (1846–1935) is widely regarded as the father of French cuisine. French cuisine, in turn, is the mother of fine cookery in Western civilization. Thus, for many decades it was a truism that the finest restaurant in any European city was a French-inspired restaurant with a menu that could have been written by Escoffier himself. The accompaniments and sauces for each entree of the *repertoire classique* were thoughtfully dictated by Escoffier in his authoritative culinary writings. Matching a wine to the meal was relatively straightforward; the French wine list covered all the bases.

Although the teachings of Escoffier are still relevant today, he lived, cooked and wrote in a time before reliable refrigeration and easy transportation. The world of fine cookery has evolved accordingly. Where French restaurants once reigned supreme, we now find Thai, Mexican, Italian and Moroccan restaurants (to give just ba few examples) of equal stature. But perhaps Escoffier's most enduring gift is the ability of French cuisine to adopt and incorporate such varying influences. If he were alive today, he might stumble upon a 'fusion' restaurant that blends many international influences, often on the same plate. If it were thoughtfully and competently prepared, Escoffier would undoubtedly approve... But he might have trouble in choosing a wine.

Among the many changes in fine cookery since Escoffier's time, the increasing complexity of food is the most troublesome for matching wine with food. Here are some guidelines (not rules) that will help.

1. Don't dwell on colour
There are enough other factors to consider; the colour will take care of itself. For instance, chicken dishes can be prepared to match any wine, depending on the ingredients. Lighter reds and strong whites can survive most food pairings.

2. Match strengths
Powerfully flavoured dishes require wines of equal fortitude. *Example:* Herb-crusted leg of lamb or garlicky ratatouille match well with a strongly flavoured wine, usually red.

Delicate dishes need delicate wine. *Example:* Simply prepared white fish (like sole) need a gentle wine, usually white.

3. Opposites attract
Example: The spicy cuisine of the Pacific Rim needs a light, sweet wine to extinguish the fire. Rich cream or butter sauces are well matched with an acidic, 'cutting' wine.

4. Regional affinity
In Europe it is a truism that regional cooking goes best with the local wine. Since gastronomy and oenology evolved side by side, it stands to reason that food and wine derived from the same soil and served on the same dinner table have an underlying affinity.

5. Simple wine with complex food
This would solve the hypothetical dilemma of Escoffier in a 'fusion' restaurant. Serve this food with a varietal not inclined to great complexity – Pinot Blanc (among whites) and Merlot (among reds) come to mind.

6. Complex wine with simple food
The best way to showcase a fabulously complex (and expensive) wine is to pair it with a simple, yet delicious, background dish. *Examples:* A super-premium Cabernet Sauvignon with plain grilled steak, or a great white Burgundy with plain grilled fish.

7. Match price
A £30 Chianti would be wasted on a pizza, but a carefully prepared dinner deserves an equally special wine.

8. Sparkling wine still goes with almost anything
Because the bubbles make up for the lightness of flavour, sparkling wine can be fine with traditional red-wine dishes.

9. And so does Rosé
Wine snobs are quick to dismiss rosé. If it tastes good, drink it. Although it is not really 'right' with any food, it isn't really 'wrong' either, unless, of course, you don't like rosé.

10. Match wine to the occasion

The above-mentioned rosé is frequently mentioned as a 'picnic wine'."Informal gatherings call for informal wine. Save the haughty bottles for smart dinner parties and/or pompous relatives.

11. Serving red wine with fish

As long as the acid level is high and the tannins are barely noticeable, red wine is fine with most seafood. Here are some suggestions:

Simple Chianti or other Sangiovese-based Italian wine

Certain Pinot Noirs – Côte de Beaune, Chalonnais, New Zealand, lighter California

Beaujolais or other Gamay-based wines

Lighter versions of Merlot (or Merlot blends) – Saint-Emilion (Bordeaux) is especially good.

Riojasfrom Spain – Though not high in acid, these Tempranillo-based wines are versatile and inoffensive.

12. White wine with beef

Certain whites are big enough to stand up to charred sirloin and other beef dishes. Consider high-alcohol and well-oaked California or Australian Chardonnay. Viognier-based whites are up for the challenge as well. This offbeat varietal can be one of the most pleasant surprises of the wine world.

13. Serve cheaper wines with cheese

The fat in cheese makes wine taste better. This makes cheese an important ingredient at receptions at which large quantities of inexpensive wine are served.

14. Fruit and wine don't match

Most fruits are acidic, and so are most wines. Fruit acids can throw a good wine out of balance.

15. Wine and chocolate don't match

And they never will, although it's fun to try!

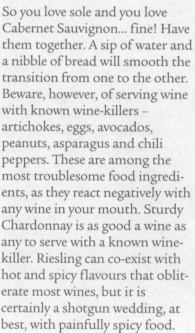

You don't need to match!

So you love sole and you love Cabernet Sauvignon... fine! Have them together. A sip of water and a nibble of bread will smooth the transition from one to the other. Beware, however, of serving wine with known wine-killers – artichokes, eggs, avocados, peanuts, asparagus and chili peppers. These are among the most troublesome food ingredients, as they react negatively with any wine in your mouth. Sturdy Chardonnay is as good a wine as any to serve with a known wine-killer. Riesling can co-exist with hot and spicy flavours that obliterate most wines, but it is certainly a shotgun wedding, at best, with painfully spicy food.

White Wine with Red Meat (Anti-Match #1)

So you all want steak and white wine... a sommelier's nightmare? Not really. There are some big, strapping Chardonnays from California's Sonoma and Napa regions that could climb in the ring with just about any dish and hold their own. The secret is wood, an important component of any big California Chardonnay.

Ripe Chardonnay fruit, high alcohol and a glycerine-charged body benefit from new-oak ageing, which seems to unify these powerful components while adding further complexity. Australian Chardonnays also qualify, but are likely to show more fruit than wood. Big French Chardonnays from the Côte de Beaune are a possibility, but their higher acidity and more subtle charms may be lost on red meat.

If you are less interested in the wine than the food, any subtle white wine can be served. However, the wine's flavours won't be easily noticed.

Red Wine with Fish (Anti-Match #2)

This is a hip way to break the rules, especially with something like a tuna or swordfish steak. Look for high-acid, low-tannin wines – Italian reds tend to be versatile, as are Pinot Noirs from New Zealand and Burgundy. California Pinot Noir is probably going to be too fruity. Rioja may be OK with fish. French Saint-Emilion, in which Merlot usually predominates, is a light take on a fruity grape and a decent match with fish. European wines are crafted to be food-friendly. This is good to remember when you are trying to make an unorthodox food/wine match like fish with red wine.

If you end up with a red that is power-fully flavoured, you are going to end up missing most of the fish's flavour. If you have a wine that is too strong for your fish or any meal, put it aside and drink it after you finish your food. The better the fish, the more you'll want to preserve the experience of the food

As a general rule, fish that is grilled takes on a charred flavour that makes it more compatible with red wines than white. It stands to reason that the fish we usually grill are quite full of flavouir to begin with – salmon, tuna, swordfish and shark.

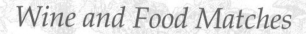

Wine and Food Matches

RED MEAT DISHES

Chili con carne	Beaujolais (an easy-drinking red); Zinfandel (a red to stand up to your chili)
Grilled steak	Cabernet Sauvignon (an ultimate match); Shiraz/Syrah (a good choice at a better price)
Hamburger	Any red wine you like that is inexpensive
Roast beef	Pinot Noir and Merlot (softer reds than for your grilled steak). If you are wild about Cabernet Sauvignon, then have a Cabernet from Bordeaux.
Steak au poivre (Steak with black peppercorn sauce)	BIG REDS! – Zinfandel from California and Rhône reds are perfect
Tenderloin	Same as for roast beef: Pinot Noir and Merlot are the best choices.

OTHER MEAT DISHES

Chicken (roast)	Almost any wine you like – this is a very versatile dish.
Chicken (highly seasoned)	Chenin Blanc and Riesling
Duck/Goose/ Game birds	Pinot Blanc or Viognier (whites); Pinot Noir or Merlot (reds)
Ham	Rosé; California Pinot Noir; demi-sec Vouvray; Gewürztraminer
Lamb (simple)	Cabernet (especially from Bordeaux); Rioja red from Spain

OTHER MEAT DISHES

Lamb (with herbs and garlic)	The herbs and garlic are going to cut into your ability to taste the wine. Try a big red (a steak au poivre wine). And go easy on the garlic.
Pork	An Italian or Spanish red; any white you like
Sausage	Gewürztztraminer or an ordinary red
Turkey	Rosé; any white you like; a very light red
Veal	Australian Chardonnay is perfect
Venison (deer)	A big red wine – Cabernet, Nebbiolo, Syrah, or Zinfandel will do

SEAFOOD DISHES

Anything with a cream sauce	White Burgundy (clean, crisp Chardonnay)
Lobster	Champagne; dry Riesling; white Burgundy
Oysters	Muscadet, a French white, is ideal with oysters; Chablis (dry French Chardonnay) or Champagne
Salmon	Sauvignon Blanc
Prawns	Light and dry white wine
Swordfish	White wine
Tuna	Versatile like chicken; anything but a big red is OK. A light red is probably the ideal match.
White fish (sole, etc.)	Sauvignon Blanc, light Chardonnay

PASTA DISHES

Red sauce	Chianti or other Sangiovese-based red
Vegetables	Pinot Grigio; light red
White sauce	Pinot Grigio

INDIAN & ASIAN CUISINE	These food cultures developed without wine, except for rice wine (saké). Beer is often a better match. German Riesling and inexpensive sparkling wines are your best wine choices, or Beaujolais if your wine has to be red.
PIZZA	Rioja red, Italian red, Australian red, any red – unless you like white, then any white. After all, pizza is *the* no-fuss food. Don't spend a lot of money on this match.
VEGETARIAN DISHES	Red beans and darker starches and vegetables go with red wine. Lighter and greener foods go better with white wine. Petite Sirah is quite good with hearty vegetable dishes such vegetarian chili.

SNACKS

Bread	Everything goes with bread.
Caviar	Champagne and money; Vodka and money
Cheese: rich and creamy (i.e. Brie, Camembert)	Sauternes or an off-dry Riesling
Cheese: goat, and feta	A Spanish or Italian red, although most wines, red or white, go well.
Cheese: other	Whatever wine you want. Cheese makes cheap wine taste better!
Fruit	Not a good match with wine. Grapes are very bad with wine.
Pâté	Gewürztraminer or light red
Rich pâté (i.e. foie gras)	Sauternes or an off-dry Riesling
Salty snacks	Something cheap. Remember to quench your thirst with water, not wine.

A Few Notes on Drinking Wine Without Food

We call wines that we drink without food 'fireplace' wines, although neither of us has a fireplace. If you like wine and you're not hungry, you can either wait until you have an appetite again, or just enjoy a glass of wine on its own. If you buy wine to be enjoyed without food, keep the following in mind.

Low-acid wine is better

High-acid wines need food to show well. The unmitigated acidity of many classic food wines is such that they cannot be enjoyed alone. Remember, acidity helps quench a thirst and cuts through the starch and fleshiness of food. A fruity Pinot Noir or Chardonnay from Chile will certainly go well solo, as will an Australian Chardonnay or Shiraz/Cabernet blend.

Have your white wine a bit warmer than usual

Good white wine is best at 8–10°C (45–50°F), which is warmer than your refrigerator. Without food to focus on, you can ponder the complexities of a good white wine, which reveal themselves more at warmer temperatures. If you open a bottle and let it warm in its own time, you can observe the wine at different temperatures. Try a white you know you like, and learn its secrets.

Keep your red wine a little cooler than usual

A slight chill takes the edge off the acidity and makes the wine more soothing on the tongue. Any red is easier to take served cooler, although not quite as easy to taste.

Avoid big, tannic wines

Unless you are a huge fan of tannin, a lot of tannin will be more overbearing without food. Save that special Cabernet for the dinner table, or at least the cheese and biscuits table.

Sweetness is okay

If you have always avoided anything but dry wines, do yourself a favour and try an off-dry wine for a change. German Riesling, Vouvray demi-sec, and most Gewürztraminers, Rieslings, and rosés are all wines that don't require food in order to show their best qualities.

Now is the time to try a fortified wine

Dry or sweet, light or dark, you can't go wrong. Remember that the fortified wines – Port, Sherry, Madeira and Marsala – are fortified with alcohol, so you should be sipping, not gulping.

Sweeter and sparkling

Off-dry Champagnes and sparkling wines that don't go well at the dinner table are quite enjoyable without food. The fruity and well-made Blanc de Noirs from California are an affordable way to try some not-so-dry bubbly.

Cooking with Wine

Many French or French-inspired recipes call for wine as an ingredient. Just as food and wine have a wonderful affinity at the table, so is the case in the kitchen. There is an adage about this (source unknown): cook with the best, drink the rest. Well, there are a lot of adages out there, and we find this one silly. The wine you cook with needs to be drinkable, but certainly not great. Here's a commonsense rule: if you wouldn't drink it, don't cook with it. This rules out the overpriced, denatured 'cooking wines' found in supermarkets next to the Worcestershire sauce.

Restaurants sometimes use the name of a wine on the menu in order to market a dish. You may see 'Pinot Noir Sauce' or 'Champagne Beurre Blanc' in the menu description. This is unreliable. If the wines used in these recipes were that great, the restaurant would be serving them by the glass, not by the ladle. Some swanky restaurant might actually say 'Dom Pérignon Sauce' on the specials menu, but the chances are that such a wine was opened in error the night before. Always consider the 'cachet value' factor when encountering anything wine related at a restaurant.

Good chefs know how to choose good quality, cost-effective wines for cooking. Here is a list of frequently called-for wines for cooking, and some tips for choosing them.

Dry White Wine

Look for simple, fruity table wines – Chardonnay or Sauvignon Blanc from the 'fighting varietal' band of wines. Avoid sharp, acidic wines, excessively woody wines and sweet wines – all these qualities become more concentrated during cooking.

Dry Red Wine

Again, fruity and simple table wines are the way to go. Pinot Noir is a good choice, as it is almost always low in tannin. You must choose your Zinfandel more carefully; look for a lighter-bodied Zinfandel.

Sherry

True Spanish Sherry adds considerable character when called for in a recipe. Avoid very dry fino Sherry and sweet cream Sherry. The safest choice is Amontillado, a light-amber-coloured, medium-bodied Sherry.

Port

Ruby port, the least expensive type of Port, is probably the best for cooking. It is fruity and sweet, and will retain its colour better than the more expensive Port types. Port is powerful stuff and should be used in modest amounts in dishes. In addition to Ruby Ports from Portugal, Australian 'Ports' tend to have a nutty sweetness reminiscent of Sherry that works very well in cooking.

Madeira

There are no substitutes when a recipe calls for Madeira. Madeira is a key component of France's rich Sauce Périgourdine: a sinful concoction of foie gras, truffles and demi-glace. Madeira sauces have a particular affinity for beef, game and mushroom dishes. For cooking, a medium-bodied Bual or a full-bodied, sweet Malmsey Madeira are best.

Marsala

This Sicilian fortified wine is a staple in southern Italian cooking. The label on a Marsala bottle will indicate whether it is dry or sweet. For cooking, the sweet style, with its richer flavour, is the better choice.

Vermouth

Always use white vermouth when cooking. The intense complex flavour of vermouth enhances many light seafood dishes. Good-quality white vermouth is widely available from Italy and France.

Brandy

It is worth splurging for a relatively inexpensive Cognac of the 'VS' grade when a recipe calls for brandy. Cognac offers reliable and intense flavours, and because 'nip'-sized bottles of brandy (as well as other spirits that may be called for in a recipe) are readily available, this ingredient won't cost you a fortune.

Sparkling Wine

When you cook any sparkling wine, you will eliminate its primary qualities – bubbles and alcohol. In most cases, Champagne as an ingredient is useful for its cachet value only. However, a simple beurre blanc sauce can benefit from the two remaining qualities of good Champagne – high acidity and yeast flavour. A good way to impress your dinner guests is to cook with the same bubbly that you will be serving with the dish. Most recipes call for only a quarter of a bottle of sparkling wine. You can then reseal your bottle with a special Champagne bottle stopper or a regular wine cork reinforced with the original wire cage. Serve it with dinner, and accept the accolades you receive from your guests with the proper amount of modesty.

Pale New World Champagne-method sparkling wines are a good choice for cooking. These tend to have a bit more fruit than their French counterparts, which makes them a bit more of a vocal ingredient in the kitchen.

Recipes

RED WINE MARINARA SAUCE

For 454g of pasta

1 tsp olive oil
2 onions, finely chopped
1 red pepper, finely chopped
100g thinly sliced mushrooms
3 cloves garlic, minced
1 tbsp dried basil
1 tsp dried oregano
400g tin tomato sauce
225g tin tomato paste
1 tbsp soy sauce
125ml dry red wine

Heat the oil in a saucepan over medium heat. Add the onions and cook, stirring, until transparent. Stir in the pepper, mushrooms, garlic, basil and oregano. Continue to cook until the ingredients are soft.

Add the tomato sauce, tomato paste, soy sauce and red wine, and continue to cook over medium heat, stirring frequently, until the sauce just boils and then thickens.

Serve hot over drained cooked pasta.

RED CLAM SAUCE

For 454g of pasta

48 small littleneck clams, well scrubbed and
*   rinsed*
60ml olive oil plus 1 tbsp for the clams
1 tsp finely chopped garlic
1 tbsp chopped flat-leaf parsley
175ml dry white wine
400g tin whole tomatoes, with the juice, or
*   454g fresh tomatoes, peeled, seeded*
*   and chopped*
1 tbsp tomato paste
Salt and freshly ground pepper to taste

Place the scrubbed clams with a tablespoon of olive oil in a large pot over high heat. Cover and steam until the clams open, about 5 minutes. Remove from the heat and cool. Pour the liquid through a sieve lined with paper towel to catch any sand. Reserve the cooking broth. The clams can remain in the shells, or be removed and returned to the liquid at this point.

Cook the garlic in the rest of the olive oil in a large saucepan until softened. Stir in the parsley. Pour in the wine and cook until the liquid is reduced by half. Add the tomatoes and the paste. Stir well to combine, then add 125ml of the clam liquid. Add salt and freshly ground pepper to taste. Simmer for 15 minutes, or until the sauce thickens. Add the clams; heat through quickly, being careful not to overcook. Remove the pan from the heat.

Add drained cooked pasta to the pan, and toss well.

WHITE CLAM SAUCE

For 454g of pasta

48 small littleneck clams, well scrubbed
60ml virgin olive oil plus 1 tbsp
*   for the clams*
2 cloves garlic, finely chopped
60ml dry white wine
Salt and freshly ground pepper to taste
1/8 tsp dried hot red pepper flakes
15g chopped flat-leaf parsley
2 tbsp unsalted butter

Place the scrubbed clams with a tablespoon of olive oil in a large pot over high heat. Cover and steam until the clams open, about 5 minutes. Remove from the heat. Pour the liquid through a sieve lined with a paper towel to catch any sand. Reserve the clam broth. *Note:* The clams can remain in the shells, or be removed and returned to the liquid at this point.

Heat the garlic in the rest of theolive oil in a large saucepan until softened. Pour in the white wine and cook about 1 minute, until the alcohol has evaporated. Add 60ml of the clam liquid and salt to taste. Simmer for 2 minutes to blend. Add the clams, and sprinkle in the pepper flakes and parsley. Heat through quickly and remove from heat. Swirl in half the butter.

Add drained cooked pasta to the pan, and toss well.

Heat the sauce, and add the pasta to the pan to finish cooking. When the pasta is al dente and most of the sauce has been incorporated, swirl in the rest of the butter.

PRAWN SOUP

Serves 4

2 tbsp unsalted butter
1 finely chopped large onion
1 chopped carrot
1 stick chopped celery
1/2 tsp dried thyme
1 small bay leaf, crumbled
225g medium prawns, peeled
*   and de-veined*
500g chicken stock
60ml dry white wine
60g small pasta shells
1/4 cup semi-skimmed milk
Salt and freshly ground pepper
*   to taste*
2 tbsp chopped parsley

In a large soup pot, heat the butter over medium heat. Add the onion, carrot, celery, thyme and bay leaf, and sauté until softened. Add the prawns and sauté quickly until just pink. Add the chicken stock, bring to the boil and simmer for 20 minutes. Add the wine, bring to the boil, reduce heat and simmer 10 minutes.

Meanwhile, in a medium saucepan, bring at least 2 litres of water to a boil. Add a teaspoon of salt. Add the pasta shells and stir to prevent sticking. Cook until al dente. Drain and stir into the soup.

Remove the soup from the heat. Stir in the milk, add salt and fresh pepper to taste, and return the pan to the heat to rewarm – do not let it boil. When heated through, sprinkle with parsley and serve.

RATATOUILLE
Serves 4

175ml olive oil
2 red onions, cut into medium dice
4 cloves garlic, chopped
1 tbsp each dried oregano, basil and thyme
1 tsp dried hot red pepper flakes
1 large aubergine, cut into small dice
60ml balsamic vinegar
80ml dry red wine
900g tinned Italian plum tomatoes with
    juice, diced
1 medium courgette, cut into small dice
1 red pepper, cut into medium dice
1 green pepper, cut into medium dice
225g mushrooms, chopped finely
2 tbsp unsalted butter
Salt and freshly ground pepper
    to taste
4 large firm tomatoes

In a large saucepan, heat the olive oil over medium heat. Add the red onions, garlic, herbs and red pepper flakes, and cook until the onions are soft. Add the aubergine and cook briefly over high heat, stirring constantly. Add balsamic vinegar and red wine, stir, reduce heat and simmer until the aubergine is tender but not soft. Add the tomatoes, courgette, peppers and mushrooms, and simmer over low heat until the vegetables are tender, about 10 minutes. Swirl in the butter. Add salt and pepper to taste. The mixture should be fairly thick. Set aside and cool.

CHICKEN LASAGNA
Serves 10

12 lasagna sheets, uncooked
2 tbsp olive oil, plus additional, if necessary
454g boneless, skinless chicken breasts, diced
350g sliced fresh mushrooms
2 thinly sliced carrots
1 sliced onion
300g frozen green peas, thawed and well
    drained
1 tsp thyme
60g unsalted butter
60g flour
225ml milk
125ml dry sherry
1/2 tsp salt
1/4 tsp cayenne pepper
400g low-fat ricotta cheese
2 cups grated part-skim mozzarella cheese

Preheat the oven to 180°C, 350°F, gas mark 4. In a large, deep frying pan, heat the oil over medium heat, add the chicken and sauté until cooked through. Remove with a slotted spoon, drain on paper towels and reserve.

Add a bit more oil to the pan if necessary. Add the mushrooms and cook briefly. Add the onion and mushrooms, and sauté until softened. Set aside.

In a large saucepan, melt the butter over medium heat. Blend in the flour with a wooden spoon to make a loose paste. Cook over low heat until light golden colour.

Gradually add the milk, stirring with a wire whisk until blended. Stir in the sherry, bring to a boil over medium heat, and cook for 5 minutes, or until thickened, stirring constantly. Stir in the salt and cayenne. Reserve 125ml of the sauce, and set aside.

In a bowl, combine the ricotta and half the mozzarella.

Bring at least 3 litres of water to a rolling boil. Add a tablespoon of salt. Add the lasagne and stir to separate. Cook only until flexible, not until done. Drain by pouring off hot water and adding cold. As the cool sheets slide into the colander, remove them to a kitchen towel to drain.

Spread 125ml sauce over the bottom of a 33 x 22cm shallow baking dish. Arrange four lasagna sheets (three length-ways, one across) over the sauce. Top with half the ricotta mixture, half the chicken mixture and half the remaining sauce. Repeat the layer. Top with the remaining lasagna sheets. Spread 125ml sauce over the last complete layer of lasagna, being sure to cover the lasagna completely.

Cover the dish with foil and bake for 1 hour. Remove the pan from the oven, uncover and sprinkle with the remaining mozzarella. Bake for 5 minutes, uncovered. Remove from oven, cover and allow to stand for 15 minutes before cutting into squares for serving.

TURKEY AND BROCCOLI IN CREAM SAUCE
Serves 4

Broccoli florets (from about one large head)
60ml olive oil
2 tbsp chopped garlic
454g turkey breast, skin removed and cut into
  12mm-thick strips
185ml dry white wine
185ml chicken stock
185ml double cream
30g freshly grated Parmesan cheese

In a large pot, bring at least 3 litres of water to a rolling boil. Add a tablespoon of salt. Add the broccoli and blanch for about 3 minutes. Remove with a slotted spoon to a bowl of cold water. Let stand briefly, drain and return to bowl.

In a large, deep frying pan, heat the oil over medium heat. Add the garlic and turkey, and sauté until the turkey is just cooked through and tender. Using a slotted spoon, transfer the turkey to the bowl with the broccoli.

Add the wine, stock and cream to the frying pan, bring to the boil and cook until thickened slightly, about 8 minutes. Add the broccoli, turkey and cheese to the sauce, and toss until heated through and evenly coated. Serve over pasta.

PASTA WITH HEARTY LAMB SAUCE

Serves 4 to 6

1 tbsp olive or vegetable oil
375g lean ground lamb
2 cloves garlic, finely chopped
1 onion, finely chopped
1/2 tsp dried rosemary
454g crushed tomatoes
250ml dry red wine
Pinch of ground nutmeg
Pinch of ground cloves
Salt and freshly ground pepper to taste
454g pasta
20g freshly grated Parmesan cheese

Heat the oil in a medium saucepan over medium-high heat. Add the lamb, breaking it up with a wooden spoon, and garlic, and cook until the meat begins to brown, about 3 minutes. Add the onion and rosemary, and cook briefly. Add the crushed tomatoes, wine, nutmeg and cloves. Bring to the boil and reduce to simmer. Add salt and pepper to taste. Cook uncovered, until the lamb is tender, about 20 minutes.

Check the lamb occasionally to make sure there is enough liquid to cover it. If not, add a small amount of water.

Meanwhile, in a large pot, bring at least 3 litres of water to a rolling boil. Add a table-spoon of salt. Add the pasta, stir to separate and cook until al dente. Drain. Stir half the Parmesan into the lamb sauce. Add the pasta, toss well and heat through over low heat. Transfer to a warm platter, sprinkle with the remaining cheese, and serve.

CANNELLONI WITH SALMON AND TOMATO CREAM SAUCE

Serves 6

300g frozen, chopped spinach, thawed and
*   drained*
510g ricotta cheese
690g salmon fillet
125ml dry white wine
125ml chicken stock
2 cloves garlic, sliced
Salt and ground pepper to taste
4 tbsp unsalted butter
2 medium tomatoes, peeled, seeded
*   and chopped*
250ml single cream
2 tbsp tomato paste
464g fresh pasta sheets or 12 cannelloni
1 egg, lightly beaten
30g freshly grated Parmesan cheese
Note: Pasta sheets can be bought in
    stores where fresh pasta is sold.

Place the salmon in a large frying pan. Pour the wine and chicken stock over the fish, and add the garlic slices. Bring the liquid to a boil over high heat. Reduce the heat to a simmer and cover. Poach the salmon until pale pink and just cooked through. Allow to cool, and break into flakes.

In a large bowl, combine the spinach, ricotta and salmon. Add salt and pepper to taste. Set aside.

Melt the butter over medium heat. Add the tomato and sauté for 1 minute. Add the cream and tomato paste, stir and bring to the boil. Reduce the heat and simmer until the liquid is reduced by one-third. Set aside.

Preheat the oven to 180°C, 350°F, gas mark 4. Lightly grease a baking dish. Cut the pasta sheets into twelve 15 x 12.5cm rectangles. Brush with egg. Place fish filling on the longer edge.

Roll and overlap the edges, placing seam-side down on the baking dish. Pour tomato sauce over and sprinkle with Parmesan.

Note: If using dried cannelloni, cook them in boiling, salted water until less than al dente. Drain and fill.

Bake for 20–30 minutes until the sauce is bubbling and the cheese golden. Serve.

GREEK PASTITSIO
Serves 6

454g lasagna sheets
2 tbsp olive oil
900g ground lamb
30g chopped parsley
1 onion, chopped
5 cloves garlic, minced
1/2 tsp ground cinnamon
225g tin tomato sauce
125ml red wine
60g butter at room temperature, in pieces
3 eggs, beaten
100g freshly grated Parmesan cheese
750ml béchamel sauce (see Chapter 4), with
    a pinch of ground cinnamon

Preheat the oven to 180°C, 350°F, gas mark 4. In a large, deep frying pan, heat the oil over medium heat. Add the lamb and brown, breaking it up with a wooden spoon, for about 5 minutes. Add the onion and garlic and sauté until softened, about 3 minutes. Drain. Add the parsley, cinnamon, tomato sauce and wine. Simmer over medium-low heat for 30 minutes.

In a large pot, bring at least 3 litres of water to a rolling boil. Add a tablespoon of salt. Place the sheets in the boiling water carefully, sliding them down gently into the water and stirring to prevent them from sticking to each other or to the pot. Cook until not quite al dente. They will cook more when baked. Drain and quickly transfer to a large bowl. Add butter, eggs and half the Parmesan, and toss well.

Place half the sheets in the bottom of a large casserole dish. Top with the meat sauce, and cover with the rest of the sheets. Pour the béchamel evenly over the top. Top evenly with cheese. Bake until the top is golden and bubbling, almost 1 hour.

WINE FONDUE

125g butter
125g plain flour
1 litre milk
500ml Chablis
2 tsp chicken bouillon powder
695g thinly sliced pieces of cheddar cheese

Melt the butter in a large saucepan. Stir in the flour and cook for several minutes over low heat. Add the bouillon, milk and Chablis, and stir frequently until mixture thickens. Stir in cheese until melted and smooth. (Use more or less cheese, according to your own taste.) Transfer to a fondue pot and keep warm. Serve with slices of bread and raw vegetables.

Dinner Party Hints

1. Don't invite people you don't like.
2. Serve two to three different wines, at least one red and one white.
3. If you are serving to a younger crowd, having two-thirds of a bottle of wine per person is a good amount. Older people tend to want to drink less. The longer the event lasts, the more wine people will want to drink.
4. If you are asking guests to bring wine, you should offer them some advice on what to bring. This will help you guide people toward wine that goes with what you are serving. The less a guest knows about wine, the more specific your suggestion should be.
5. Don't force a food/wine combination. Wine does not go readily with soup, salad or fruit.

A dinner party usually begins with guests trickling into your home. Rather than having the early arrivals sitting on your sofa, twiddling their thumbs and complimenting you on how dust-free the corners of your rooms are, you should have a pre-dinner stand-up course of wine and wine-friendly snacks. If your guests are likely to stand, these snacks should require only a single hand, since the other is reserved for wine. When planning a small dinner party with guests who are usually punctual, you need not have a stand-up course.

Because some people are *red-wine-only people*, and some others are *white- wine-only people*, you will want to offer both at all times. A sparkling wine is a good stand-up-course wine. Offering sparkling wine with sparkling water as the alternative during this course is probably OK, too.

At the dinner table each guest should, in a perfect world, be given two glasses. Having a non-identical pair of glasses is a good idea for keeping track of what is in what glass. Don't dictate what a guest should drink. You may think the white goes with the first sit-down course and the red with the main course, but some of your guests may not want to see things that way.

If you don't have a stand-up course, be daring and serve a dessert wine for dessert. Because such a wine is sweet, it is best served alone. Offer coffee and tea after the dessert wine to help rouse your guests from what has become hours of eating and drinking. Don't let people drive when they are drunk or obviously drowsy.

Wine Drinks

MIXED DRINKS WITH WINE

There is no substitute for a wine that you truly enjoy, but there is a place for wine as an ingredient in a mixed drink. Combine wine with the bubble of sparkling water for a refreshment with less overall alcohol content. Combine the flavour enhancement of a liqueur with fruit juice. These are light-hearted drinks with unpretentious ingredients and flexible proportions. That's what makes them appealing.

MULLED WINE

180ml.	red wine
splash of	brandy
1 tbs	fine sugar
splash of	lemon juice
2 whole	cloves
1 dash	cinnamon

Combine ingredients in a saucepan and heat to simmer. Do not boil. Stir well. Pour into a coffee mug.

SANGRIA

1 bottle	dry red wine
60ml	Triple Sec
30ml.	brandy
60ml.	orange juice
30ml.	lemon juice or juice of half a lemon
60g	fine sugar
10 oz.	soda water
	chilled orange and lemon slices

Chill all ingredients together except soda water for at least 1 hour. Before serving, pour over ice into a jug or punch bowl and add the soda water. Makes approximately ten servings.

WHITE OR RED WINE COOLER

125ml.	wine
60ml	pineapple juice
60ml	soda or sparkling water
	wedge of lemon or lime

Pour wine, juice and soda water over ice into a large wine glass. Stir gently. Garnish with a wedge of lemon or lime.

RED OR WHITE WINE SPRITZER

125ml.	wine
60g.	soda or sparkling water
	wedge of lemon or lime

Pour wine over ice into a large wine glass. Add soda water. Stir gently. Garnish with a wedge of lemon or lime.

KIR

| 15ml | crème de cassis (or to taste) |
| 125ml | dry white wine |

Pour the cassis into a large wine glass. Add the wine. Do not stir. The cassis is meant to be at the bottom so the drink gets sweeter as it diminishes. More white wine can then be added if desired. Serve with a lemon twist.

BISHOP

125ml	red wine
60ml	orange juice
15ml	lemon juice or juice of half a lemon
1 tsp	fine sugar

Pour juices and sugar into a mixing glass nearly filled with ice. Stir. Strain into a high-ball glass over ice. Fill with red wine. Garnish with a fruit slice.

VALENTINE

125ml	Beaujolais
1 tsp	cranberry liqueur
60ml	cranberry juice

Combine ingredients in a shaker half filled with ice. Shake well. Strain into a wine glass.

MIMOSA

| 90ml | chilled champagne |
| 90ml | orange juice |

Combine in a champagne flute or white wine glass. Stir gently.

How to Ruin Your Wine-Drinking

1. Serve your wine at the wrong temperature. Reds should be slightly cooled; whites and sparkling wines should be cold, but not too cold.

2. Brush your teeth and rinse your mouth with mouthwash prior to drinking wine. The acidity of the wine will be very noticeable in this situation.

3. Serve wine in a non-wine glass. There is no reason for this. Sure, in theory the wine will taste about the same, but part of the wine experience will be lost. Wine glasses encourage us to sip.

4. Break the cork when trying to remove it from your wine bottle. This is very easy to do with a cheap corkscrew.

5. Drink too much wine and get drunk and/or fall asleep.

6. Drink wine with someone you don't like, or someone who talks too much about too little.

7. Drink your good wine after having too much bad wine.

8. Start drinking wine late at night to ensure a hangover.

CHAPTER 9

STORING AND
SERVING

Wine Bottles

Most of the wine you'll buy in the shops comes in a standard bottle size of 750ml, three-quarters of a litre. You'll also find half bottles (375ml) and magnums (1.5 litres) fairly easily.

Dessert wines often come in half bottles, as they tend to be sweet and alcoholic, and are drunk in moderation and only on special occasions. Most decent wine stores have a small section of half bottles of regular wine. These are good when you don't want a lot of wine, and don't want to worry about saving what is left over.

The magnum is used to sell large quantities of wine. Champagne is often promoted in magnums, in double magnums and in even larger sizes. A wine bottle that is triple magnum, six regular-size bottles' worth of wine, is a Rehoboam; a double magnum, or four bottles of Champagne is known as a Jeroboam.

There are many cheap wines sold in magnums, but there are also some very good wines available in this size. A good wine in a magnum-sized bottle makes a great impression on any dinner table. Anything larger than a magnum, regardless of what it's called, isn't practical.

Speaking of practical, if you want to christen your new yacht with a bottle of Champagne, you need to order a special bottle. What? The carbonation in sparkling wines puts so much pressure on the bottle that they are made with extra thick glass so as not to break from internal pressure – or from a collision with the side of your nice new yacht.

Ageing and Storing

Wine needs to be aged. Everyone takes this to be a truth, even people who don't drink wine. Wine happens to be one of the few agricultural products that can improve with age. If you think back to the time when people didn't have refrigerators and freezers, you'll realize how important this quality really is.

The fact that wine could be bottled and stored (aged) was a primary reason why it was aged. Since wines could age over a period of years, and wines from different years could be aging in the same cellar, the wine's vintage year became of consequence. Because weather is such an important factor in the growing of grapes, and because it varies from year to year (especially when you consider that the growing season is nearly six months long), each year's wines vary.

Whether a particular year was a good or a great year for a certain wine may not be known until two or more years after the harvest, when people start drinking some of the bottles from that harvest. However, generally favourable weather during a growing season usually ensures a good year for winemaking. It does not, however, guarantee a great year.

Most red wines, and almost all whites, do not benefit from more than four years of ageing. This is because a winemaker cannot usually make a bottle of wine that tastes good after only two or three years and also will be able to evolve into something even

better a decade later. Few products are manufactured with the intent that they will be sold ten months later, never mind ten years later.

Wine that is produced with its components in a drinkable balance doesn't need to be aged much at all. Wines with bolder components need one or more years to allow the components to mellow. However, wines can be, and some are, made in such a way that they will be unapproachable for a decade. These are rare and expensive wines that are crafted with great skill and aimed at a small audience. Most of these wines are red, and much of the ageing process involves the relationship between fruitiness and tannin. The truly ageworthy wines are made from the noble-red varieties: Cabernet Sauvignon, Nebbiolo, Sangiovese, Syrah and, to a lesser extent, Pinot Noir and Merlot.

WELL I GUESS IT'S ABOUT READY.

WARNING! WARNING! SPORTS ANALOGY AHEAD!

Let's take a look at the evolution of an expensive and ageworthy red wine as if it were a top-league footballer whose career is broken down into four phases.

1. The wine is tasted by experts straight out of the barrel when it is produced. Praise emanates. 'Powerful tannin, overwhelming fruit, great length,' they say. 'What power! What potential!' A young striker comes up from a small team to the Premier Division. Although he misses the odd kick, the ball usually goes straight to the mark at a speed that amazes the opposition. Sports commentators exclaim, 'What power! What potential!'

2. The wine goes into its dormant phase. Roaring fruit subsides and becomes masked by the tannin. The flavours are out of balance. The footballer injures his knee, develops a drug or alcohol problem, and ends up back in a lower-division team.

3. Given time, the wine reemerges from its slumber with mature fruit flavours of tobacco, cedar, figs, etc – well worth the wait and the price. The footballer successfully completes a drug rehabilitation programme, discovers religion and gains family life, and eventually returns to the Premier Division with pinpoint control. He is Captain of England.

4. The wine loses its redeeming qualities. The fruit and tannin are gone. It tastes like weak tea. Because it's from a great year, it has cachet value on a wine list; it's worth more unopened than opened. The footballer still fills stadiums, especially when playing away. At home, however, the crowd knows he's washed up and prays for him to be injured and be taken off.

Any wine you choose to put away should be kept away from light and, ideally, in the range of 9–15°C (48–58°F). Keeping a typical wine at 21°C (70°F) for six months isn't going to be much of a problem.

If a wine is stored in a warm environment, it matures too quickly; in too cool an environment it will mature too slowly. If your home gets warm in the summer and you do not have air conditioning, it is probably a good idea to drink any good wines you have been saving.

If you are storing wine, lay each bottle on its side; this keeps the cork moist. Whether you are saving a wine for a month or a decade, it is always a good idea to do this. Cork will contract if it is allowed to dry, possibly allowing air to get into the bottle.

It would probably never occur to you to shake your wine bottle, but if it does, don't do it. Some wine experts have made an observation, although unconfirmed by scientists, that vibrations adversely affect wine. This doesn't mean you should carry an expensive wine home from the shop with the gentleness with which one carries a newborn baby, but if you dream of building a wine cellar someday, don't buy a house next to the railway line.

Serving Temperature

Sparkling wine should be served chilled, possibly with an ice bucket to keep it at the right temperature. White wine should be chilled, but not ice-cold. Most wines are allowed to warm up from a stay in a refrigerator for a little while before being served. Red wine should be served a little cooler than normal room temperature.

Unless you own a wine thermometer, the notion of serving a wine at a specific temperature is silly. If you are serving white wine, the chances are you have been refrigerating it. Unless your home has a temperature around 17°C (63°F), you need to manipulate the temperature of every bottle of wine, using the air in your refrigerator (or freezer!), the air in your home and possibly ice, if you are drinking sparkling wine.

To chill a wine, put it in the refrigerator. To warm it, take it out. Where you live, what season it is and how you regulate the temperature in your house determines how warm your home is. On a hot summer night, in a city house or flat or a restaurant that doesn't have air conditioning, you may find yourself and your wine sitting in a 30°C (86°F) room.

General rules of thumb regarding serving temperature allow most people to enjoy wine without needing to be both a physicist and a meteorologist.

- You can drop the temperature of a warm full bottle of wine roughly 2°C (4°F) every ten minutes it sits in your refrigerator. You can chill it about twice as quickly if you put the bottle in your freezer. The fastest way to chill wine is in a mixture of ice and water. Add salt to the water if you are in a *real* hurry.

- If you are taking a bottle of white wine from your refrigerator, you can raise its temperature in a cool room roughly 2°C (4°F) every ten minutes, more quickly if you pour some into a glass. If you are in a very warm room, it will probably warm at twice that speed.

- You can manipulate the temperature of wine bottles with warm and cold water faster than with warm and cold air. However, guessing the temperature of such water is iffy, especially a warm-water temperature. If you are drinking an ordinary wine or are in a hurry, you may want to consider placing your wine bottle in a pot or pan of warm or cool water. After all, it's only wine.

- Using the freezer: A bottle of white wine will go from normal room temperature to drinking temperature in 40–45 minutes if you put it in your freezer. This is about half the time it takes via the refrigerator.

Now let's build some guidelines on all this.

Red Wine
You want to drink this at about 18°C (64°F). If you are drinking a red of questionable quality with bad elements you might want to numb a bit, or a Beaujolais (good or bad), serve it at 15°C (60°F).

If your home is at 21°C (70°F), then you want to put your wine in the refrigerator for 15 minutes. If it is at 30°C (86°F), then you should keep your wine in the refrigerator for about 40 minutes to bring it down to 18°C (64°F).

White Wine
You want to drink white wines at about 9°C (48°F). If it is a really expensive white wine, you will want to taste it more, and you should serve it at 14°C (58°F). Let's assume your refrigerator is at 6°C (42°F). This is cool for a refrigerator, but not uncommon in this era of good home appliances. We'll also assume you didn't spend £70 for your bottle of white wine and would like to drink it at 9°C (48°F).

To get your white wine warmed up to drink, reckon that it will warm at 2°C (4°F) every ten minutes if your home is at 21°C (70°F), and twice that speed if it is at 30°C (86°F). So take it out 15 minutes before serving, or eight minutes prior in a very warm setting.

Sparkling Wine
This should be served at about 6°C (42°F) (about the temperature of your refrigerator). It's probably ideal a bit warmer, but unless you are drinking in a very cold room, it will warm up fairly quickly. So if you plan on taking your bottle out of your refrigerator for any length of time, you will want an ice bucket around. Warm sparkling wine is anything but festive.

Sherry
Light Sherry should be served like a white wine. Sweeter, darker Sherries should be served like red wine – even normal room temperature is OK.

Port, Marsala and Madeira
Same as red wine.

Dessert Wines
Same as white wine.

Trial and error will help you perfect the timing for the temperature in your home, refrigerator and freezer, but the guidelines above are a good place to start. Even if you get the serving temperature thing perfect, you'll always need to deal with the fact that wine warms up every minute it sits in your glass.

Letting Wine Breathe

What is breathing? It is exposing wine to air, aerating it. Oxygen is the element in the air that affects wine. White wines don't seem to react right away to oxygen, so when we talk about letting a wine breathe, we are talking about a red wine. If this were a chemistry book, we would be explaining a set of complex reactions and processes. Let's stick to how the air changes the flavour of wine.

Practically all wine is crafted in a way that causes it to evolve over time. If this were not the case, then we'd be buying and drinking month-old wine like we buy month- old beer (if we're lucky). A large part of the evolution is the mellowing of the wine. Tannins and acids are the components that most need to mellow. Without suffi- cient exposure to oxygen, wines can taste harsh. Eventually, as the tannins and/or acids fade a bit, the fruit begins to exert itself and the wine's components become more balanced. After too much exposure, wine – especially red wine – begins to taste like vinegar. This is caused by the development of acetic acid.

A Cabernet Sauvignon, Shiraz/Syrah or Nebbiolo may need to breathe for an hour or more, depending on how the wine was made and how mature it is. Equally important are the personal tastes of the people who will be drinking the wine. Some people like to taste wines right out of the bottle and experience the evolution over time. A Beaujolais Nouveau doesn't need to breathe much. This makes sense, as it is crafted not to evolve but to be drunk just weeks after harvest.

Generally speaking, all red wines taste better ten minutes after you open the bottle and pour it into the glass. Just taking the cork out and leaving the wine in the bottle is ineffective, since so little of the wine is exposed to air. Let your wine breathe in a glass. Wines that are still before their peak when the cork is removed may taste much better after half an hour or more in a glass.

Letting your wine breathe doesn't have to be a controlled scientific experiment. It is interesting merely to observe how bad some good wines may taste when you first open the bottle. Just keep in mind that a red wine will probably be better (and unlikely to be worse) after ten minutes of aeration.

A white wine may also benefit from some air and is unlikely to taste worse. Some wines actually taste better the next day. We've had some £4 bottles of red wine that tasted like £8 bottles the next day. It's important to note that these wines were in a recorked bottle and not left out for a day in a wine glass.

If you ever have an expensive bottle of wine 15 or more years old, you don't want to give it much air time. These wines can change drastically literally from minute to minute. Because a lot of the mellowing has already been done by sitting in the bottle for years, these wines may run out of steam an hour after the bottle is opened. However, that can be an incredible hour, in which a seemingly static bottle of liquid changes dramatically. Don't bother saving part of an old wine for the next day unless you want to experiment: It will probably be dead.

£30 Bottles of Wine That Are Worth the Money

1. *Château Pichon-Lalande (Pauillac, France).* These wines are a delicious, ageworthy Cabernet Sauvignon–based blend.
2. *Louis Jadot Gevrey Chambertin (France).* This is a large, reliable producer of Red Burgundy, which is, of course, Pinot Noir–based. The Clos St-Jacques version of this stuff costs more than the regular version, which is good enough to impress you and anyone else you might want to impress.
3. *Mumm Renée Lalou Champagne.* If you've read this book, you know this stuff comes from Champagne, France.
4. *Chablis Grand Cru Les Clos.* This is simple, elegant, excellent French Chardonnay.
5. *Silver Oak Cabernet Sauvignon from California.* These bottles are hard to find, harder not to like.
6. *Penfold's Cabernet Sauvignon Bin 707.* This is a great wine from Australia.
7. *Domaine Zind Humbrecht (Alsace, France).* This is a single-vineyard Grand Cru-Riesling and Gewürztraminer.
8. *Château Raymond Lafon Sauternes (France).* A full bottle of this is delicious dessert wine is an expensive bargain.
9. *Château Smith-Haut-Lafitte Blanc (France).* This is the finest Sauvignon Blanc–based wine in this price range.
10. *Beaune Clos de Mouche from Joseph Drouhlin (France).* A bottle of this is as good as any Chardonnay, especially with food.

Wine Glasses

All wine glasses have stems that connect the base to the bowl or cone of the glass. It is proper etiquette to hold the stem of the glass. This keeps your hand from heating the wine, and it keeps fingerprints off the bowl.

There are three main styles of wine glasses: all-purpose white-wine glasses, large bulbous glasses for red wine, and a third style for sparkling wine, a flute, which is tall and very slender.

There are many wine-glass styles to investigate at upmarket wine shops and houseware shops, but sticking to the three styles makes the most sense for most people. There are even wine glasses for individual grapes. The Burgundy glass, theoretically, is designed for the enjoyment of Pinot Noir wines that come from Burgundy.

If you don't own any decent wine glasses, get a set of the all-purpose glasses. The Burgundy glass has a bulbous bowl, some more wide than tall, on a stem that is used almost exclusively for red wines. Burgundy-style glasses look good but are less practical than white-wine glasses. White wine shouldn't be served in a Burgundy glass, but the all-purpose white-wine glass is perfectly fine for red wines.

If you entertain guests, or yourself for that matter, and you like red wine, it is nice to have a set of both the all-purpose and the larger red glasses. This allows you to serve two different wines without there being any confusion about which glass holds which wine – the better wine goes in the bigger glass.

Wine glasses come in different sizes. It is possible to buy a glass that holds 500ml or more. A good-sized glass holds 375ml, and you probably don't want to buy a glass that holds less than 310ml. We recommend your everyday glass be an all-purpose one that holds about 310ml. Larger glasses do add an exclamation point to a festive occasion and are a good way to go when choosing a second set, but they are a bit ostentatious and more likely to get broken.

Stay away from odd colours or shapes for your wine glasses. Wine is meant to be looked at through clear glass and to flow out of your glass smoothly, without nooks and crannies to negotiate.

Wine glasses do break. Because you are going to lose some glasses in time, you should buy glasses that are easy to replace and that you can afford to break on occasion.

Don't serve wine in plastic glasses or cups. If you are having a large reception, you can hire wine glasses for the occasion, usually at a reasonable price. It adds a little class to the occasion, regardless of the wine in the glass.

SPARKLING WINE   CHAMPAGNE FLUTE   WHITE WINE   RED WINE

Pouring Wine

Is this something you really need to worry about? No, but there are a couple of things to remember. If you work at a restaurant, you have quite a few things to keep in mind.

First, when pouring, it is polite to serve yourself last.

You shouldn't fill a wine glass more than half full; one-third is considered optimum. The fuller the glass, the more difficult it is to swirl your wine, which people do in order to smell the aromas in the wine and thus enhance their enjoyment. Even if the people at your table aren't big wine sniffers, don't fill the glass up past halfway. By not over-filling the glass you can see if your wine is viscous and leaves legs (tears) on the glass.

You should always aim to pour 155 or 180ml, regardless of the size of the glass. When pouring non-sparkling wine, aim for the centre of the glass; it's not going to bubble up. Sparkling wine should be poured slowly and against the side of the glass so it doesn't bubble over.

When you have poured enough, give the glass bottle a slight twist as you lift it upright, which helps prevent a drop or two from dribbling down the side of the bottle.

If you are *serving* wine by the bottle in a restaurant, you will first be expected to present the bottle to your customers before opening it. You are supposed to make the presentation to the person who is most likely to be paying for the wine, usually the person who ordered the wine. This ritual is to show the customer you are serving the wine that was ordered. Most restaurants have a wine-serving policy that may even include how you hold the bottle when pouring it.

Some wine bottles have a touch of sediment that tends to emerge from the bottle when it is almost empty. This is because the sediment is heavier than the wine. If you are drinking a red wine more than a few years old, the chance of there being sediment increases.

Sediment isn't going to kill you, but you are likely to be surprised when you see it in the bottom of your wine glass. Sediment will make your wine cloudy and can adversely affect the flavour of it. A simple rule of thumb is to avoid trying to get every last drop out of a bottle of wine (especially a red) by turning the bottle vertical when pouring the last of it into a glass.

If you see some sediment in your wine glass, there's no need to worry. The chances are that most of it will end up at the bottom of the glass.

Affordable Wines Worth Aging

Sauternes (France) Dessert Wine from the Bordeaux subregion of Sauternes. A good producer is Château Raymond Lafon; there are also others. Age for a long time, but play it safe and pull the cork before its 25th birthday. *Cost: £18 half bottle*

Petites Châteaux, (the plural of Petite Château). These are lesser châteaux of Bordeaux (France), with good red blends, usually of Cabernet Sauvignon, Cabernet Franc and Merlot. Age for 4–5 years. *Cost £5–12*

Moulin-a-Vent (France). This is one of the ten premier villages for Beaujolais. Age for 4–5 years. *Cost: £7–10*

Riesling from Alsace (France). Purchase wines from one of these top producers: Trimbach, Hugel or Domain Zind Humbrecht. Age for 4–5 years. *Cost: £12–24*

White Burgundy (France), a Chardonnay-based wine. Look for wines produced by Joseph Drouhlin, Louis Latour and Domaine Laflaive's Bourgogne Blanc. Age for 5–10 years. *Cost: £15–30*

Chianti (Italy). Buy Sangiovese-based reds from Castello di Ama or Ruffino. Age for 5–10 years. *Cost: £7–15*

Vintage Port (Portugal). A port with a vintage year is one made from grapes from a particularly good harvest. Prices vary widely on these. Half bottles are available. Unless you are immortal, you'll have a difficult time over-ageing one of these. Two reliable producers in this category are Dow and Croft. *Cost £12 and up*

Chateauneuf-du-Pape (France – both a place and a wine name). These are red wines based on any number of 13 grape varieties of various combinations and percentages. They are a perfect example of why the French are less interested in grape variety than place of origin. These are very good wines and can be aged a long time. Two top producers are Vieux Télégraphe and Beaucastel. *Cost: £12–25*

The Right Cabernet Sauvignon. This, the premier red-wine grape, is meant to be aged. Ask a wine person whose judgment you trust for a suggestion for a Cabernet worth aging. Tell him how long you are willing to wait and how much you are willing to spend.

Decanting

Decanting is not an everyday necessity for any wine drinker. Many wine drinkers go a lifetime without needing to decant any wine.

Decanting is the process of pouring wine from its bottle into a carafe or a decanter. The main purpose of this is to leave the sediment behind. Sediment can be a problem with older red wines, especially Ports. If you are serving such a wine, you need to consider a few things.

Let the wine sit upright for a couple of days. When you serve the wine, you should pour it slowly out of the bottle, so as not to disturb the sediment that has settled to the bottom. You will need a bright light, candle or torch to shine through the bottle to monitor the sediment as it drifts toward the neck of the bottle.

Decanting also aerates the wine. If you are decanting a Port, aeration isn't a big deal. But if you are serving an old red table wine, the clock is ticking. These wines generally don't last long after opening before their fragile components begin to fade.

If you don't have a decanter, you can either pour your wine slowly and carefully, which will leave much of the sediment behind, or pour it into an old but clean wine bottle. Having a steady hand is always important when decanting, and it becomes that much more important if you try to decant from bottle to bottle. Some people choose not to bother with decanting and deal with the sediment on a glass-by-glass basis. This approach is fine, so long as the amount of sediment doesn't detract from your enjoyment.

A 'quick and dirty' method of decanting wine is to filter it through cheesecloth or a coffee filter. This is foolproof, although purists might protest against the wine's touching a foreign object.

Sometimes it is desirable to decant a young wine solely for aeration. This should be done quickly, almost violently, to expose as much wine to as much air as possible. Let the wine rest for about an hour before serving. This method will make young reds, especially New World Cabernet Sauvignons from top producers, more enjoyable.

If you've invested in a wine that will need decanting, it is hoped that you will have remembered to invest in a decanter, or at least saved a wide-mouth carafe and its top for the occasion.

Corks

The usual way to keep air, more precisely oxygen, out of an unopened bottle of wine is with a cylindrical piece of cork. Cork expands in the neck of the bottle and provides an airtight seal, unless the cork dries out. If an unopened bottle of wine is left in a very cold place, the cork can be forced out of the bottle.

When you buy a wine, feel the cork through the plastic or lead wrapper on the top of the bottle. Make sure the top of the cork is about level 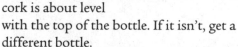 with the top of the bottle. If it isn't, get a different bottle.

While plastic corks achieve their main aim – to prevent wines from becoming corked – they can be difficult to remove from the bottles, and they're impossible to get back in the neck of the bottle .

Once looked down upon as being fit only to seal the cheapest of wines, screwcaps are considered to be highly desirable bottle closures by many producers and retailers who want to prevent their wines from any possibility of cork taint.

You still won't find the classiest, most age-worthy reds with screwcaps. That's because, although the argument for screwcaps is well on the way to being won when it comes to wines intended for early drinking and aromatic white wines, the case has yet to be proven that a really good screwcapped bottle of, say, Bordeaux would be at its best 20 years down the track.

Corks may have imperfections that can cause a wine to go bad in the bottle. An imperfect seal allows oxygen to interact with the wine, prematurely ageing it. More commonly, the cork may be tainted with a chemical known as TCA. This causes the wine inside the bottle to smell damp and mouldy, a bit like a long-neglected basement. If you find a bottle of 'corked' wine, take it back to the shop you bought it from.

It is a good idea to have a couple of good corks from bottles already consumed lying around your kitchen in case you encounter a cork problem. A broken or brittle cork should be replaced with a better one if you recork your wine. Eventually, old corks will reexpand and won't fit in a wine bottle, so replace your saved corks with newer ones from time to time.

Corkscrews

Corkscrews are used for removing the cork from the bottle. They are not used to open sparkling wines; this would be both dangerous and unnecessary, as the pressure behind the cork will help you to remove it and perhaps send it flying. Believe it or not, there are actually organizations for corkscrew collectors. These people buy, sell and trade rare and/or expensive corkscrews, have newsletters, etc. But let's talk about the corkscrews that people actually use to open a bottle of wine.

Worm (or Auger)

This is found on some penknives; you just never knew what to call it. The worm and a handle (the penknife body doubles as the handle) doesn't work very well. Do not buy one of these things. The worm, however, is the main part of most corkscrews. Unless you are using the butler's corkscrew (see page 222), you will need to bore your way into a cork before you can pull it out of the bottle. Sometimes plastic versions of these are given away as promotional items. *Cost: Free–£2*

Screwpull

This device is considered to be the most effective and practical corkscrew. It is designed to ensure that the worm bores straight into the cork. All you do is put the screwpull in position on the bottle and start turning the handle. At first you are boring the worm into the cork. Then, when the worm is deep enough in the cork, you suddenly find that your turning of the handle is pulling the cork out of the bottle. It seems like magic, until you use one and figure out how this clever device works. (*Hint:* The cork 'rides up' the thin, teflon-coated worm.) *Cost: £20 for a good one*

Winged Corkscrew

This is the metal corkscrew with wings and a bottle-cap opener at the end of the handle. Some people don't like these because they don't have control of the direction of the worm as it bores into the cork. However, once you are comfortable with this type of corkscrew, your success rate will be very high. Also, having a bottle-cap opener on your corkscrew is a nice convenience.

To use a winged corkscrew, you align the worm perpendicular to the top of the cork. Then you start twisting the handle while keeping the corkscrew as vertical as you can. The hand you use to steady the bottle should be positioned so as not to impede the wings that lift as the worm bores into the cork. When the wings get to the five to one position, you stop turning the handle and, instead, press the wings down. This brings the cork up and out of the bottle. Ideally, the cork will still be in one piece. If the cork doesn't come all the way out of the bottle, you will be able to yank it out of the bottle while holding the corkscrew. *Cost: £5*

Waiter's Corkscrew

This corkscrew has a little knife on it to cut the wrapper off the top of the bottle before removing the cork. This is a nice feature, but the mechanics of getting the cork out of the bottle leave a lot to be desired. However, practice makes near-perfect. The worm is manually turned into the centre of the cork. A swinging arm attached to the corkscrew is then placed on the lip of the bottle. This provides leverage so that the wine server may pull up on the other end of the corkscrew and thus pull the cork out. If you don't plan to work in a restaurant, don't buy this type of corkscrew; splash out on a screwpull. *Cost: £5–10*

Butler's Corkscrew

Also known as the 'Ah-So' corkscrew, this style is the only one that doesn't use a worm to bore through the cork. You slide the two prongs down the sides of the cork, and then twist and pull the cork out of the bottle. One of the prongs is longer than the other, and you need to get this one between the cork and the edge of the bottle before positioning the other prong. This is not an easy device to use without a lot of practice. However, for people who buy a lot of old wines whose corks may have deteriorated a bit over the years, this device is the best way to get a bad cork out of a bottle in one piece. *Cost: £4–8*

Port Tongs

The fanciest and most dramatic device for opening bottles is a set of port tongs. As the name implies, this contraption is designed for opening very old port bottles whose corks have disintegrated. The tongs are heated red-hot in a fireplace and then closed around the neck of the bottle. This heats the glass in a narrow band just below the cork so that, when brushed with a feather that has been dipped in cold water, the glass neck neatly cracks. The top of the bottle and the crumbly cork are then removed and the port is decanted. *Expect to pay over £80, if you can find them.*

Champagne

As we mentioned earlier, a champagne bottle does not require any type of corkscrew to remove its cork. It should, however, be opened with the same caution used in handling a dangerous weapon. Imagine the bottle as a gun and your finger as the safety catch. Always keep a thumb or finger over the cork. First remove the foil and wire, with your thumb hovering over the cork. Then point the bottle at a 45° angle away from everybody. Grip the cork firmly in one hand and pull with the other. Never turn the cork. As the internal pressure loosens the cork, continue to hold it firmly.

Saving Leftovers

Leftover wine is an issue that stirs controversy. Products have been made to keep leftover wine 'fresh'. These devices either pump out the air in the bottle, or replace the air with inert gases. The goal is to keep oxygen away from leftover wine in the bottle. The effectiveness of these products varies from study to study.

Restaurants that serve premium wines by the glass must sometimes choose between serving a questionable wine and throwing it away. White wine, kept chilled, keeps well, but a red wine that was opened a day or two ago may no longer be worth drinking.

If you open an old bottle of red wine, it is best drunk within an hour or two before it loses the qualities that made it worth ageing all those years in the first place. Leftovers from these wines aren't worth saving. Fortified wines and dessert wines, on the other hand, will last quite a while without much effort.

The question is, how does one best save table wine for future consumption?

PLAN 1

The easiest and, in our opinion, best thing to do is the following. Get yourself a half bottle of wine. Drink it. Enjoy it. Save the bottle and the cork. Clean the bottle by rinsing the inside with hot water a couple of times. Let it dry; then put the cork back into the empty bottle.

You now have a surrogate half bottle for future wines. When you open a bottle of wine that you know you won't finish, it's time to use your half bottle.

Step 1. Open the new bottle.
Step 2. Pour half of its contents immediately into the half bottle. Fill it high into the neck, leaving little or no room between the top of the wine and where the bottom of the cork will be.

Step 3. Cork the half bottle.
Step 4. Refrigerate it (optional for
red wines).

You now have a half bottle of wine that received very little exposure to oxygen, and is not receiving much, if any, in its new home. This will preserve many red wines, especially young ones, for up to two weeks. If you refrigerate the bottle, the wine will last longer. Because wines vary and room temperatures vary, the ability of your wine to hold out in its new home will vary.

What does refrigeration do? It slows down the biological activity going on in the wine. Oxidation is the biological activity that turns wine to vinegar.

Half bottles, for the most part, are shorter than full bottles and fit better when they are standing up in refrigerators, even on a door shelf.

Note that the bottle that stores your leftovers doesn't need to be a wine bottle. You can use a soda bottle or even a ketchup bottle. If your bottle is clear glass, then it is easier to inspect it for cleanliness on the inside. Green or clear-glass half bottles are preferable to brown; it is difficult to see the wine level as you pour into a brown bottle.

If you have saved a red wine, you will need to remember to remove the wine from the refrigerator 45 minutes before you plan to drink it. A half bottle of wine will warm up somewhat more quickly than a full bottle.

If you end up drinking some of the leftover wine from the half bottle that day or on a subsequent day, it is a good idea to refrigerate your red because there will now be oxygen in your bottle.

PLAN 2

Recork and refrigerate leftover wine in its original bottle. The sooner after opening, the better.

No matter what you do to save your wine, you don't have to lay the bottle on its side. In fact, this is a bad idea because the wine may be able to sneak past the cork, causing a mess and a loss of wine.

All of this fuss is unnecessary for inexpensive box wine. The process of pasteurization, usually used on such wines, kills everything in the wine that can make it go bad.

This wine vacuum pulls air out of a open wine bottle to preserve leftover wine.

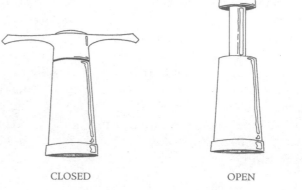

CLOSED   OPEN

Saving Sparkling Wine

If you drink sparkling wine more than twice a year, and you find yourself having some left over, you might want to invest in a sparkling-wine bottle stopper (shown at right). This little device does a good job of retaining the carbonation. A standard wine cork also works, although unless you secure it with the original metal cage from the sparkling wine bottle (or aluminium foil), it can pop out. When saved properly, sparkling-wine leftovers will keep pretty well for a day or two.

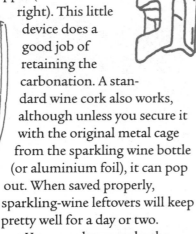

You can always make the following mixed drinks with your leftover champagne or sparkling wine.

CHAMPAGNE COCKTAIL

1 tsp.	fine sugar
3 dashes	bitters
180ml	champagne, chilled

Dissolve sugar in bitters in the bottom of a champagne flute. Add champagne. Stir. Top with a lemon twist.

MIMOSA

90ml	chilled champagne
90ml	orange juice

Combine in a champagne flute or white wine glass. Stir gently.

MIDORI MIMOSA

60ml	Midori
1 tsp.	lime juice
125ml	champagne, chilled

Combine in a champagne flute or white wine glass. Stir gently.

BELLINI

60ml	peach nectar
15g	lemon juice
	chilled champagne

Pour juices into a champagne flute. Stir. Fill with champagne. Stir gently.

CHAMPAGNE MINT

15g	crème de menthe
	chilled champagne to fill

Pour crème de menthe into a champagne flute. Add champagne. Stir gently.

CHAMPAGNE CHARISMA

60ml	champagne, chilled
30ml	Vodka
15ml	peach-flavoured brandy
30ml	cranberry juice
1–2 scoops	raspberry sorbet

Combine all ingredients except champagne in a blender. Blend well. Pour into a large red-wine goblet. Add champagne. Stir.

CHAMPAGNE FIZZ OR DIAMOND FIZZ

60fl	gin
30fl	lemon juice or juice of half a lemon
1 tsp.	sugar
125ml	champagne

Combine gin, lemon juice and sugar in a shaker half filled with ice. Shake well. Strain into a highball glass over ice. Add champagne. Stir gently.

BUCKS FIZZ

155ml	champagne, chilled
15ml	Triple Sec
30ml	orange juice
1/2 tsp.	grenadine

Pour champagne, Triple Sec and orange juice into a champagne flute. Add grenadine. Stir. Garnish with an orange slice.

SCOTCH ROYALE

45ml	scotch
1 tsp.	fine sugar
dash	bitters
	chilled champagne to fill

Dissolve sugar in bitters and scotch in a champagne flute. Fill with champagne. Stir gently.

KIR ROYALE

30ml	crème de cassis
	chilled champagne to fill

Pour ingredients into a champagne flute or wine glass. Stir gently.

Cleaning Wine Glasses

There are different approaches to the goal of having a truly clean wine glass. By clean we mean no dust, no odour, no visible or invisible caked-on liquids from previously contained beverages – no soap residue.

If you choose to run your glasses through a dishwasher, you then must clean the glasses by hand using hot water to remove soap residue, which you may or may not be able to see or smell.

If you clean your glasses by hand using dish soap and water, the same thing must be done. When you clean your glasses by hand, you can better regulate the amount of soap you use. Less is better.

Your third option is to use no soap at all. A thorough cleaning is possible using only hot water, clean fingers and maybe a sponge that has no soap on it. This is the method we use.

If you don't own many glasses, or you're lazy or just don't care, you can use a wine glass for other beverages like juice or water. This is acceptable. We do it, and many other people do it too. A wine glass has an elegant functional shape, and it is difficult to resist the urge to use it when it is the most convenient glass and you want some juice, water or other liquid refreshment.

Wine Stains

This topic isn't fun, because a good piece of clothing or a carpet may be at stake, and there is no sure answer. Red-wine stains are tougher to remove than white-wine stains.

Salt and water is the best home recipe for removing wine stains. We have used both hot and cool water with salt and had some success. If you have a piece of clothing that you can remove right away, you might want to try to clean it yourself with salt and cool water if the label reads *dry clean only*. Do this your own risk to the fabric, but not all dry-clean-only fabrics are as delicate as their labels suggest. We suggest you use about 310ml of water with two tablespoons of salt, and less salt for better fabrics.

On cotton, a lot of hot water poured from a foot away onto a wine stain primed with salt works pretty well, even when this is done the next day.

If you spill wine onto a carpet or rug, you can use salt and water. Cool water is safer, so if you have an expensive carpet or rug, restrict these efforts to cool water and conservative amounts of salt.

We have also heard that white wine poured onto a red-wine stain can be effective in neutralizing the staining elements in red wine. We make no promises with this solution.

Bottle Shapes

The French didn't invent wine, nor did they perfect it. They did, however, define the standards to which all other wines are held. As such, French wines have served as role models for New World wines. It is a tribute to the primacy of France that her regional bottle shapes are imitated around the world to indicate the intended style of the wine.

In the Bordeaux region of France, Merlot and Cabernet Sauvignon are the dominant red varieties, whereas Sauvignon Blanc and Semillon are used to make white wine. Thus in the New World, the easily recognizable Bordeaux bottle shape, with its full, rounded shoulders, is normally used for these varietals. A variation of this classic shape is tapered to a narrower width at the base, making the bottle both prettier to look at and more difficult to stack. The Bordeaux bottle is the most widely used bottle shape in the world

The wine producers in Burgundy use a slope-shouldered shape for both reds and whites. Accordingly, many New World versions of the Burgundian varieties – Chardonnay, Pinot Noir and Gamay – are offered in Burgundy bottles. A similarly shapes bottle is used in France's Loire region and yet another variation is common in the Rhône valley.

The wines of Alsace, nearly all white, are sold in tall, slender bottles nearly identical to those in neighbouring Germany. Many New World Rieslings are sold in similar bottles. Germany has a long tradition of wine making. Her two major fine-wine-producing areas lie along the rivers Rhine and Mosel. In order to better distinguish

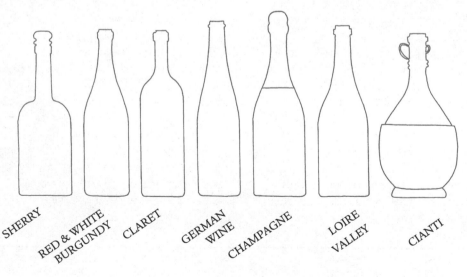

SHERRY   RED & WHITE BURGUNDY   CLARET   GERMAN WINE   CHAMPAGNE   LOIRE VALLEY   CIANTI

between these approximately equal rivals, the Mosel-Saar-Ruwer bottles are bright green, whereas the Rhine bottles are brown. These two regions agree on the nobility of the Riesling grape, which is used for the finest wines of each.

The bottles used for Champagne require an important structural consideration: They must be able to withstand six atmospheres of pressure. Thick and sturdy glass is therefore required, as is a protruding 'lip' around which the wire basket may be secured. Other than those differences, the classic Champagne bottle is just another variation of the ubiquitous Burgundy shape. However, the bottles used for tête de cuvée, the super-premium Champagnes, are usually different. The relatively squat bottle used for Dom Pérignon and others in the highest price range has historical roots in the Champagne region. It is likely that the long, thin neck associated with this shape made easier the hand-disgorging (removal) of the dead yeast, a labour-intensive process used today only for these fabulously expensive premium Champagnes (for lesser Champagnes it is usually done by machine). The tête de cuvée Champagne bottle type is increasingly used for cheap sparkling wine.

Italy and Spain usually use the two basic shapes, those of Bordeaux and Burgundy, with no apparent pattern. Whereas the wines of Rioja are usually offered in a Bordeaux bottle, perhaps as a nod to their oenological mentors, they are sold in the Burgundy shape as well. Chianti, the flag-ship wine of Tuscany, used to be sold in bulbous straw-clad bottles. Thankfully, as the quality of Chianti has improved, so the rustic style of bottling has diminished. These days, you're more likely to find a Chianti in a Bordeaux bottle. Barolo and Barbaresco, the twin pillars of Piedmont, are sold in either the Bordeaux or Burgundy shapes, with no apparent pattern.

Just as there are 'wines from the edge', there are bottle shapes so far out of the mainstream that they merit mention. The Italian wine Pescovino is sold in a fish-shaped bottle – the better, perhaps, to suggest an appropriate food pairing. Portuguese rosé was popular early in the wine boom, and Mateus, the most popular, comes to our shores in bottles far more distinctive than the wines within.

As a result of intense marketing efforts, some new trends have emerged. Brilliant blue bottles, usually used for Riesling or other light wines, certainly stand out in the store. Sillier yet is the 'collar' now appearing at the top of many bottles. This protrusion is there supposedly to prevent drips. The bottles still drip, however, and they are more difficult to open with standard corkscrews.

Afterword

THE HANGOVER: TOO MUCH OF A GOOD THING

You're having dinner out and the waiter keeps refilling your wine glass. You're at a party and the host insists on refreshing your glass... again. Who's counting? Your stomach, your head and those tiny red blood cells that rush alcohol to the rest of your body. They're ringing the hangover bell, but you aren't listening. Unfortunately, you hear it in the morning when it's clanging right between your eyes.

Too much alcohol causes a hangover, but no one knows exactly why. Everyone has their own personal barometer; the quantity that brings on the symptoms is personal (age, weight and sex count) and so are the circumstances. One prevailing theory is that dehydration is the culprit because, as the body processes alcohol, it uses up a great deal of water. Another hypothesis describes a hangover as a minor withdrawal episode from an addictive substance. How minor are a great thirst, a nauseous stomach, a pounding head and an all-round feeling of anxiety? That may depend on whether you can wrap yourself around your favourite pillow and go back to sleep. A nap is as good a remedy as any.

If wakefulness is required, you will probably have to face the fact that there is no cure, only helpful possibilities. Drinking lots of water helps, and doing so before bed is even better. A non-aspirin painkiller may be good for your head and kinder to your stomach than aspirin. Anyone who mentions pickles or bacon fat is talking about remedies that are peculiar to them, or just plain peculiar.

RESPONSIBLE DRINKING: MORE DOES NOT MAKE IT BETTER

The thirst-quenching embrace of a cold white wine on a hot day, the mellowness of a good port after dinner – these are near-perfect sensory experiences. Link them with good friends, lovers and favourite places, and they capture life's truly satisfying moments. Alcohol enhances our lives.

But alcohol is a drug, pure and simple, and it is foolish not to be aware of its dangers. It affects our bodies and brains, our judgment, coordination and perception. The amount of alcohol that brings on these impairments is entirely individual, depending on size and weight, metabolism and age, even on the variables of a single day.

The greater tragedy is that most traffic fatalities are not confined to the drinker. Drunk drivers are involved in a significant proportion of all traffic fatalities, and the innocent are often the victims. Awareness and responsibility are the only factors that will make a difference.

Enter law enforcement; the police are working hard to get drunk drivers off the road. Their primary weapon is the Breathalyzer, which can count your BAC, blood alcohol content – the percentage of alcohol in your blood. A BAC percentage as low as .05 has been found to increase the normal risk of accident by two to three times. So while you may not feel that your reflexes or judgment are impaired, if you are drinking you should not be driving. Period. No argument.

The legal alcohol limit in the UK is 80mg of alcohol in 100ml of blood. This can represent as little as two glasses of wine on an empty stomach, so remember to take it easy. If you get caught, the chances are that your driving licence will get taken away from you and you will be fined. And that's the best possible outcome – at the worst, you may cause an accident you will regret forever.

'Responsible drinking' is not an oxymoron. Moderation is the key to most pleasures. It is our responsibility as hosts, friends and even citizens to keep people from driving drunk. In fact, it is our *legal* responsibility to do so.

To drink in moderation is not to have less fun, but to savour the drink we do have. We raise our glasses for so many joyous and solemn occasions – to the bride and groom, to the job well done, to the friend we have lost – and to the pure pleasure of the drink itself.

Glossary

AC/AOC: An abbreviation for apellation d'origine contrôlée; the set of French wine laws that has established winemaking standards for quality French wines. AC is the top level of quality; VDQS is a set of laws with slightly lower standards; vin de pays is the lowest set of standards.

ACETIC: Vinegary taste or smell that develops when a wine is overexposed to air and acquires a trace (or more) of acetic acid.

ACID: One of the taste components of wine. Acidic wine is sometimes described as sour or tart. The taste buds for sensing acidity are found on the sides of the tongue and mouth.

ACIDITY: All wines naturally contain acids that should be in proper balance with fruit and other components. Sufficient acidity gives wine liveliness and crispness, is critical for wines to age, and gives wine thirst-quenching qualities.

AERATING: Letting wine breathe. Aeration occurs upon opening a bottle, by exposing wine to air that can help it develop and mellow, especially red wine.

AFTERTASTE: The aroma and taste that linger at the back of the throat and nose after the wine has been swallowed.

ALCOHOLIC FERMENTATION: Natural, chemical process that turns the sugars of grapes, and any added sugars, into alcohol through the action of yeast. The better sparkling wines undergo a second fermentation in the bottle. This happens because developing bubbles are trapped when the carbon dioxide produced during the fermentation process has nowhere to go.

ALOXE-CORTON (Ah-LOHSS Cor-TAWN): A village in the Côte d'Or in Burgundy, France.

ALSACE: Major wine range in France, on the border with Germany, noted for its white wines.

AMONTILLADO: A style of Sherry, amber in color and fairly dry.

APÉRITIF: A before-dinner drink. In theory, it stimulates the appetite (and the conversation).

APPELLATION: A specific geographic area. For instance, a wine from Bordeaux may be labelled as Bordeaux or by progressively more specific areas, if applicable – Médoc, then, for example, Margaux.

AROMA: The smell of a wine. Aroma seems to generate a surprising number of adjectives among wine people discussing a beverage made from grape juice.

ASTRINGENCY: A lip-puckering sensation caused by sharp acidity and tannin. A wine's astringent quality often diminishes as the wine ages.

ATTACK: The first impression a wine makes on the palate.

AUSLESE: German white wines made from very ripe grape bunches. These wines tend to be sweet.

AUSTERE: Wine that has very little fruity flavour and high acidity. Some very good wines – French Chablis and Italian Gavi – may be described as austere.

AVA.: An abbreviation for the American Viticultural Area. AVAs are officially recognized names that are used to indicate the area from which a wine comes. (*See* APPELLATION.)

BALANCE: Harmony among the wine's components – fruit, acidity, tannins, alcohol.

BARBARESCO (bar-bar-ESS-coh): A full-bodied DOCG red wine from Piedmont, Italy, made from the Nebbiolo grape. This type of wine can be a great one. Barolo and Barbaresco are the top two Nebbiolo-based wines from Piedmont, Italy.

BARBERA (bar-BEAR-ah): A red grape grown in the Piedmont region.

BAROLO (bar-OH-lo): A full-bodied DOCG red wine from Piedmont, Italy, made from the Nebbiolo grape. Barolo and Barbaresco are the top two Nebbiolo-based wines from Piedmont, Italy.

BEAUJOLAIS (bo-zho-LAY): A light, fruity red Burgundy wine from the region of Beaujolais, France, made from the Gamay grape.

BEAUJOLAIS NOUVEAU (bo-zho-LAY new-VOH): The 'new' Beaujolais that comes out in the third week of November.

BIG: Powerful in aroma and flavour; full-bodied wine. Such wines are also said to be chewy.

BLACK MUSCAT: A wine grape used to make funky, raisiny, dark red wine. These wines are usually somewhat sweet.

BODY: The weight and texture of a wine. Glycerine is the component of wine most responsible for body.

BORDEAUX: The most important wine region in France, if not the world. The reds from this region are usually blends of Cabernet Sauvignon, Cabernet Franc and Merlot. White wines are primarily blends of Sauvignon Blanc and Semillon.

BOTRYTIS CINEREA: An affliction that occurs in white wines. It helps make them into dessert wines by concentrating juices and sugars in rotting grapes that have lost some of their water. Also known as 'noble rot'.

BOTTLE AGING: Process of ageing a wine in the bottle to help refine its flavours.

BOTTLE FERMENTED: While *méthode champenoise* sparkling wines could be called 'bottle-fermented', this term is only used to pass off transfer-method sparkling wine as being something special. The term 'naturally fermented in the bottle' is also used – for which 'the bottle' doesn't mean 'this bottle'. *Méthode champenoise* is the way superior sparkling wines are made.

BOUQUET: The collection of different aromas from a wine is called its bouquet. It is also called its 'nose'.

BOURGOGNE: The French name for what we call Burgundy, the famous wine region of France, known for its Pinot Noir and Chardonnay.

BOX WINE: Inexpensive wine sold in sealed bags contained in a cardboard box.

BREATHE: Exposing wine to air to allow it complete its evolution before drinking. The wine drinker's term for 'aerating'.

BRILLIANT: Describes a wine that has a bright, clean appearance, with luminous reflections. To impress your friends, hold your glass up to the light and say, 'Brilliant', without smiling.

BRIX: Term used to measure the sugar content of grapes prior to harvest.

BRUT: Term for dry Champagne or sparkling wine.

BULK METHOD: (*See* CHARMAT METHOD.)

BURGUNDY: The anglicized name of Bourgogne, a major wine region of France. This region is noted for its Chardonnays and Pinot Noirs.

BUTTERY: An adjective used to describe wines with a lot of flavour and a smooth texture, referencing the oiliness and flavour of butter. This term more often refers to oak-aged white wines than reds; many Chardonnays and white Burgundies are said to have buttery aromas and flavours. 'Almondy' is another adjective that is often used in the same sentence as buttery. The malolactic fermentation is largely responsible for this flavour.

BYOB: Bring your own bottle. This term may be used by a restaurant that does not have an alcohol license.

CAB: Nickname for Cabernet Sauvignon.

CABERNET: Longer nickname for Cabernet Sauvignon.

CABERNET FRANC: Red wine grape used primarily as a blending grape. It is popular in France, where it is blended with Cabernet Sauvignon. Château Cheval Blanc, considered by many to be the finest wine from the Saint-Emilion region of France, is 66 per cent Cabernet Franc and 34 per cent Merlot.

CABERNET SAUVIGNON: The most noble of red-wine grapes. Cabernet Sauvignon makes big, complex, and powerful red wines, the greatest of which are very expensive.

CACHET VALUE: The pleasure you get from drinking a trendy or famous wine. Restaurants experience cachet value by having such wines on their menus. The quality of the wine is not part of its cachet value. Dom Pérignon Champagne has a lot of cachet value in many social circles. Cachet value may be defined as the pleasure you get from drinking a wine when you know what it is *minus* the pleasure you would get if you drank it without knowing what it is.

CARAMELY: Used to describe wines, usually white, that have been aged for a long time and have a rich, burnt-sugar flavour. Oak also contributes to this flavour.

CARBONATED WINE: Sparkling wines of inferior quality that have been injected with carbon dioxide, like soda.

CARBONIC MACERATION: Special technique for fermenting young red wines to make them drinkable. Widely used for Beaujolais, this process involves crushing the grapes in a carbon dioxide environment, thus preventing oxidation.

CASK: A wooden cask is used to age wine. Casks are bigger than barrels.

CAVA: Spanish sparkling wine made using the Champagne method, undergoing its second fermentation in the same bottle in which it's sold.

CHABLIS (shah-BLEE): Chardonnay-based, somewhat austere white wine from the Chablis district of France.

CHAMPAGNE: A major region of France known for its sparkling wines of the same name. In most countries this word is not allowed to appear on any bottle of sparkling wine not made in Champagne, France. The Champagne method, or *méthode champenoise*, was invented in this region.

CHAMPAGNE METHOD: English for *méthode champenoise*, this is the labour-intensive process by which carbonation is added to still wine. This is the superior way to make sparkling wine.

CHAPTALIZATION: The adding of sugar to wine in order to achieve the right alcohol level. Wine grapes grown in cooler climates often don't achieve enough ripeness, thus they lack sufficient sugars to be converted into alcohol.

CHARACTER: The combination of a wine's features that make it distinguishable from other wines. It is a term usually used as a compliment.

CHARDONNAY: The most popular of all white-wine grapes, and the primary white grape of France's Burgundy region.

CHARMAT METHOD: An inexpensive process for producing huge amounts of sparkling wine. It is also called the 'bulk method'. Unlike the Champagne method, the second fermentation takes place in a vat, and the resulting product is filtered under pressure into bottles. Serving charmat-method sparkling wines is an excellent way to avoid impressing people.

CHÂTEAU: A piece of land. For instance, Château Latour is a specific plot of vines in Pauillac, France. This term means the same thing as 'domaine'. 'Domaine' is more frequently used in Burgundy, and 'château' more in Bordeaux.

CHÂTEAUNEUF-DU-PAPE (shah-toe-NUFF doo PAHP): The name comes from a period of time in the 14th century, when the papal court relocated to Avignon. It is a district in the southern Rhône region of France where quality red wine is produced. These wines may be made from up to 13 different grapes, but Syrah and Grenache are the primary two.

CHEWY: A term used to describe red wines with unusual thickness of texture or tannins.

CHIANTI (K'YAHN-tee): A famous red wine made in the Tuscany region of Italy from primarily Sangiovese grapes.

CHIANTI CLASSICO: The core subdistrict of Chianti in Tuscany. There are other sub-districts, the best known of which is Rufina.

CINSAULT: A minor red wine grape, often used as a blending grape in the Rhône region of France.

CLARET: Medium-light red wine. In Britain, 'claret' is also used to mean red wines from Bordeaux.

CLOSED: Young, undeveloped red wines that do not yet reveal their positive qualities and are sometimes harsh. Breathing can help, but oftentimes the wine is ruined by being opened, and nothing can really help.

COMPLEX: A wine with a lot of different flavour and aroma components. Complexity is good.

COOKED: Burnt-fruit flavours resembling raisins. This quality is often found in wines from very hot growing regions.

CORK: Two definitions: (1) the cork that is used to seal the bottle, or (2) an unpleasant smell and/or taste given to a wine by a bad cork (also known as 'corked' or 'corky').

CORKAGE FEE: If you go to a restaurant that serves wine but allows you to bring your own special wine, the restaurant will often charge an additional fee for bringing your own. This fee is called the corkage fee. It covers having the staff uncork and serve you your wine in the restaurant's wine glasses, which will be cleaned later by restaurant personnel. It also covers some or all of the profits not made on the wine you might have bought had you not brought your own.

CÔTE: A French word for slope, as in the slopes of a river valley. Many vineyards in France are on slopes.

CÔTE D'OR (coat dor): A French region that includes the most important Burgundy vineyards.

COUNTRY WINES: France, Italy and Germany, whose top-quality wines are tightly regulated by their countries' wine laws, also produce light, simple and inexpensive 'country wines'. These are known as *vin de pays* in France, *vino da tavola* in Italy, and *Tafelwein* in Germany.

COUPAGE: The adding of one wine to another to improve or enhance its qualities. This is a somewhat derogatory term.

CRISP: Fresh, brisk character, usually associated with the acidity of white wine.

CRU: French for growth. In French usage the word means a vineyard of high quality, usually considered worthy of independent recognition under the laws of classification. An officially classified vineyard is *cru classé*.

DECANTING: Pouring a mature wine from its bottle into another bottle or container. This allows the wine to breathe. It is also the best way to separate wine from its sediment.

DELICATE: A wine that is light in texture with subtle flavours. Such wines are easily overwhelmed by powerfully flavoured foods.

DEMI-SEC: A term used to indicate moderately sweet to medium-sweet sparkling wines. It is also used to indicate off-dry versions of Vouvray.

DEVELOPED: Wine that has undergone positive changes during its years of ageing. Wines can also develop after a bottle has been opened.

DISTINCTIVE: Elegant, refined character that sets the wine apart.

DOCG/DOC: The abbreviations of *denominazione di origine controllata (e garantita)*. Of the three tiers of government-regulated Italian wines, DOCG wines are the top rated, and DOC wines make up the second tier. VdT, *vino da tavola*, is the lowest rating for wines shipped abroad.

DOMAINE: A specific plot of land. This term means the same thing as 'château'. 'Domaine' is more frequently used in Burgundy, and 'château' is more frequently used in Bordeaux.

DOUX: The sweetest of Champagnes.

DRY: Opposite of sweet. By definition, this means the wine has little or no residual sugar left following the fermentation process or processes.

DULL: Lacking flavour and/or enough acidity. Sometimes wines go through a dull phase in their evolution process, and may emerge as a good or even great wine.

DUMB: A wine that doesn't reveal its flavours and aromas. This is because the wine is too young or being served too cold.

EARTHY: Smell or flavour reminiscent of earth. European wines are more apt to be earthy than wines from other continents.

ELEGANT: A wine with flavour, quality, and style, and that isn't heavy, tannic or acidic. A balance of components is also implied.

EXTRA DRY: Term used on sparkling wine labels to indicate a wine that is fairly dry, but not as dry as brut.

FAT: Full-bodied, low-acid-flavoured wines are said to be fat.

FERMENTATION: Process in which yeast turns sugar into alcohol. Heat and carbon dioxide are by-products of this process.

FILTERING: Elimination of the deposits formed in a sparkling wine during its second fermentation in the bottle.

FINISH: Aftertaste or final impression a wine gives as it leaves your mouth for your stomach or bucket (if you are at a serious wine tasting). Long is good; short is bad.

FINO: A dry, pale style of Sherry.

FIREPLACE WINE: A wine that is as good, if not better, without food than with food. Low acidity, high glycerine content,

residual sweetness, moderate-to-low tannin and fruitiness are characteristics that make for good fireplace wine.

FIRM: This is a serious wine term. It means the elements of a wine's structure are tightly wound together, and also implies the wine has quite a bit of flavour. This is not a good word to bluff wine snobs with. 'Firm tannins' might indicate a red wine that is well made and has a bright future.

FLESHY: A wine with a lot of big, ripe fruitiness. These wines are thick on the palate. Glycerine can also give a fleshy impression in the mouth.

FLINTY: A dry, mineral-like flavour component that comes from soils containing a lot of limestone. It is an interesting flavour that is a big selling point for French white wines.

FLOR: A layer of mould that forms in some, but not all barrels, during the Sherry-making process. This development is a good thing. Unfortunately, man hasn't figured out how to make it happen; its formation is still a secret of nature.

FLORAL: A term used to describe the floral scents found in some wines. Riesling is often described as floral.

FLOWERY: See FLORAL.

FLUTE: Special glass for sparkling wines. It's tall and skinny, mainly because this is the best shape to keep the carbon dioxide bubbles from vanishing too quickly.

FORTIFIED WINE: Wines with alcohol added. Port and Sherry are the best-known examples of fortified wines. Madeira and Marsala are the major types.

FORWARD: A term that has two meanings: (1) a wine that develops ahead of similar wines from the same vintage, and (2) a wine that has fruit as the flagship of its components.

FREE RUN: Fermented grape juice obtained not by pressing grapes but rather by letting the juice run freely, thus avoiding the extraction of harsh tannins.

FRESH: A white or rosé wine with a good balance between alcohol and acidity. May also be applied to young red wine.

FRUIT: One of the taste components of wine. The interaction of alcohol and organic acids results in the development of fruit esters. These compounds imitate the flavours and aromas of other fruits.

FRUITY: Refers to prominent fruit flavours and aromas in a wine. Blackberries are often referenced in the aromas of Cabernet Sauvignon and Zinfandel wines.

FULL-BODIED: A lot of flavour, alcohol and thickness.

GAMAY: The red-grape variety used to make Beaujolais. Not grown very much in any other region of the world.

GEWÜRZTRAMINER (geh-VURZ-tra-MEANER): In German, literally, 'spicy Traminer'. Grape used for white wines in Alsace, France; Germany and the New World.

GLYCERINE: A complex alcohol that gives wine its thickness. This is very desirable, up to a point.

GRAND CRU: Literally means 'great growth'. In France's rating system of Burgundy, this is the top designation of any vineyard.

GRAN RESERVA: Name given to Spanish wines that have been aged in oak barrels for at least two years, prior to a bottle ageing period of at least three years.

GREEN: Term used to describe a young wine that hasn't developed enough to balance out its acidity.

GRENACHE: A workhorse grape of the southern Rhône. Known as Garnacha in Spain.

GRIP: A function of tannin. The slightly bitter and dry taste of moderate tannin seems to give the other flavours 'traction' in the mouth. Young reds with a lot of tannin may have too much grip.

HALBTROCKEN: German for 'half-dry'. This term is sometimes found on German wine bottles.

HARD: A red wine with tannin showing more than its fruit is often said to be hard. A hard wine may soften with time.

HARMONIOUS: Wines whose elements – fruit, alcohol, acidity and tannin – are not totally balanced but appear to blend seamlessly.

HARSH: Rough, biting character from excessive tannin and/or acid. Excessive tannin or acid may be perceived due to a lack of fruit.

HEADY: Strong, aromatic wine with a high concentration of alcohol and other components.

HERBACEOUS: Wines with herbal undertones. This is a serious wine term, and not a good one to bluff with among wine people. Mint, sage and eucalyptus are three herbs often detected in wine.

HONEST: A relatively flawless but simple wine. It is implied that the wine sells for a fair price.

HYBRID: A cross of two grape varieties of different species.

JEREZ: The town on the coast of Spain after which Sherry is named.

LANGUEDOC: A source of good, inexpensive wine (mostly red), located on the Mediterranean coast of France.

LEES: Dead yeast left by the wine after its first fermentation. Sometimes a bottle will brag that the wine was allowed to age on its lees before it was clarified and bottled.

LEGS: Traces of oiliness left in the glass by a wine with at least average amounts of alcohol, sugar and glycerine. The more alcohol, sugar and glycerine, the bigger the legs. Also known as tears.

LENGTH: A good wine displays its progression of flavours across the palette as you sip it. If this display seems to take a long time, the wine is said to have length.

LIGHT: Refers to a wine that is light in alcohol and/or to its texture and weight in the mouth. Sometimes lightness is desired, and sometimes it is considered a weakness; it depends on the wine. Great Pinot Noirs from Burgundy are often light; great New World Cabernet Sauvignons are never light.

LIVELY: When a wine is lively, it has a clean aroma and fresh acidity. This term is also used for sparkling wines that have a good amount of carbonation without being too carbonated.

LOIRE VALLEY: One of the major regions of France, and the source of Muscadet, Vouvray, Rosé d'Anjou, Sancerre and Pouilly Fumé.

MACERATION: The soaking, for a greater or lesser period, of the grape skins in the must that is fermenting.

MADEIRA: An island under Portuguese rule off the coast of Africa, on which the fortified wine with the same name is produced. This fortified wine is usually used in cooking, but not always.

MAGNUM: A bottle size of 1500ml, rather than the normal 750 ml.

MALBEC: A minor red grape, most often used for blending with more popular red grapes like Cabernet Sauvignon.

MALOLACTIC FERMENTATION: The second fermentation of some wines through bacterial action, whereby the malic acid is converted into lactic acid and the acidity becomes milder.

MANZANILLA: A very dry Sherry style said to have a slightly salty tang acquired during its maturation close to the sea.

MARSALA: A fortified wine produced from local white grapes on the island of Sicily. Available in dry and sweet styles, Marsala is a common ingredient in Italian cooking. Marsala is named after the Sicilian city of Marsala.

MATURE: Fully developed, ready-to-drink wine. Ideally, wines are aged until they mature. Different wines need varying amounts of time to mature. Many great estate wines are crafted to require a decade or more to mature.

MEATY: A wine with a chewy, fleshy fruit; sturdy and firm in structure. This is a wine adjective applied to big red wines such as Cabernet Sauvignon.

MÉDOC: Bordeaux's largest district, home of the communes of Saint-Julien, Saint-Estéphe, Margaux, Moulis, Listrac and Pauillac.

MELLOW: A wine adjective describing a low-acid wine that is smooth and soft, rather rough around the edges. Well-made Merlot tends to be a mellow red wine.

MERITAGE: A term coined by American wine producers to indicate a wine blended from Bordeaux grapes.

MERLOT: A red grape that makes easy-drinking wines.

MÉTHODE CHAMPENOISE: This translates to 'the Champagne Method'. The best sparkling wines undergo their second fermentation in the same bottle in which the wine is sold. This laborious process is the *méthode champenoise*.

MINTY: A desirable aroma in some wines, particularly Cabernet Sauvignon.

MISE EN BOUTEILLE AU CHATEAU: This French term translates to 'bottled at the estate'. This often denotes high quality, as the winemaker has a personal relationship to the grapes he or she uses in crafting a wine.

MOSEL-SAAR-RUWER: A major wine region in Germany that lies along the connected rivers of these names.

MOURVEDRE: A red blending grape from the southern Rhône area.

MUSCAT: A type of grape that yields a raisiny fruit-tasting wine. Muscat wines are almost always sweet. Black Muscat makes wines that are dark purple, whereas orange Muscat makes bronze-coloured wines.

MUST: The combination of crushed grapes, skins, and pips from which red wine is drawn.

NAPA VALLEY: A highly regarded wine region in California where the top US wines are produced.

NEBBIOLO: A red grape grown primarily in the Piedmont region of Italy. This is an important red-wine grape, capable of producing great red wines. Unlike Cabernet Sauvignon, which is found on many continents, Nebbiolo is rarely found outside Italy.

NOBLE GRAPES: Grapes that produce the world's finest wines: Cabernet Sauvignon, Pinot Noir, Merlot, Syrah, Nebbiolo and Sangiovese are the noble red grapes. Chardonnay, Sauvignon Blanc and Riesling are the noble white grapes. The exact set of grapes considered to be 'noble' is a moving target, varying from person to person.

NOBLE ROT: This is the nickname for *botrytis cinerea*, a mould that affects certain white grapes and helps make them suitable for dessert wines by concentrating juices and sugars.

NON-VINTAGE: A wine made from grapes from more than one harvest.

NOSE: The smell of the wine; it may have a 'good nose' or an 'off nose'. It could also have a big nose.

NUTTY: Nut-like aromas and flavours that develop in certain wines such as Sherries or old white wines.

OAK: Smell and taste produced in a wine that's been aged in oak barrels. Oak is a very popular tool of the winemaker, and sometimes it is overused. Oak flavour is occasionally added via oak chips thrown into the vat. It adds a vanilla flavour to wine.

OENOLOGY: The study of wine.

OENOPHILE: One who loves, appreciates and studies wine.

OFF-DRY: Wine with noticeable residual sugar, usually above 1 per cent by volume.

OLOROSO: A dark Sherry that may be sweet or dry. The sweet versions are usually called cream or brown Sherry.

OXIDATION: An alteration wines undergo after exposure to oxygen. Some exposure to oxygen is good for the wine and its flavours. Eventually, however, oxygen helps turn wine into vinegar.

PALE: Used to describe wines with less color than similar-styled wines.

PALE DRY: The style in which Fino Sherry is made.

PALOMINO: The primary white grape used to make Sherry.

PEPPERY: Red wine that has a hint of black pepper flavour, such as Syrah/Shiraz, is said to be peppery.

PHYLLOXERA: A vine louse that kills grape vines.

PIEDMONT: The great red-wine region of northern Italy, famous for its Nebbiolo wines. Also called 'Piemonte' on wine labels.

PINOTAGE: Unique to South Africa, this grape is a cross between the Pinot Noir and Cinsault grapes.

PINOT BLANC: A somewhat dull but reliable white wine grape used to make simple wines in Italy and Alsace.

PINOT GRIGIO: White wine grape, also known as Pinot Gris. This grape produces good white wine in Italy and Alsace.

PINOT NOIR: The noble red grape of Burgundy. This grape isn't easy to grow, but it produces wonderful light- and medium-bodied wines that go well with food.

PIPS: Grape seeds; two per grape. Pips are a source of tannin in red wine.

PORT: Fortified red wine from Portugal, where it is known as Porto. This class of wine is available in a variety of styles, including Ruby, Tawny and Vintage.

POUILLY-FUISSÉ: (POO-yee FWEE-say) A white wine with a good reputation, made from Chardonnay grapes in the commune of Fuissé (or one of four other neighbouring communes) in the Mâcon subregion of Burgundy.

PREMIER CRU: Literally meaning 'first growth', this is the highest level of quality in Médoc, Bordeaux, but it is the second-highest level behind *grand cru* in Burgundy.

PRICKLE: Presence of tiny natural bubbles in some young wines.

PROVENCE: A minor wine-producing region of France, often lumped together with the neighbouring Rhône region. Provence is best known for high-quality, dry rosé wines.

PUNT: The mysterious indentation in the bottom of many wine bottles. This feature was originally intended to collect sediment before effective clarification techniques came into widespread use.

QUALITÄTSWEIN BESTIMMTER ANBAUGEBIETE (QbA): The middle quality of German wine. (*See* QUALITÄTSWEIN MIT PRÄDIKAT.)

QUALITÄTSWEIN MIT PRÄDIKAT (QmP): The highest quality level of German wines. The 'prädikats' are the designation of sugar content at harvest. From driest to sweetest they are Kabinett, Spätlese, Auslese, Beerenauslese and Trockenbeerenauslese. QmP wines don't have any sugar added to them. The second level of wine is the QbA wines. *Tafelwein* is the lowest level.

RAISINY: Smells reminiscent of raisin, found in wines made from very ripe or over-ripe grapes. Australian red wines are often raisiny. Muscat wines are inherently raisiny, irrespective of the ripeness of the harvested Muscat grapes.

REGION: A large subdivision of a wine-producing country. For instance, France has seven major regions: Bordeaux, Burgundy, Rhône, Loire, Champagne, Languedoc and Alsace.

RESERVA: This word on a Spanish wine label indicates that the wine has been aged in a barrel and/or a bottle longer than regular wines from the same region. *Riserva* with an i' is the Italian equivalent.

RESERVE: Reserve wines are implied to be aged longer than and superior to their contemporaries.

RHÔNE VALLEY: Region in France noted for big, strong reds and some interesting white wines.

RICH: An adjective used to describe a wine that has a lot of flavour, body and aroma.

RIESLING: A white wine grape that is not as popular as it deserves to be. This grape is every bit as noble as the Chardonnay grape. The best of these wines come from Germany and Alsace, although the Australians are making some pretty stunning versions, too.

RIOJA: A wine region in northern Spain where the local Tempranillo grape is often blended with a little Garnacha to make red wines bearing the name Rioja. Some white Rioja is also produced.

ROBUST: Full-bodied, full-flavoured and high in alcohol.

ROSÉ: Pink-coloured wine, usually made from red-wine grapes fermented with minimal contact with grape skins, which produces a lighter colour. Some rosés are made from mixing a small amount of red wine with white. White Zinfandel is a rosé made from the red Zinfandel grape.

ROSE D'ANJOU: A rosé wine from the Loire Valley in France, made from Cabernet Franc, Cabernet Sauvignon and other red grapes.

ROUGH: Describes a wine with harsh edges and one that is biting and sometimes unpleasant. Rough wines are sometimes a good match with garlic.

ROUND: Describes a wine with balance and harmony among its various components: fruitiness, acidity, alcohol, tannin, glycerine and sweetness

SAINT-EMILION: A major subregion of Bordeaux, France.

SANGIOVESE: A red-wine grape grown primarily in Italy. It is the primary grape in Chianti.

SANGRIA: A wine drink that is served chilled. It is made from wine and fruit.

SAUTERNES: An important subregion of Bordeaux, France, famous for dessert wines.

SAUVIGNON BLANC: Generally a notch below Riesling and Chardonnay in terms of the high end of the wine spectrum, this white grape makes some excellent food wines.

SCREWPULL: The most effective and easy-to-use cork extractor available. (*See* corkscrews section in Chapter 9.)

SEC: Literally means 'dry'. However, in terms of Champagne it actually means noticeably sweet.

SECOND-LABEL WINE: Many top producers in France and the New World maintain the quality of their flagship wines by using slightly lesser grapes in their notch below top wines, known as second-label wines. In bad years, these producers may not make their first-label wines.

SEDIMENT: The stuff found at the bottom of a bottle of red wine, which comes from the wine itself.

SEMILLON: A white-wine grape often used in France as a blending grape with Sauvignon Blanc, and in Australia with Chardonnay. It is also used quite a bit for making dessert wines.

SHARP: A wine with high acidity level is said to be sharp. Sharp wines can cut through rich, creamy sauces.

SHERRY: A type of fortified wine from Spain. Sherries can be sweet or not, heavy or light in body, and dark or light in colour.

SHIRAZ: The Iranian town where the red-wine grape Syrah supposedly originated. masny New World countries refer to the Syrah as Shiraz. This grape makes some interesting and affordable red wines.

SHORT: Refers to when the finish, or aftertaste, ends abruptly.

SILKY: An adjective describing wines with a smooth texture and finish. Glycerine is the component most closely related to silkiness. 'Silky' is not very different from 'velvety'.

SIMPLE: Opposite of complex. Straightforward, inexpensive wines are often referred to as being simple. It is not a negative term when describing a £5 bottle of wine, but it's certainly an insult to a £50 bottle.

SMOKY: An aroma sometimes associated with Sauvignon Blanc and Pinot Noir.

SMOOTH: Describes a wine somewhat rich in glycerine and usually light in tannin and acidity, which feels good in the mouth.

SOAVE: The name of a white-wine-producing region of Italy.

SOFT: May refer to soft, gentle fruit in delicate wines, or to a lack of acidity in wines without proper structure. It may used on a label to indicate a low alcohol content.

SOLERA: System of mixing wines that consists of improving young wine with the addition of older wine (and vice versa). It is the aging system used for the Sherry wines of Jerez. *Solera* wines are bottled without a vintage year, because these are wines from multiple years.

SOMMELIER: A restaurant employee who purchases wine for the restaurant and assists customers wishing to order wine. A broad knowledge of matching food and wine is essential for this job.

SPARKLING WINE: Wines with bubbles created by trapped carbon dioxide gas, induced by a second, enclosed fermentation.

SPICY: Having the character or aroma of spices such as clove, mint, cinnamon or pepper. Gewürztraminer is particularly noted for its spiciness.

SPUMANTE: Inexpensive, sweet sparkling wine from Italy.

STEELY: Firmly structured; taut balance tending toward high acidity.

STEMMY: Indicates a harsh, green, tannic flavour.

STRAW: Used to describe a white wine with a colour like straw.

STRAWBERRY: A fruity aroma that appears in certain red or rosé wines and some Ports.

STRUCTURE: The framework of the wine, made up of its acid, alcohol and tannin content. Great wines must have a good underlying structure to support the other flavour components, such as fruitiness.

SULFITES: Both naturally occurring and added to wines, they are used as a defense against oxidation and other woes.

SUPER-TUSCAN: Usually a blend of grapes that does not conform to Italian wine law, but many such wines are of superior quality. Cabernet Sauvignon and Sangiovese are usually the components of a Super-Tuscan.

SWEET: Usually indicates the presence of residual sugar, retained when grape sugar is not completely converted to alcohol. Even dry wines, however, may have an aroma of sweetness, the combination of intense fruit or ripeness. It is considered a flaw if not properly balanced with acidity.

SYLVANER: A workhorse white grape of Germany, often blended with Riesling. It is often found in QbA wine such as Liebfraumilch.

SYRAH: Known as Shiraz in many New World countries, this red grape is used to make some great wines and some great-value wines. The northern Rhône of France is a hotbed for good Syrah.

TANNIN: A natural component found to varying degrees in the skins, seeds and stems of grapes. It is most prominent in red wines, where it creates a dry, puckering sensation in young reds. Tannin mellows with aging and is a major component in the structure of red wines.

TART: A sharp taste that comes from a wine's natural acidity. Not necessarily a negative term.

TARTARIC ACID: The predominant wine acid that occurs naturally in grapes.

TEARS: Traces of oiliness left in the glass by a wine with at least average amounts of alcohol, sugar and glycerine. The more alcohol, sugar and glycerine, the bigger the tears. Also known as legs.

TEMPRANILLO: The major red grape of Spain's Rioja wines, this grape is not widely cultivated in other countries.

TERROIR: A French word that refers to the influence of soil and climate, rather than grape variety, on winemaking.

THIN: A negative term for a wine (usually red) with insufficient body, flavour and/or colour.

TINTO: This is Spanish for red wine.

TIRED: A wine that is past its peak of flavour development. Such a wine should have been opened at an earlier time.

TOBACCO: An aroma that is noticeable in some mature wines. This is considered to be a good thing, especially in Cabernet Sauvignon.

TROCKEN: German for 'dry', this is a word to look for on German wine labels. Germany is fighting its reputation for sweet wines with this term.

TUSCANY: One of the major wine regions of Italy, it is the home of Chianti and Brunello di Montalcino.

UNCTUOUS: An adjective to describe a thick, rich, and glycerine-laden wine with an equally rich aroma.

VANILLA: A spicy aroma and flavor imparted to a wine by oak-aging.

VARIETAL: Wine that is made from one dominant grape variety and is labeled as such is a varietal wine.

VARIETAL CORRECTNESS: A wine that exhibits the signature characteristics of the grape variety with which it is labelled is considered to be varietally correct. Many cheaper varietals are not varietally correct, although they might taste good.

VARIETY: Type of grape.

VELVETY: A wine that is smooth and silky in texture is often called velvety. This is a signature characteristic of Merlot. Low acid, low tannin and generous glycerine make for a velvety wine.

VIN: French for 'wine'.

VINEGAR: When a wine begins to go bad from exposure to oxygen, it turns to vinegar. Some wines have a natural vinegary quality to them – not high praise.

VINIFICATION: The process of winemaking from harvest to bottling is called vinification.

VINO: Spanish and Italian for 'wine'.

VINTAGE: The year in which the wine was harvested. This information should appear on the bottle.

VIOGNIER: A white grape that does well in the Rhône, with apricot-like fruit.

WOODY: A wine that has absorbed too much oak flavour from casks or barrels is described as woody. However, some wood is good, because it adds complexity to wine.

YEAST: Single-cell organisms found in the grape skin that facilitate the alcohol-fermentation process. Extra yeast is often added by the winemaker during the wine-making process.

YEASTY: A bready smell, sometimes detected in wines that have undergone secondary fermentation, such as Champagne. This can be used as either a positive or negative adjective.

Index